The Latin American University

The Latin American University

Edited by

Joseph Maier and

Richard W. Weatherhead

UNIVERSITY OF NEW MEXICO PRESS

Albuquerque

Library of Congress Cataloging in Publication Data
  Main entry under title:

The Latin American University.

   Bibliography: p. 221.
   Includes index.
   1. Universities and colleges—Latin America—
Addresses, essays, lectures.   I. Maier, Joseph,
1911–   II. Weatherhead, Richard W.
LA541.L33   378.8   78-55708
ISBN 0-8263-0487-7

To Our Parents
Quid rides? Mutato nomine, de te fabula narratur

Preface

This book grew out of an awareness that little attention has been given to the Latin American university as an institution with a particular history and definite role in relation to the other great institutions of society: the state, the church, the family, the military, and the economy. This is not to say that there is no bibliography on the subject. Indeed, there are many articles, some monographs, and a few full-length books. But most have treated the university partially, examining it in a particular historical period or intellectual climate, or have described the origins and growth of a specific university in one country. The present volume looks at the Latin American university from a variety of viewpoints.

The research for the book began in 1966–67 and involved several trips to Latin America, Europe, and Japan. During these trips many interviews were held with scholars and students to discuss the outline of the proposed study. The comments they made were all useful in amending and expanding the original prospectus.

We are grateful to the Midgard Foundation, which provided an initial grant to launch the project and has given generous subsequent assistance. We are indebted to many people for their suggestions and helpful comments along the way. We can only mention a few, but our gratitude extends to many. Florestan Fernandes made valuable suggestions about the university in a developing society. He has since published an essay entitled "A Universidade em uma sociedade em Desenvolvimento" in *Circuito Fechado*. Juan Marsal, of the Instituto Torcuato Di Tella in Buenos Aires, offered advice about the intellectual and his influence on the university in Latin American Society. George Waggoner, of the University of Kansas, discussed parallels and differences between the university in Latin America and the United States, and his essay has since been published elsewhere.

Another valuable and suggestive paper was by Gustavo Andrade Lleras, of Sophia University in Tokyo. It dealt with distinctions to be seen in the role of the university in Japan, following the Meiji

Restoration (1868), and in Latin America. His comparative study of institutions provided a useful perspective. Gregory Rabassa, of Queens College, the City University of New York, explored new ground in his research into the way the university and its personnel are mirrored in late nineteenth- and early twentieth-century Latin American novels. Both subjects are worthy of treatment in separate books.

The translations in this book were made in the interests of greater readibility and unity of style and thought, always bearing in mind the Italian adage *traduttore, traditore.*

For editorial suggestions, we are indebted, once again to Sally Rogers, whose careful commentary helped smooth many a sentence, and to Stanley Salmen for his kind assistance.

Joseph Maier
Richard W. Weatherhead

Contents

1

The Latin American University:
An Introduction

Joseph Maier and Richard W. Weatherhead

I

Serious attention is seldom given to Latin America unless it is struck somewhere by human, natural, or political catastrophe. Newspapers and periodical magazines—this is particularly true for the United States—will report at length on the havoc of a terrible earthquake or the turmoil following a political coup. In the 1970s, soaring inflation and birth rates, and a spate of kidnapping by guerrilla groups, have been covered but largely in a superficial or sensational manner. An event is usually discussed out of context without being related to Latin American environment and history. For example, the context and etiology of the political instability of given countries is seldom part of reports on the widespread military or dictatorial regimes in Latin America. A student strike, responsible for shutting down an entire university, or the massacre of a group of students who have elected to become martyrs for some special cause, are events that take place within a particular setting whose cultural and political realities should be part of the account reporting them.

One reason for the hasty explanations of what happens in Latin America is that North Americans in general are ignorant about the region's language, history, literature, religion, and educational systems. Much has been written about North America and South America sharing the New World, and about how the experience of establishing new societies in the Western Hemisphere somehow endowed those who live in it with a similar outlook. Most North Americans, for instance, confuse Latin America with South America, having gained a passing acquaintance with Latin America during visits to Mexico, Central America, or the Caribbean. These are the geographical areas that shape the North American view of Latin America. (Choosing Puerto Rico as the *puente*, or bridge, between North America and South America during the early days of the Alliance for Progress in the 1960s was part of this superficiality.)

There are other important reasons for our inability to understand Latin America. Much of it is very distant from the big cities of the United States. Think, for example, of the five thousand miles, largely over water and jungle, that separate New York, Boston, and Washington, D.C., from Rio de Janeiro, Santiago, Buenos Aires, La Paz, Asunción, and Montevideo.

There is also a cultural distance separating the United States from Latin America. An inventory of the factors which distinguish Latin American societies from those of the United States or Canada would be lengthy. Adding to the generalities, the significant differences among the Latin American countries would become tedious for authors and readers; Brazil, Mexico, Argentina, Peru, Costa Rica, Haiti, and Cuba, while fitting into the same immense geographical area, have little in common with one another.

Contemporary American historians still point out the sharp dissimilarities between the cultures and institutions that arose in Latin America and those existing in British America. In a general history of the United States, *The Great Republic* (1977), Bernard Bailyn, for example, explains that Spain's American empire

> was most elaborately *bureaucratic*. Several echelons of full-time salaried officials enforced detailed decrees and laws governing the behavior of rulers and ruled. And the system was *patrimonial;* that is, it was hierarchical in structure, all authority ultimately centering in the patriarchal figure of the monarch of Castile.

The whole of Latin American political culture was shaped by the crown's dominance and by the flood of writing that rationalized it. There were no competing intellectual centers from which contrary ideas could develop. The Catholic church engrossed the intellectual life of Latin America, and it was a church that was conservative in doctrine and royalist in politics. Far from Spanish America proving to be a legitimate refuge for religious dissenters, as British America would become, it developed into a more tightly controlled bastion of Catholic orthodoxy than Spain itself. Dissenters and heretics of all kinds were barred by law from emigrating to America.

Latin America, after about 1500, was an extension of Mediterranean Europe, specifically of the expanding empires of Spain and Portugal. The population mix included Spaniards and Portuguese, imported African slaves, *criollos* (American-born offspring of the Iberian settlers), *mestizos* (those with Iberian and Indian blood), and other blendings. The language was Latin-derived with infusions of indigenous words. The colonials were cared for and frustrated by an elaborate bureaucratic organization designed to keep the empires intact, growing, and prosperous. The imperial experience of Spain and Portugal in the Americas lasted about 300 years, and the law, polity, religion, language, education, family structure, sexual attitudes, types of food and their preparation, notions of time and punctuality, and observance of holidays in Latin America still show its shaping influence.

The faith of the Iberian conquerors was a militant one that justified seizing the new territories in the name of God and the Emperor. One of the main designs in settling the new lands was to save the Indian by means of conversion to the one true faith. The Catholic Church was the universal house of orthodoxy and zealous missionaries were roving the world to save the uninitiated. St. Francis Xavier was in Japan and China not many years after Bartolomé de Las Casas was active in Latin America.

The religion established in Latin America was intended to hold its adherents firmly together. The creed, not to be contaminated by alien faiths, was an expansive and intolerant doctrine. This unitary religious organization of society was a principal factor in the survival of the Iberian empires in the Americas. The religion bred suspicion of outsiders. The Inquisition (the Holy Office) generated attitudes hostile to heresy (dissent in its most unspeakable form). It was an effective agency of thought control, whether the thought was political, religious, or philosophical. Church teaching tended to view history in chiliastic terms. Colonial education relied almost exclusively on books authorized by the church and religious texts predominated in the classrooms. The religious orders—chiefly the Jesuits, but also the Dominicans, Franciscans, Augustinians, and Mercedarians—were responsible for the spread of books and printing, both secular and sacred, in Spanish America.

A cursory look at the purposes and consequences of the Inquisition suggests lasting influences on the university that are religious, educational, and political. The Holy Office was instituted to preserve the integrity of the faith and to watch over its keepers and followers. In this sense it was wholly benign and gave the believer a code to live by, a set of rules prescribing what was off limits, and the punishments to be meted out to those who transgressed. The Holy Office was a political instrument that kept track of the King's subjects by compiling dossiers on leading citizens in important communities, by conducting investigations of some of them, and by punishing (or *in extremis*, executing) them. The Inquisition acted also as a censor of public knowledge with its Index of forbidden books determining what books were available for instructional purposes and private enlightenment. Bibliophiles had to be on guard about what volumes to keep on their library shelves lest they run afoul of the censorious eye of the Holy Office—as did Melchor Pérez de Soto. Arrested on January 10, 1665, in his Mexico City home, he was to die two months later in a secret prison of the Inquisitors. His offense was having possessed outlawed books, *"1,502 cuerpos de libros en latín y en romance."*

The university became an orthodox institution whose main task was to provide society with an oligarchy wedded to the purposes of church and state. Universities were established soon after the initial settlements of American lands. In an examination of the early charters of incorporation one will find two rationales repeated time and again: loyalty to the King and purity of the faith.

By contrast, in the United States during the seventeenth and eighteenth centuries, no one religious establishment succeeded in becoming the only church for all the colonies. The colonies had been founded on the principles of English Common Law and the idea that it was salutary to allow religious dissenters to create their own societies far from the established church. Only in Massachusetts, where the protestors against the Church of England had created an even more rigid religious life, was there anything comparable to the Holy Office. (The anticommunist crusades of A. Mitchell Palmer and Joseph McCarthy were attempts to purge society of heretical thinking and activities but, happily, both were short-lived and are generally viewed as deviant behavior in American political life.)

Contemporary politicization of the Latin American university derives its legitimacy and authority from this early convergence of church and state. At the time of its creation in the New World, the Spanish-American university was an imitation of Salamanca or Alcalá. The Portuguese never exported their university to the colonies. Brazilian colonial education was at first under Jesuit control and later under royal supervision, with the Brazilian university being established only in the twentieth century. Those in Brazil who wanted a university education had to go to Coimbra, in Portugal, while almost all Spanish Americans who had higher education attended universities in Spain's American empire. These institutions had the imprimatur of the Holy See *and* the official blessing of the Spanish Crown when the first was established in Santo Domingo in 1538.

A politicized university is a peculiar institution that exists in an already highly politically charged environment. In the nineteenth century, the newly independent states abolished the university and replaced it with academies and institutes. They followed the Napoleonic pattern of creating a more secular, open, progressive, educational system that would slough off the domination of the clergy and scholastic learning. The new educational structures, whatever their designations, were still creatures of the state.

The university continued to be embroiled in religious and political controversy in the transition from the colonial to the national period. People within the university took sides, divided themselves up as liberals or conservatives, *blancos* or *colorados*, *pipiolos* or *pelucones*, and so forth. Once sides were chosen, political groups were formed and parties developed. At the time of Independence, 1810–30, political dogmas, party doctrines, clandestine operations against the imperial powers and local juntas, circulation of revolutionary literature, and discussion of constitutional theories all derived in a measure from the politicized colonial university. The university might be disbanded by decree, but intellectuals and politicians and scholars still met and drew inspiration from one another or found out that they were at political swords' points.

The politicized university is highly sensitive to ideology and party. Teachers and students, both full-time and part-time, seek recruits to their cause. One reason for such missionary activity is the belief that the university is the one place to preserve the ideal, if not the practice, of the democratic state. This view would describe the university as potentially the ideal republic, the image of what society should be, and would hold that the university should be at least tolerant of the critical mind to counteract the authoritarian and antiacademic tendencies of the state. The university has developed an attitude of being in active, articulate, and sometimes militant opposition to the state—whose apparatus is often in the hands of military leaders.

On November 30, 1976, the *New York Times* published an article entitled "Latin American Universities, Once Strong, in Political and Academic Decline." The reporter perceptively noted that in many countries the university had virtually lost its autonomy. The current rector of the National University of Buenos Aires was quoted as saying:

> The concept of an independent university left to its own affairs is unthinkable today. If we want order, we need professionals who know how to handle weapons to defend us. We need policemen in the university. In fact, I cannot imagine what would happen if they left.

The military regime had intervened in the name of educational and social order; autonomy, for the moment, had atrophied. The same article quoted a Peronist rector of a few years earlier: "We Christians possess the truth and we do not share it. The rest do not have it, and we shall treat them accordingly."

Both quotations are better understood against a historical background broader than it is possible for any news report to provide, no matter how responsible and alert the reporter or editor. Neither statement could have been made without appreciation of such institutions as the Holy Office and of the frequent convergences of church and state. The Latin American student seems to have the idea that his educational experience is part of a larger mission to save society from this religious background. The idealistic critique of the university, as developed in the twentieth century, has an expansionist reach and redemptive tone in its statement of goals. Its rhetoric is directed against those in opposing camps—the heretical and the dissenting.

II

Paradoxically, although the Latin American university system is older than the colleges and universities of the United States, at the same time it is more recent in development. The first universities in the Spanish colonies were founded about a century before Harvard College but there may be some rough similarity in the colonial evolution of higher education in the British and Spanish empires. In both cases, the institutions served church purposes and were chartered by the Crown. The differences, however, are greater than the resemblances. In each of the American colonies, the legislatures and the churches had different outlooks and influences, and in some colonies the position of the King was more respected than in others. In the English colonies all education tended to be more locally autonomous and supported by private centers of power than in Latin America.

Higher education in Latin America throughout most of the nineteenth century had two goals: to forge a national identity and to create a national culture under the banner of positivism. For Latin American countries, Comte's positivism—and, more particularly, his theory of the three stages of history—provided a convenient and respectable scheme for interpreting their national development and cultural identity. One encounters these themes early or late in the last century. They are the principal concerns of Andrés Bello and Justo Sierra, Mariano Moreno and Domingo Faustino Sarmiento. Gabino Barreda and José Martí in Spanish America, and of Benjamin Constant and Miguel Limos in Brazil. "National" meant placing the university in the position of guardian of the nation's ideals and, therefore, making it a combatant in the political arena. Throughout the nineteenth century, as many Latin American countries adopted French educational reforms, the university came under attack. The French models, however, only partially replaced the traditional university as an institution for training people and for the transmission of knowledge and skills, collective values and wisdom.

In the United States, meanwhile, the process of incorporating continental lands into the federal union on an equal footing was proceeding rapidly. The Civil War reaffirmed the principle that diverse sections of the nation must live together in one political union and vie with each other for political hegemony without recourse to warfare. Two congressional acts of the 1860s—the Homestead Act and the Morrill Act—respectively provided for the rapid settlement of the lands west of the Mississippi and the establishment of vocational and secular education to train the settlers to use the new lands productively. The land-grant colleges predominated over the private colleges in the West and Southwest because they were the civilizing complement to the physical occupation of the land; they trained the young to be better farmers, planters, veterinarians, railroad builders, and later, agronomists and earth scientists. These schools did not aim at creating a national identity for the United States, nor were they especially involved in national politics. In fact, most of the land-grant colleges—and later, in the 1890s, the graduate schools—were politically unexciting and institutionally quite literal in carrying out their educational functions.

Between 1890 and 1910, graduate schools, mostly in the social sciences, were set up at leading universities such as Johns Hopkins, Columbia, Harvard, and Chicago. The North American college, with its graduate school, was becoming the equal of the great European universities. Increasing specialization within disciplines and greater emphasis on independent or collaborative research (through the seminar and tutorial techniques) distinguished graduate studies from the liberal arts orientation of the undergraduate years. Even before graduate schools became familiar divisions of the American university, a rudimentary kind of professional school in law, medicine, engineering, business, architecture, pharmacy, agricultural sciences, dentistry, and nursing had started to develop. Their growth as integral and at the same time autonomous parts of the university was attributable to the flexible and nonideological organization of the university, to generous support by private individuals and foundations, and to the interest of the federal and state governments in the independence of higher education. Tax laws encouraging private giving to universities have for almost one hundred years reflected this interest. The constituency primarily charged with the responsibility for insuring the survival of these universities was their large and growing number of alumni. The "old grad network" kept most of the universities afloat financially and provided the trustees, regents, or overseers who would pass the institution on the next generation.

In the twentieth century the Latin American university began to change and grow rapidly. The name "university" was fully reinstated and a long list of reforms—institutional, pedagogical, demographic, and political—were proposed for all universities in the Argentine Reform Movement of 1918. There are strong echoes of Bello and Barreda in the Reform leaders' call for the creation of a national identity and the establishment of true national independence, and it was through the university that these aims were to be realized. Two specters haunted the authors of the Reform manifestos: one was imperialism, especially that of the United States; the other was oligarchic capitalism. Separately or together they threatened to encroach on indigenous culture and national treasure. Something radical had to be done to forestall their perilous effects. The industrial process had brought into dominance an oligarchic class that ignored the educational and social needs of the masses of peasants, tenant farmers, immigrants, and Indians. Exclusion of these masses from the educational system deprived the national culture of richness and vitality.

The young leaders of the 1918 Reform wanted to liberalize the traditional university and open its doors to all members of society. They asked that professors be promoted on the basis of merit and achievement. They wanted full-time professors and full-time students, sensitive to the great ideas of the West and their own cultures, and aware of what was "relevant" to the contemporary university and modern society. The student was to be given an expanded role in the governance of the university. Autonomy was to be guaranteed by constitutional law and observed by all governments. University life was to be a more truly communitarian experience of master and student living in an ideal republic (a state within a state) than had ever existed.

The university was to be the conscience of the nation. All "reformed" universities were to be linked together to provide a hemispheric conscience and enlightenment for all Latin Americans. The Reform was to infuse national universities with an awareness of national cultures and awaken all Latin Americans to the peculiarities of the Latin American experience. In Anisio Teixeira's words, the university was and is the "master institution of national culture."

The 1918 Reform could not avoid being a political event. It attempted to reform a politicized institution, at times a friend and more often a foe of the government in power. Generally in Latin America, governments increase their power at the expense of other institutions. There is seldom a strong move to diffuse political power, to expand the constituencies on which it is based, to share it with contending parties, or to grant immunities to potential adversary groups. Hence, one finds the authoritarian state—whether in the guise of one-party rule (as with the PRI in Mexico), or in the form of a military regime (as in Brazil, Peru, Argentina, Uruguay, or Chile), or following the Cuban example of a combination of authoritarian state, ideological credo, *caudillismo,* and a revolutionary commitment to create a new society.

Ironically, the 1918 Reform and the contemporary authoritarian state profess a similar goal: the creation of a national society and a national culture in which the masses will actively participate. But while there may be agreement on ends, there are invariably differences on the means to achieve them. Among the difficulties in the relationship between state and university is the university's tendency, as an institution based on the 1918 Reform, to assume too many functions and responsibilities for itself. The university cannot fully define what the culture of the nation will be. Culture creation is cumulative and sometimes individuals are as important or more important, in given periods, than are institutions. German culture, insofar as poetry and elevated language and thought are concerned, owes more to Goethe and Schiller than to Heidelberg. Nor can the university stand alone as the conscience or arbiter of what is and should be the nation. The young and the old, the religious and the agnostic, the plutocratic and the unemployed, by various means, literate or not, organized or not, contribute collectively to a nation's conscience. Determining the national conscience is almost as hard as taking the nation's temperature at any given moment.

The Latin American authoritarian state, given its descent from Spanish and Portuguese colonial institutions, does not tolerate the autonomous republic envisioned by the 1918 Reform; it will not condone criticism and subversion from within the protected walls of the university. Both the government, whatever its strengths, and the university, whatever its weaknesses, know that one will infiltrate the other. Both are highly charged political institutions and both are engaged in political battles.

The Latin American university faces new challenges for which its older structure does not adequately equip it. The Reform of 1918 sought to modernize the colonial university by wedding it with the Napoleonic educational innovations, thus helping it to deal with the issues of urban and mass society in the twentieth century. In their attempt to create a modern national university, the authors of the 1918 Reform showed they were aware of many of the problems of the twentieth century. What they did not see so clearly was that the university as an institution could not escape its political history; nor did they realize that expanding the social obligations of the university would time and again cause it to come into conflict with authoritarian governments.

III

One may examine the ways in which politics enters the university by looking at the leading actors inside, and also by viewing the university in relation to other institutions. The rector, as the title of the office implies, must give direction. Often he does so because he is beholden for his appointment to various ministers of the state, or because he is a person with political and ideological force of his own, or because he has won support inside the university among partisan factions of professors and students. The values of the rector are almost always ideological and partisan; he is not chosen simply for his managerial and administrative capabilities. He comes to the office because of his willingness either to keep the university subservient to the state or to maintain its antagonistic posture toward the state.

Professors are not wholly academic creatures; they retain only part-time posts in the university while performing other professional work on the outside. Teaching is a demanding exercise and monetarily an unrewarding one. The professor does receive compensations, however: he is considered a *maestro* or becomes one, revered and honored by students. Such reverence, however, often is accorded him not because of the incisive brilliance of his lectures but rather because of his ideological zeal and oratory. The professor as well as the intellectual must have the gift of the word; he must be a rhetorician, harking back to his scholastic forebears of the sixteenth and seventeenth centuries.

The Latin American intellectual is an ideologue and polemicist, and influences the university because of the reach of his ideas and the glitter of his prose and poetry. The *pensador* of the nineteenth century and the intellectual of the twentieth century write of the glories and unity of the Latin races, extolling the noble values and virtues of *"nuestra América."* They are beacons for a whole generation, whether that of 1898, 1918, or any other epochal year.

There are many examples of the *pensador* and the intellectual in Latin American history. The *pensador* was a figure primarily of the nineteenth century as the French *philosophe* was of the eighteenth, and the two shared similar attributes. Juan Montalvo, Manuel González Prada, José Martí, Rubén Darío, Justo Sierra, Víctor Raúl Haya de la Torre, and José Enrique Rodó are best classified as *pensadores* in the nineteenth-century mold although some lived into the present century. José Vasconcelos, Alfonso Reyes, Pablo Neruda, César Vallejo, José Carlos Mariátegui, Pablo González Casanova, Daniel Cosío Villegas, Gilberto Freyre, Jorge Amado, Carlos Fuentes, Gabriel García Márquez, and Alejo Carpentier, whatever their métiers, are better categorized as intellectuals. The intellectual today is a more professional critic of society than was the *pensador*. He is also more cosmopolitan, and his criticism is more widely read. Intellectuals do not always associate themselves with partisan callings as did the *pensadores*.

All wrote extensively, and virtually no subject was foreign to their pen. They addressed themselves to their generation and to the young of the next, exhorting them to fulfill their ideals and to found the perfect society. The fact that the Latin American *pensador* —and on occasion the intellectual—so often take the road of exile attests to the political force of their writings. Governments fear the effects of their hortatory presence on the internal political process and the influence of their voice upon student and professor partisanships.

Latin American intellectual history has been dominated by two basic attitudes toward the United States. One was represented by Domingo Faustino Sarmiento, who saw much in the United States to be emulated. The other and more enduring view was developed by José Enrique Rodó.

Rodó is well known for his parable *Ariel,* written in 1900. Laced with literary allusions from antiquity to the present, it is addressed to the nobler spirits of all future Latin American generations and not just Rodó's Uruguayan compatriots. Ariel, the ethereal sprite, Prospero's willing servant of civilization, epitomizes the purest essence of Latin America. Caliban, the brutish slave of his own impulses and the symbol of the materialism, imperialism, utilitarianism, and practicality Rodó associates with the United States. Rodó wanted to draw basic distinctions between two civilizations he saw as opposed to each other but forced to live together disharmoniously in the Western Hemisphere. He was afraid that Latin America might lose the unique values and purposes of its cultural inheritance and what it could contribute to western civilization, and noted its endangerment by the imperious sway of Anglo-Saxon America. As *pensador* and *maestro,* beacon of a generation, he took his mission to be literally a continental one; the task he assigned himself was pedagogic, missionary, grandiose, political, and idealistic all at the same time.

Rodó and some of the others already mentioned wrote between the Spanish-American War (1898) and the completion of the Panama Canal (1915). Today Latin American intellectuals have concerns as well as means of communication that did not exist fifty and seventy-five years ago. It is unlikely, however, that the United States will cease to be a prime object, an almost necessary ingredient, of their criticism. One may anticipate that in the last decades of this century, Latin American intellectuals will scrutinize U.S. policy on at least three crucial matters—the border with Mexico, the Panama Canal, and U.S. relations with Cuba.

The rector, the professor, the student, and the intellectual form an overlapping but not uniformly cooperative elite or series of elites. Whether they support or oppose one another and regardless of their relationship or lack of it with the state or church, peasant or labor groups, all four have an elite or superordinate view of their calling in society. Coming from an academic community, they are all more or less in favor of proclaiming a democratic society, but one in which they will maintain leadership positions and in which the masses will be led to enlightenment and enfranchisement. In most of Latin America, the members of the university community, in spite of the democratic declarations of the Reform of 1918, remain aloof and distant from the masses they want to lead. Academic experience does not give them the language of the masses, although the academics may articulate the needs of the masses and exercise the dialectics of revolution.

The irony here is that those who affirm the principles of democracy are scions of society's authoritarian elites. This irony is compounded when the academic leader or prominent intellectual, as shaper and guardian of the national ethos, develops the rationale used by the military to legitimize its control throughout so much of Latin America. Furthermore, where scientific progress and industrial modernization are the keystones of national development, the university, by insisting on its autonomy and by indulging partisan factions, becomes liable to the charge of being irresponsible and irrelevant in the pursuit of these goals.

IV

Since World War II, social scientists have redefined the world we live in and have given us such terms as "the atomic era," "the space age," "the post-industrial society," "the global village," "emergent nations" and "dependent economics," "ecosystems," "the population explosion," and "the end of ideology." Within this society, the university has become physically enlarged, a real city containing a large and heterogenous population, no longer possessed of its earlier medieval, communitarian solidarity. Especially in the developed countries, the university has tended to become a knowledge factory with many of the attributes of an industrial enterprise: the application of technology and managerial expertise, the production and distribution of knowledge, and a division of labor determined by a growing number of functions and specializations.

As the university grows, and becomes more diverse in its constituents and more diffuse in its purposes, so it will diverge from its function as a place for the accumulation, creation, and dissemination of knowledge and the formation of character. Already its learning constituency includes minority groups, consumers, and the growing population of the elderly. As it becomes increasingly interconnected with other universities and educational centers, such as U.N. agencies or specialized "think-tanks," it will grow more international in outlook, more cosmopolitan in personnel, and more dependent upon technology and managerial competence.

The worldwide student protests of the late 1960s and the early 1970s may be seen as responses to the depersonalization of the traditional and familiar ties binding the members of the university community together. A sense of alienation led to calls for greater "relevance" of the curriculum to improve the social order. Student protests of this kind could not have been generated in the university of fifty or even twenty-five years ago. The so-called "multiversity" was the unintended setting for the student discontent and protest.

It may have seemed that in the 1960s the universities in France, Germany, Japan, and the United States were being "Latin-Americanized" and that even the young leaders of the S.D.S. had read about the 1918 Reform. The earlier Latin American reformists were prescient in anticipating the "multiversity," in foreseeing the feelings of alienation, and in articulating demands for scholastic "relevance" and social activism. The Latin Americans, however, were operating in a university environment that was historically sensitive to the political climate and involved with it, whereas the S.D.S. leaders entered and left a university that was essentially apolitical.

The Latin American protest was directed against what was thought to be an inbred and inflexible institution at a time when flexibility and openness were needed. In the Latin American context, the student manifestos and demonstrations possessed a historical logic. The protests of the 1960s, in the United States anyway, were anguished and somewhat impertinent cries against an institution already deeply changed and largely apolitical.

Today, the 1960s student protest movement in the United States is largely defunct and university students are more concerned with improving their lot through a good education. As Martin Trow observed in a 1977 Carnegie report on changes in student and faculty attitudes between 1969 and 1975, the trend has been toward political moderation and economic self-advancement. It may be symbolic of the eclipse of academic radicalism that in the 1976 California race for U.S. Senate, it was S. I. Hayakawa, the representative of the traditional university and the grammarian who opposed the "free speech" movement, who won. The 1918 Reform, on the other hand, retains some of its permanence because its demand for changes in the university and society was issued within an entirely different political context.

Whether one looks at all universities in the world or only at the Latin American university, it is well to remember the historical limitations of the institution, as well as what changes in size and the introduction of technology portend. The university, anywhere, cannot be expected, as Prospero or Merlin, to produce solutions to abiding or immediate problems in society. Regardless of demands and changes pressing in from the outside, it will have to adhere to its traditional inheritance of educating—that is, providing basic knowledge for students, who will later become, one hopes, useful citizens. It is they, shaped by their university experience, who will solve—or not—the social and political problems of their generation. The university remains a special institution with particular educational functions and historical determinants beyond which it cannot safely go.

In order to perform its traditional functions and at the same time respond to society's needs, the university must retain a safe measure of institutional independence. Only then can it remain an acute critic of itself and society. It cannot be at odds with the state nor can it be a handmaiden to the state's momentary purposes. The vision the university has of society and man's role in it derives from accumulated past experience, and the university tends to be skeptical of progress, or at least to raise basic questions for responsible leaders to consider.

The Latin American university does not exist outside of these universal currents, although it develops and operates within a specific social, cultural, political, and economic environment. The purpose of this book is to describe the special institution that is the Latin American university and the particular place it holds in its society. The university will remain one of the basic institutions of Latin American society along with the church, the state, the family, and the military.

2

Origin and Philosophy of the Spanish American University

Mario Góngora

The New World received from Spain the state, the church, and the university, institutions reflecting the threefold medieval division of power into the temporal, the spiritual, and the academic. Of these, the state, over a period of four centuries, has been most subjected to a thorough process of "Americanization." The university is the institution that has retained to the largest degree the features of the medieval European model imported to the New World in the sixteenth century. Our concern here will be with the European—and especially Castilian—models from which the contemporary university of the Spanish-speaking countries in Latin America has derived.

Universities originated in the twelfth century, having evolved out of the monastic and the urban episcopal schools of earlier centuries. By 1100, courses of General Studies had developed, around which were grouped the basic divisions of "liberal learning"—as distinct from vocational or guild learning, which stressed proficiency in the mechanical trades. Philosophy, theology, law, and medicine were to stand for centuries as the pillars of higher education, resting on a foundation that was episcopal, municipal, royal, and papal. General Studies, however, represented only the intellectual pursuits of the university. To be complete, the university needed a structure, and this it acquired during the last years of the twelfth century as an autonomous corporation, conforming to the strong medieval trend of social corporatism. By 1230, it was firmly rooted in both Paris and Bologna, the two international universities of the Christian world and, for this reason, bound to the power of the Papacy.

Paris was prototypical of the university run by masters, the *universitas magistrorum,* in contrast with Bologna's largely student-controlled institution. Under the aegis of the Cathedral Council of Paris, the masters of arts and theology taught an international student body with a measure of freedom and autonomy, even though they were under the jurisdiction of a chancellor who served as a representative of ecclesiastical power. The university emancipated itself progressively from the control of the Cathedral Council after much strife and student brawling, but only did so with sustained and decisive support from the Pope. The Bull *Parens Scientiarum,* promulgated in 1231, defined the new corporation in such a way that the chancellor's authority would diminish as that of the masters increased. The masters organized themselves into faculties according to their scientific disciplines, while the students grouped themselves into "nations," depending upon their birthplace and language—or, more loosely, their ethnic background. Although at the beginning the rector was only the magistrate of the student nations, he soon became president, albeit with limited powers, of the whole institution. General Studies at Paris was the European center for the study of philosophy and theology throughout the thirteenth century.

The second university model, at Bologna, became the European capital for legal studies in the twelfth century. As such, doubtless owing to Spain's marked concern with the study and cultivation of the law, Bologna, rather than Paris, exerted the greater influence in Spain. Students came to Bologna from all over Europe. The "universities" or "nations" of students elected the rector and his counselors. The rector's authority was reflected in the fealty oath all the students swore to him, paralleling the practice of oath-taking between lords and vassals. Supported by the Pope, the students defended their autonomy against incursions by the City Council. The masters of law were under certain obligations to the City Council, and were aligned with it because the Council had brought them to Bologna. The bishop was represented by a chancellor. Because the students' movement for autonomy had the support of the Pope himself, none of these contending groups was able to frustrate it. Bologna, thus, was a model in which the word "university" clearly meant a corporation of students as against a collegium of masters and doctors.

Basic to the university was the corporate hierarchy of its members. Paralleling the masters, officials, and apprentices of the artisan guild were the university's masters of learning and their subordinate licentiates and bachelors. The bachelor was a qualified apprentice who had taken courses and passed examinations. The licentiate, although he held the license to teach, *licencia docendi*, which was the goal of his studies, committed himself to another two years of study under his master's tutelage to avoid the stigma of sloth. Thereafter, he received the title of Master of Arts, or Doctor of Theology, Law, or Medicine. It eventually became clear, however, that not all those who held the title of doctor could teach, but rather only those who were the titular occupants of chairs (*cátedra*). The nonteaching doctors were members of the university senate, but they were not *catedráticos*, holders of chairs, and, unlike them, drew no salary or other compensation.

In Castile and León, by the end of the twelfth century, courses of General Studies were offered at Palencia and Salamanca, universities founded by royal charter. Palencia went into an institutional decline by the middle of the thirteenth century; Salamanca, however, is much better known because of the preservation of the royal documents of 1243 and 1252–55. The violent struggles for autonomy observed elsewhere did not occur at Salamanca, although there were the inevitable altercations between students and townspeople. The King would establish and confirm universities, and the Pope would extend coveted privileges to them, such as that of teaching in other kingdoms, exclusive of Paris and Bologna. The royal documents (1254) speak of a *"universidad del estudio de Salamanca,"* which comprised all members of the university; but in 1282 there was reference to a *"universidad de los escolares,"* suggesting the predominance of the Bologna model. The *maestrescuela-canciller* ("headmaster-chancellor") represented the bishop of Salamanca, but the Pope gave the university its seals, symbolizing its autonomous powers. The financial power remained in the hands of the King, who paid the masters' salaries.

The Castilian conceptualization of the university was distilled in the great body of laws known as *Las Siete Partidas* (1256–65), compiled under the direction of Alfonso X, the Wise. Learning, it said, was "the coming together of masters and students in a given place with the intention and purpose of acquiring knowledge." The nature of General Studies was determined by the King and the more specialized subjects by the prelates or municipal authorities. Basic matters relating to the establishment of a university—such as the healthfulness of the site, the soil, the possibilities for recreation —were outlined. There was to be at least one master for every discipline. "Well and faithfully," *Las Siete Partidas* ruled, "must the masters display their knowledge to the students, reading to them and making them understand the books as best they can." Teaching, until the eighteenth century, meant "reading" the basic texts of European culture—the Bible, the Summas of St. Thomas Aquinas, the works of Aristotle, Justinian, Galen, and Avicenna—all of them in Latin, the medium of universal culture.

Las Siete Partidas authorized the students to organize councils and fraternities for the purpose of "advancing their studies and well-being" and to elect a superior of all called a "rector." Originally, the rector, as in Paris, was only the head of the student body, while the *maestrescuela-canciller* controlled the examinations and the granting of degrees. Though this university structure had a number of obvious parallels with Bologna's, papal was decidedly less than royal authority. The relative strength of kingly authority was in accord with medieval Castilian tradition, which made Spain unique among the great Christian states in its relations with the Papacy.

As further evidence of Bologna's influence, theology was not taught in Spain until 1355. Great emphasis was placed on the teaching of law, which was deemed more valuable than "that of any of the other sciences," according to *Las Siete Partidas*. The master of law enjoyed at the same time the title of *caballero*. From the thirteenth century on, the Castilian monarchy recognized, honored, and depended upon the *letrado*, the learned man of law.

In 1254, Alfonso the Wise made annual donations to Salamanca for the following masterships: one in law and two in Papal Decretals, 500 *maravedís* each; one specialized in the exegesis of Gratian's Decree for canonists, 300 *maravedís*; and in the Faculty of Philosophy, two in logic, 200 *maravedís* each. The King's purpose was to confer distinction on each of the schools. Two physicians taught medicine for 200 *maravedís*; the arts had two masters of grammar, each earning 200 *maravedís*; an organ master (in plain chant and music) received 50 *maravedís*. A bookseller and an apothecary rounded out the university's staff. In 1254, also, the King specified that a master of law was to have a bachelor at his side.

Salamanca was the principal university model in Castile. The Ecumenical Council of Vienna of 1312 named it along with Paris, Bologna, and Oxford as a place where Greek, Hebrew, Arabic, and Chaldean should be taught. Salamanca's prestige was reflected by the attention given to it by a number of popes. The famous Aragonese Benedict XIII reorganized the Faculty of Theology. Martin V issued a series of Bulls in 1421, requested by the university corporation itself, that sought to reform Salamanca, whose members were always desirous of maintaining its link with the Papacy and of enjoying the privilege of teaching anywhere in Christendom (*jus ubique docendi*).

The founding of Alcalá, endowed with university privileges in 1513, produced another model, of the collegiate type, that had its origins in Paris. Cardinal Cisneros's grand plan for San Ildefonso de Alcalá was conceived with the idea of improving ecclesiastical scholarship, and, indeed, ultimately, great distinction was achieved at Alcalá in Biblical and philosophical studies. Alcalá, with the town of San Ildefonso and a group of satellite colleges for poor students, was known for its concern with the scriptures, arts, and grammar.

All of the colleges had their own curricula and, in their best moments, provided the most cloistered life possible. There were openings or scholarships not only for students, but also for recent graduates and young masters. At each college, courses leading to a degree were offered by tutors (*pasantes*) or professors (*regentes*). At Alcalá, where college and university were identical, the collegians would elect a rector and his counselors from among themselves. Collegial autonomy was always somewhat limited by the office of a chancellor appointed by the archbishop of Toledo. The monastic style of life, inherent in the conception of these institutions, led to their development by the religious orders. First the Dominicans, and later the Jesuits, were active in founding colleges and subsequently in obtaining for them the rank of university. Such institutions, originally set up to aid poor students, were soon transformed into closed guilds, demanding of their entrants lineal purity (*limpieza de sangre*) and noble parents. The point of these requirements was to ensure as far as possible the purity of the faith and to shut out heresy. The unattached day student (*manteísta*) was ignored by and excluded from these guilds, which controlled university life. Later, under the Bourbons, university reform (1760–70) was in great part directed against the aristocratic colleges.[1]

The Indies received from Spain the idea of the European university, with its well-defined types of autonomous organization, its articulated structure of authority, and its system of degree-granting, curricula, and scholastic exercises. The university was one of the most enduring and socially prestigious European institutions brought to the New World.

The Formative Period: The Sixteenth Century

The first university in the Americas was founded by the Papal Bull of 1538, requested by the Dominicans living on the island of Hispaniola. Organized as a pontifical university, it was located in the city of Santo Domingo. The Dominicans had had the means of teaching their novices for some twenty years but did not possess the right of graduating them. They wanted to establish a university along the lines of Alcalá and Salamanca, with the same privileges and immunities enjoyed by those institutions. (Valladolid, the other great Castilian university, is rarely mentioned as a model in Spanish America.) Four doctors appointed jointly by the Dominican prior and the rector were authorized to grant degrees to individuals who had taken courses and passed examinations. Permanent doctors of the university—and this title could be held only by those graduated from it—and *catedráticos*, the principal constituents of the university, could come from anywhere. The reason behind requesting such a privilege was that while men came to the island from many varied places to trade or to reside, Hispaniola was a remote place to send one's sons, an area *"totalmente ignara en las letras sagradas."* The natives had to be indoctrinated in the Christian faith, and for this task a goodly number of properly trained ecclesiastics was needed. Santo Domingo would have more "honor" if it had a full-fledged university with all its appurtenances. Pope Paul III, when he approved the petition to set up a university, had yet another reason in mind: he recognized that the clerics would find a fair compensation for their efforts in academic honors and prizes made available by the university.[2]

Around 1550, when Inspector-General (*visitador*) Tomás López was in Guatemala, he drew up a rough plan for a university. This document, recently discovered by the French scholar Marcel Bataillon, sheds new light upon the founding of universities after the turbulent period of conquest had ended and the time of imperial stabilization had begun. The plan's basic objective was to create missionaries who would convert the Indians. The university was to train them first in Latin grammar, then in logic (uncontaminated by sophistry), the Holy Scripture, and basic theology, free of scholastic disputations. In addition, judges of the *audiencia* might read some Canon Law to them. Apparently, those young Creoles not destined for a church career could study grammar, and furthermore, some Spanish physicians were there to teach them medicine. Seemingly, López had absorbed some of the humanistic thought of Erasmus and the reformers of Charles V as well as their ideals of an antimedieval and antischolastic Christianity.

Of equal interest is the plan's silence on the teaching of Civil Law and the training of lawyers, despite the fact that this was a common concern among the Creoles. (There is a curious tendency among Spanish reformers to avoid criticism of the law and its practitioners.)[3] Shortly after López's *visita*, the Augustinian Fray Alonso de la Veracruz, in his *Dialéctica* of 1554, gave a critical review of the newly founded University of Mexico. As a professor of the university, he denounced the superfluities of logic and dialectics. A new land, he implied, should be an appropriate setting for a renovation of faith and education.

The Dominicans were in control of educational affairs in Lima after 1548, directing a college with a chair in grammar. The *cabildo* of Lima petitioned for the establishment of a school of General Studies in 1550 because of the city's enormous distance from Spain. A royal university was founded in 1551 on the site of the Dominican college and was closely tied to the convent. When Viceroy Francisco de Toledo arrived in Peru and restructured the royal university, he justified this undertaking with the claim that it would provide the training of both the clerics, who would proselytize the Indians, and the prebends, who would work in the

Spanish cities with a bishopric and a cathedral. By this means it would also be possible to reward the conquistadors' descendants with a broader repertory of offices. This was to be decisive in the development of a higher bureaucracy of the Spanish Empire: legal studies would produce competent lawyers to serve in judicial offices; theological and canonical studies would produce the needed ecclesiastic personnel. Both branches of the bureaucracy —judicial and ecclesiastical—were filled by drawing upon the aristocratic families who claimed to be the descendants of the conquistadors and the early settlers.

The reasons adduced for the founding of universities were almost invariably of a practical sort: remoteness from peninsular universities or from others in the Indies; the need to train a ruling professional class for the Creole church and state; urban population growth and its consequent needs; and conversion of the Indians. As will be seen, however, these practical reasons did not imply any really utilitarian approach to teaching itself.

From the very first, the royal university was distinguished from the pontifical university, even though both insignias could adorn the same institution. The first University of Santo Domingo was Dominican; yet municipal governments and church officials were petitioning for a royal university so that "the sons of those who have come here," as the resident Bishop Fuenleal said in 1529, "would find masters in all the disciplines." Or as Hernando de Gorjón, a prominent citizen, said in 1537, on leaving a substantial legacy to implement his wishes: "All fields of knowledge necessary to the preservation and diffusion of our holy Catholic faith be taught without charge." In 1550 this grant was officially received and eight years later dispensed in accord with the statutes of Salamanca. In Mexico City, which had a Dominican college for the arts and theology, all the authorities from 1530 on recognized the need for a university. Bishop Zumárraga stressed one purpose of the university: its competence to render judgments on intricate and knotty matters affecting the Indians. "Each day brings more and more complex problems," he complained, "and there is no university to which one can turn; the ones in the Indies are so far away that before we can receive information from them on a given matter we might well have made a mistake in our duty." A group of Dominican friars wrote to Charles V asking for a university, saying that "if everything always has to come from Spain, the situation is harmful and is becoming insufferable." Nevertheless, it took until 1551 for the incorporating charter to arrive.[4]

These founding charters extended the privileges enjoyed by Salamanca, with two important qualifications quite in tune with the strong absolutist tendency of the sixteenth-century monarchy: autonomy was not immediately conceded to the university; nor was the institution exempted from paying taxes or other tributes (*pechos*). On the latter point, it is interesting to observe that the exemptions enjoyed by the Spanish subjects living in the Indies were then so broad that the failure to make the graduates of the university tax-exempt had no practical significance.

It was not long before the universities won their autonomy. In 1562 the University of Mexico succeeded in this endeavor. In 1582 an official order (*cédula*) approved a viceregal request from Lima for control over masters and students. Subsequently, the *Recopilación de Leyes de los Reynos de las Indias* contained a summary of the orders from 1587 to 1589 limiting the authority of the rector. Reference was made to offenses committed within the university as long as they were not major crimes; reference was made also to matters concerning studies, even if outside the premises of the university (such as squabbles over a scholastic controversy or a dispute over the payment of board). The rector could take disciplinary action in cases of student excesses and impose punishment on those *catedráticos* and doctors who violated university rules and ordinances. In the case of a major offense, the rector's jurisdiction was limited to the preparation of a brief and remand of the transgressor to the civil authorities. Apart from such cases, members of the university did not have broader personal freedoms (*fueros*) than nonmembers. For instance, if a *catedrático* committed an offense not related to the business of the university corporation, and if it happened beyond the university's physical limits, he was subject to regular court procedures. In any event, the authority of the rector (and not that of the headmaster or the chancellor, as in Castile) was one of the key elements in the autonomy of the university. Another key element, as in Salamanca, was the university's authority to formulate its own rules and to enforce them fully.

The precise delimitation of royal authority, of the *patronato real*, over the university had posed problems from the very beginning and especially so in Lima, where the royal university was housed in the quarters of a Dominican college and its convent. The college was at least partially endowed with funds supplied by the royal treasury. The monks oversaw the election of the rector and the *catedráticos* (amid continuing difficulties in marking out the boundaries between convent and university). Nevertheless, the university gradually extended its prerogatives in teaching by establishing new chairs. Francisco de Toledo, in justifying the charters he issued in 1571, which sought to end the overlap with the Dominican convent and college, wrote in the same year to Spain:

> It is not appropriate for Your Majesty to found a university in a monastery whose clerics would be distracted by it and I am not sure that they profit from doing things which are not strictly related to their profession, such as the study of Law, Medicine, Grammar, and other branches of Learning. Their practical training and education in Theology are sufficient as means and end of their profession, which is to enlighten and save souls. I am persuaded that it is better for universities to be separate and not under the auspices of any monastery, as are the universities in Spain and, I think, in the rest of the world.

Toledo issued such a decree, physically separating the monastery from the university, even though "controversy and passion were aroused over the matter."[5] Thus, the University of San Marcos was born and formally opened in 1574. None of this interfered with bringing before the Pope a measure designed to sanction the status of the already established royal institutions. One of the basic requirements of the charters of 1571 was that the rector not be a cleric. In the following decade, under the Count of Villar, a provision was added stipulating that the rectorship alternate yearly between regular and secular ecclesiastics—between the ordained and the unordained. The contest for power in the colonial period was not so much between church and state, as it was in the nineteenth century, but rather between the state and the religious orders. The latter were as anxious to assert themselves against regal prerogatives as against the established church order, and quite frequently this assertion was directed mainly against the church establishment itself.

A much more persistent conflict, both in Mexico City and Lima, was the one between the Jesuits and the university—a conflict that surfaced in Chile in the middle of the eighteenth century. It was toward the end of the sixteenth century that the Jesuits reached the apex of their activity in the church and Catholic countries. In Lima they had founded the College of St. Martin to train young lay students and secular ecclesiastics. The founding of the royal university there as in Mexico City raised the problem of the validity of the college's courses as against those offered by the university. This dispute did not arise with the other religious orders, which by and large restricted themselves to the education of their novitiates. Because of the long-drawn-out dispute in Lima, we know that in 1578 Francisco de Toledo finally directed that all students take their courses in the university. And from then on, this was the policy of the university. The Jesuits, however, defended their right to continue giving, in their college, courses in grammar and rhetoric, aboriginal languages (which allowed them to control the training given to those priests who would proselytize the Indians), art, and moral philosophy. They tried to mitigate the university's opposition by scheduling their classes in such a way as to avoid conflict with it. Furthermore, they saw to it that such activities as public debates, examinations, and theatrical performances—in their view, basic elements in the educational scheme of things could be practiced in the college as well.

The compromise settlement proposed by the Council of the Indies in 1604 authorized the Society of Jesus to give courses in grammar and rhetoric and literary exegesis, in all of which the Jesuits had unquestioned and unrivaled competence. These courses were considered minor disciplines within the university curriculum. The students were to matriculate in the university, although the classes might be given in the college. The chair in the arts was freely assigned to the Society of Jesus, but it was located in the university. The Jesuits, however, were unyielding in their demands. In 1608 and 1610, with the support of the viceroy and the archbishop, the Jesuits were still insisting that their demands to teach art and theology at different hours from the university be fully met. Here was an interminable conflict between contending powers over the right to educate.[6]

Courses of Study

The inspection tour (*visita*) of the University of Lima,[7] conducted by Dr. Arteaga Mandiola in 1581–82, casts some light on
the state of studies in the Indies toward the end of the sixteenth
century. There were chairs in grammar, the arts, basic and
advanced theology, sacred scriptures, the philosophy of St. Thomas
Aquinas (given without charge by the Dominicans), basic and
advanced law, canon law and Decretals, and finally the study of
Quechua, the language of the Incas. There was no one to teach
medicine (as required by the university statutes), nor was there any
demand for it by the students. In 1589, shortly after this *visita*,
other courses were added, including, in the Faculty of Law, the
Institutes (a digest of civil law); and in the Faculty of Canon Law,
Commentaries. The courses given were determined annually by the
rector on the basis of requests submitted by the students. The
courses in grammar were based on the *Exercitatio Linguae Latinae*
of the great humanist, Juan Luis Vives.[8] In other parts of the Indies,
the basic Latin text was the *Arte de la Lengua Latina* of Antonio de
Nebrija.

In the arts, so we are told by a Mercedarian occupant of a chair,
it took three years to complete a course of studies, covering the
Súmulas (a compendium of logic), logic and philosophy, using
Domingo de Soto's work as the required text. De Soto was an
eminent Dominican theologian who had written several *Summulae
Logicales* and a commentary on Aristotle's *Dialectics* that appeared
in many editions. Owing to his close relationship with the order, de
Soto's books were employed as manuals for the first two years of
instruction. In the third year there were lectures on physics, the
heavens and the earth, growth and decay, the soul, and metaphysics, as was generally the case in the educational system.

Many students of civil and canon law willingly participated in
the review of university affairs conducted by Dr. Arteaga Mandiola. He asked them if the professors merely repeated their
lectures, whether they gave them in Latin or in Spanish, whether
they were there in person or had somebody substitute for them, and
how much time they spent with their students. From the answers
given, it appears that the *catedráticos de Prima*, the professors who
worked in the morning, lectured for one and a half hours, and

catedráticos de Vísperas, those who held class in the afternoon, lectured for one hour. The courses in law were organized around specific subjects derived from the *Corpus Iuris Civilis:* for example, in one year, Interdicts, Evidences, and Last Will and Testament. In canon law, the subjects dealt with sections in the Papal Decretals, and the Institutes were given by the *catedrático* as basic instruction.

Arteaga's study indicated that the professors would "present the case in Latin and, after making a commentary on the text and drawing conclusions from it, they would then frequently spend time on learned theories in such a way as to elaborate on these and other texts and commentaries." If a student signaled for repetition, the professors would repeat the matter in question. They would lecture in Latin, but give examples in Spanish. One of the student respondents stated that the professors—after having presented the case, explained the fundamentals, and noted several pertinent things on the subject matter—would send the students to study the works of the scholars who had written about it. A number of students asked that a chair in the Institutes be established to offer introductory instruction. In 1589 such a chair was founded at San Marcos.

If one can judge from the students' answers, the emphasis on textual study of legal glosses in Lima seems to have been very strong, although reference was made to the important commentators. The chair in scriptural studies had just been vacated by the famous Jesuit scholar José de Acosta. Theology was taught in the morning session by the Dominican friar Bartolomé de Ledesma, who stated that he used Book III of Peter Lombard's *Sentences* to comment on Part III of St. Thomas's *Summa* (Lombard was also used as the guide at Salamanca). The afternoon session was conducted by an Augustinian friar who discussed the *Secunda Secundae* of St. Thomas.

If the records of Arteaga's *visita* give us an accurate picture of the situation in Lima, the textbooks published by the professors at the University of Mexico suggest the caliber of teaching there. Aside from the works of Alonso de la Veracruz, the most widely used texts were those written by the Jesuit Antonio Rubio, especially his commentaries on Aristotle's *Dialectics,* first published in 1605 and reissued several times until 1615. He was also known for his commentaries on Aristotelian physics and psychology.[9]

The Statutes of the University

The texts of the statutes and ordinances of San Marcos (1581), and those drawn up by Bishop Palafox for the University of Mexico in 1645, were widely used during the colonial period as models for other universities.

In Spanish America, the authority of the *maestrescuela-canciller* as the bishop's representative was virtually nil, although his presence was necessary when degrees were conferred, to symbolize his jurisdiction in all Spanish royal universities. The real power in university affairs was vested in the rector. The rector and the counselors (*consiliarios*), who assisted him in governing the university, were elected annually by the *claustro*, the corporate academic community, at Lima; in Mexico City, the rector was elected by the counselors. The *claustro pleno* was made up of the doctors, the licentiates, and the masters of arts who had graduated from the university or whose degrees entitled them to teach there. According to the medieval concept of the corporation, the nucleus and motor force of the university were the graduates, for upon them had been conferred a virtually sacrosanct degree that allowed them to transmit knowledge to others.

The *catedráticos* were salaried functionaries, but they were not members of the *claustro* unless they were graduates of the university, and even in this case, at least in Lima, they were not eligible for election as rector. The doctors and other graduates, beyond their active and passive voting rights, received financial remuneration from the recently matriculated students. There were four counselors in Lima and eight in Mexico City. Half of them were doctors and masters. In Lima, the other half were students who had just received their bachelor's degrees. In Mexico City, of the other half, one of the counselors was a master of arts (a rank always somewhat inferior to the other major degrees) and the other three were recent recipients of the bachelor's degree. Thus, through the council the students participated in governing the university, but the rector had to be a member of the *claustro;* he was not, as in the "more democratic times" of the Middle Ages, a student. The annual rotation of the rectorship between the laymen and the secular ecclesiastics was practiced everywhere.

An important and highly regulated aspect of the university statutes was the one covering the institution of *cátedras*. Once an announcement of the terms for filling a chair had been made, the process would begin with a public disputation (*concurso de oposición*) and end with a vote. Doctors, masters, licentiates, bachelors, and students of the respective *facultad*—provided that they had twelve years of grammar and fourteen years of study in other *facultades*—participated in the competition. The votes of the students and the bachelors were not counted individually, but computed and evaluated according to a set of complex rules. In any event, student participation was noteworthy, and by the seventeenth century it had become turbulent and colorful, with the students forming voting blocs (*caudrillas de votos,* as they were called in Palafox's *Ordenanzas,* which sought to prevent them). The examination or oral testing, which preceded the actual voting, consisted of reading a passage, selected at random, from one of the great writers of western civilization (Justinian, Thomas, and so on) and responding to questions put by the examiners. Occupying a *cátedra* was independent from the possession of higher degrees in such a way that even a bachelor could hold one, provided that within a two-year period he would earn his licentiate and doctoral degrees.

Some of the most important articles in university statutes dealt with academic degrees, the prerequisites for entering upon a course of higher studies, and the procedure for final examinations. The normal curriculum, after three years of grammar (or four years, if one studied rhetoric), included a three-year program of study in the arts. The bachelor's degree in the minor *facultad* was awarded at a public ceremony in which the candidates had to prove themselves apt in the handling of textual interpretations and in responding to the arguments presented by the examining doctors. From this point on, the student could elect to work in one of the major *facultades* of theology, civil law, canon law, and medicine. He could spend four or five years in any one of them before receiving the bachelor's degree if he had submitted to a similar procedure of presenting a thesis and taking an oral examination.

It took three or four years to obtain the licentiate degree, serving either as a teaching assistant (*pasante*) or submitting to a public examination in order to prove one's competence for the degree. The degree was awarded in a solemn academic ceremony that included a long exercise in questioning and answering, the *pique de puntos;* the purpose was to discover the theoretical niceties and required the candidate to produce a defense of those subtleties within twenty-four hours. The granting of the doctor's degree took place in a comparable setting but was more purely a ceremonial function.

In the *facultad* of arts, the equivalent degree was that of a master's. The early medieval influence was revealed in the long and involved rules, analogous to the requirement of producing a masterpiece in order to become a guild member, which even included a session of ridicule and tease, the *vejamen.*

The graduation fees, the gratuities given to the examiners and their assistants, and the *de rigueur* festivities made academic life rather costly and constituted outright economic discrimination against the many who could not afford it. The colleges already were exacting a heavy tuition fee, although some scholarships were available. Black slaves, and Indians tributaries of an encomienda, could not attend, although, at least in principle, all who were nominally free could be admitted. In 1577, Bishop Lertundo of Cuzco asked that freed Indians, mestizos, negroes, and mulattoes be admitted to the study of grammar and the arts, leaving the other *facultades* for the scions of the affluent. It was possible, at least in the beginning, for a few nonwhite students to gain admission, but as the process of *mestizaje* accelerated, proof of *limpieza de sangre* was increasingly demanded in the university as in so many other colonial corporate organizations of the seventeenth and eighteenth centuries. John Tate Lanning mentions as a rarity one such graduate in canon law at the university in Guatemala in 1803.[10]

Not only among the students but also among the graduates there were differences in rank. For example, the masters of arts and the doctors of medicine could not become rector at the University of Mexico. In Lima, however, the masters of arts could become rector if they were priests, bachelors of theology, and over thirty years of age. The courses in aboriginal languages were obligatory for the proselytizing priests, but they did not lead to any degree.

1600–1767: The Importance of the Religious Orders in Colleges and Universities

During the century and a half before the expulsion of the Jesuits, royal universities were founded in Guatemala (1676); Guamanga

(1677); Cuzco (1692), previously a seminary; Caracas (1725) and Havana (1728), formerly Dominican universities; and Santiago de Chile (1738). Santiago de Chile had Dominican and Jesuit universities in the seventeenth century. But a request was made in 1713 for the founding of a royal university, governed by the *Leyes de Indias* and the Charters of Lima, with the rectorship alternating between laymen and secular clerics, for the purpose of training lawyers, who until then had gone to Lima or Caracas for their education. The petitioners claimed that the presence of university *cátedras* would be an added stimulus to the jurists and the clerics resident in Santiago.[11]

From 1600 to 1767, the Dominicans and Jesuits—and to a minor degree the Augustinians, Franciscans, and Mercedarians—deployed their energies primarily in the populated capitals. Not only did they teach grammar, the arts, and theology, but the last two *facultades* enjoyed the privilege of granting degrees, with the bishop acting as chancellor, in colleges at least two hundred miles from the nearest established universities.

The Bulls and royal edicts for the Dominicans and Jesuits were promulgated in 1621 and 1622 respectively. The courses were attended by secular clerics and young lay students. The Jesuits segregated the resident and nonresident novitiates. The main goal of these colleges was to attain the right to teach civil law, canon law, and medicine, as the Dominicans had succeeded in doing in 1652 at the Colegio del Rosario in Bogotá. In this, they surpassed the Jesuits in academic appeal for young lay students, because the Jesuits had to be content with teaching only grammar, the arts, and theology at San Bartolomé. At Quito in 1683, the Dominicans founded the Colegio de San Fernando, intended for the instruction of lay students in the same subjects offered at San Bartolomé. By 1692, they had managed to round out their teaching program and offered a full university curriculum, but only after a long rivalry with the Jesuits, who had their Seminario de San Luis at Quito. Having colleges with lay students enabled the order to broaden its recruitment for its convents and, at the same time, to enhance its power and popularity among key social groups.

Time and again the great doctrinal dispute of the epoch resounded over the local quarreling among the orders. From Quito, the Dominican friar Juan Mantilla de los Ríos wrote in 1681 to a coreligionist that he had in his hand the text of deviant statements of backsliders recently condemned in Rome, and that he anticipated preaching from the pulpit against the Jesuits who "had corrupted the conscience of the faithful."[12]

There were rivalries among the orders not only in the colleges, but also within the precincts of the royal universities. The accommodation arrived at was to establish free *cátedras* granted to each order, a sort of pluralistic arrangement that permitted the Dominicans to teach Thomas, the Franciscans Duns Scotus, and the Jesuits Francisco de Suárez. The principal orders, together with their masters, students, and followers, formed power groups in the big royal universities. On the other hand, the pontifical universities founded in colleges could insure doctrinal unity. This explains the specific concern shown in the founding of the Dominican universities in Bogotá, Quito, Santiago de Chile, Santo Domingo, Manila, Havana, and Caracas, and of the Jesuit universities located in Bogotá, Santiago de Chile, Córdoba, Caracas, Santo Domingo, and elsewhere. Sometimes it was not the orders themselves that founded universities; the bishops were known subsequently to have assigned the institution to a given order (as was the case in Córdoba with Bishop Trejo, and in San Bartolomé de Bogotá, which was assigned to the Jesuits).

The royal universities continued to defend themselves zealously *vis-à-vis* the religious orders. In Havana, for example, when the university founded by the Dominicans in 1722 was converted into a royal university in 1728, the Dominicans sought to retain control of it against the protestations (contained in a lengthy memorial to the King) of Rector Diego Rubí de Celis, who was himself a priest in Havana. The university, he wrote, was "a common property serving the public purposes of both the religious and secular inhabitants of the city of Havana and of the island of Cuba." The priests had proceeded on their own initiative in removing professors. The King, according to Rubí de Celis, could establish universities without the consent of the Pope, whose role was that of cosponsor in setting aside prebends for graduates and in validating the degrees. The university, he went on, was not anything clerical but a "*facultad* to award those who study there and to license them to teach;" it was a lay affair, although the ecclesiastics living there had certain personal privileges. The rector was to be elected by the *claustro* and not by the prelates of the order.[13]

In Santiago de Chile, when the royal university of San Felipe began to function around 1758, a conflict developed with the

Jesuits, who attempted to maintain degree-granting authority at the Colegio Convictorio de San Francisco Javier. The writings of Rector José Valeriano de Ahumada were full of vitriol and contained only slightly veiled allusions to the laxness of the Jesuits. To be sure, we are approaching the fateful year of the expulsion of the Society (1767).[14] This conflict parallels the conflict of a century and a half earlier at the University of San Marcos.

The colleges, with their handful of aristocrats and scions of the well-to-do, were the most important formative centers in the educational life of the colonial period. Only those who could go on to the doctorate were graduated, thus excluding the sons of the artisans and the *castas* (mulattoes, mestizos, and quadroons). Only the day students (*manteístas*) attended the university. The seminaries, on the other hand, could take in students of modest means, mere candidates for the priesthood, and some lay students.

The 1683 statutes of a Dominican college, the University of San Fernando de Quito, give us an idea of the organization of comparable institutions. There were only seven ecclesiastics, five *catedráticos*, the rector, and vice-rector. The *catedrático* of the *prima de teología* was chosen from among his peers to be the dean of studies. The collegians had uniforms and insignias. They paid a fee of eighty pesos annually. The religious exercise included a daily Mass after arising at four in the morning, a half-hour of meditation, thanksgiving, the progression of the seven Holy Sacraments, confession, and communion every two weeks and during the major festivals and holidays. On Thursday afternoon they would have time off and go to the countryside. In addition, they had three other holidays and the long summer vacation.

Discipline was strict and there was a pillory in the college. Meals were taken at eleven in the morning and at seven in the evening; there was a recess from seven to eight, followed by an hour of study in the cells, and bedtime at nine. Classes were given by professors and lecturers from seven-thirty, beginning with a half-hour of grammar and continuing with the other courses until eleven, and then in the afternoon from three to five. Within this schedule there were lectures in which a student defended his thesis and others challenged points contained in it. On Friday afternoons, there was a major lecture during which the *catedráticos* presented a similar display of erudite skills and wit.

When a college was not part of a university (because a royal

university already existed nearby), the way of life would lose some
of its cloisterlike atmosphere. Thus, when the Universidad de San
Felipe was founded in Santiago de Chile, there were classes for two
months at the end of the year at the university, which both lay and
clerical students attended. Furthermore, the daily lectures, the
public defenses, and the presentation of one's thesis to qualify for
graduation all took place on the university's premises and the
collegians in a body were obliged to attend. In such *facultades* as
medicine, courses were only offered in the university itself, and so
students pursuing this course of study could not become members
of a college.

Colonial education included scholastic-type disputations that
aimed at sharpening the intellect. The thesis and the various forms
of interrogation of the candidates for the licentiate and other
degrees were printed at the expense of the candidate himself.
While this system served the ends of dialectical (or scholastic)
education, it also allowed for intellectual showing-off, flights of
fancy, and mental acrobatics. The Jesuits were the undisputed
masters of this educational formula—the others were merely
imitators.

The Jesuits excelled especially in Latin studies. Far from limiting
themselves to grammar (which included the three levels of
elementary, intermediate, and advanced), they generally added
rhetoric to their curriculum. In Bogotá, rhetoric was studied for
two years and comprised Horace's poetry, the great orators,
literary forms, and composition. This, at least, was the ideal
program; there were many instances, however, in which fathers
could see their sons at the age of ten promoted to the *facultad* of
the arts after having studied only grammar. The rhetoric notes that
have been preserved at the Convictorio de San Francisco Javier in
Santiago de Chile show a series of short poems composed as a drill;
themes of secular and mythological history; the lives of Jesuit
saints; common poetical phrases arranged alphabetically; and short
theatrical pieces—all of which were copies of materials written by
the Jesuits in Brussels between 1653 and 1654 and used in Chile.
Assessing the results within New Granada, a province in which the
Jesuit influence was very extensive, Rivas Sacconi observed that
Latin had become an academic but not a conversational language.[15]

Dictation was one of the important exercises of the university and collegiate system because it insured the orthodoxy of opinions with regard to official instructions of the order. In addition, the procedure was indispensable, given the scarcity of printed texts, particularly in the poorer regions of the Spanish Empire. In order to prove that they had attended the courses, the graduates had to have their notebooks with them, signed by a professor.

In summary, the century-and-a-half period 1600–1767 was one of ideological diffusion rather than intellectual creativity. The leading Creole classes needed the university and this was a socially decisive factor. A formalistic and dialectical intellectual style became rooted in the main professions; it had been developed by a habitual use of disputation and led to an intellectual disposition both scholastic and legalistic.

Apart from the numerical increase of *cátedras* in the different *facultades*, the seventeenth century witnessed the introduction of still other chairs, marking something of an educational innovation. To the study of theology and scholastics were added moral theology and ethics (*casos de conciencia*). This illustrated a trend toward a practical consideration of matters of personal conduct and daily life that were to be taken up by the casuists and would influence social relations. Again, the Jesuits were to show their brilliance in this exercise of mind.

Medicine, as a professional course of study, became more elaborate and formal. Lima, which had disparaged the importance of medicine in the preceding century, introduced morning and afternoon classes under the prodding of the Viceroy Count Chinchón. In Mexico we see a similar process at work: along with anatomy and surgery, Palafox's statutes of 1645 refer to the usefulness of teaching methodology.

In the seventeenth century, mathematics was introduced as a course of study. It had been developed by the Jesuits toward the end of the sixteenth century at the Imperial College in Madrid. In accordance with Palafox's statutes, we find a *cátedra* in mathematics and astronomy at the University of Mexico, and in 1672, the famous scholar Carlos de Sigüenza y Góngora held the chair. The same chair was established in Lima by Viceroy Alba de Liste. In the colonies in the seventeenth century, these subjects were of interest mainly because of their relationship to the study and practice of navigation.

The manner in which *cátedras* were established gave rise, both in

Spain and in the Indies, to all sorts of student maneuvers and riots. In Spain, the Conde Duque de Olivares did away altogether with student participation. For the New World, a Royal Edict of 1676 stipulated that the competitors for the *cátedra* be selected by a committee made up of the archbishop (in the case of Lima and Mexico City), the chief justice (*oidor decano*) of the *audiencia*, the *maestre-escuela*, the dean of cathedral, the *cátedratico* who taught the morning classes in the *facultad* where the vacancy occurred, and the most senior doctor of the same *facultad* (*Recopilación* I. 22, 40). This rule was followed henceforth in Mexico, Guatemala, Caracas, and elsewhere. But, in Lima and those universities, such as Chile, governed by statutes derived from San Marcos, the original and more democratic electoral right was upheld, because the doctors refused to accept a regime that in any way would curtail their power or importance. An edict of 1684 and especially another of 1687 placed the decision-making power entirely in the hands of the masters and doctors of the respective *facultad* together with a limited number of students who were taken at random from the three colleges in Lima and from among the *manteístas*.[16]

The guild outlook of the universities became most obvious when they felt their monopolistic hold over the students of a region threatened. When it came to setting up universities at Quito and Charcas in the 1620s, recourse was made to León Pinelo's *Por la Real Universidad y los Estudios Generales de San Marcos*. Other defenders of the Lima model would argue that "by going to the city of Lima, the students' intellect was awakened and sharpened, leaving behind the timidity and provinciality of small town life. They learned how to argue urbanely about political matters, and they were weaned from the vices and the peculiar ways of speech of the Indians among whom most of the socially important people had been raised."[17] The *catedráticos* of the proud, even haughty, University of San Marcos were to defend with equal zeal the claims of the Creoles for ecclesiastical and judicial offices, since they were graduates of the faculties of San Marcos.

The social advantage for which academic honors were sought was shown in a less dignified light in the frequent requests for dispensations from courses for the purpose of getting through them as rapidly as possible. These dispensations were liberally granted by viceroys, governors,and rectors; this partly explains the extreme youth of many of the university graduates and also tells us much about the realities of teaching in the colonies.

1767–1810: The Catholic Enlightenment and the Intellectual Reformers

While the expulsion of the Jesuits in 1767 left an enormous vacuum in the educational world, at the same time it caused a spate of ideas and plans concerning higher education both in Spain and in her American colonies. In many instances they came from the same sources and sometimes even the same author. The plans for the universities of Salamanca and Alcalá, the Royal Institute of San Isidro and the Seminary of Nobles in Madrid, as well as the educational programs of the Franciscans drawn up by Commissioner General Fray Manuel María Trujillo in 1786, were all models that inspired reform projects for universities, colleges, seminaries, and novitiates in the New World. The intellectual contacts between the mother country and the colonies showed themselves strongest in the declining decades of the Empire. In addition, the growth in transatlantic trade during the eighteenth century led to an increase in the number of Spanish books available. The naturalist José Celestino Mutis wrote in 1802 that the new program of studies at the colleges in Bogotá had been shaped "according to Spanish ideas for the university," and that it would not be possible to return to the older forms; the youth of the land could no longer be enticed to follow them "as long as there was a free and open interchange with the mother country and with the learned world at large."

The ideas transmitted by the Spanish Enlightenment, whether by means of the free flow of literature or the several reform plans adopted under the aegis of Pedro Rodríguez de Campomanes, did not originate in Spain. The Iberian peninsula had become a disciple of the rest of Europe. The intellectual movement that began with Benito Gerónimo Feijóo, the Benedictine monk, in the 1730s, and came to fruition with Count Campomanes, could be called "the Catholic Enlightenment," analogous to the broader European trend that manifested itself in other countries in the course of the century—in the Italian and German principalities, Austria-Bohemia, and Portugal—and whose earliest roots were in seventeenth-century France. An eclectic philosophy, the knowledge and applications of the new science, a nonbaroque religious culture inclined toward moralism and fundamentalism, an anti-papal Gallicanism, a renewed belief in natural law—all these particulars characterized the Catholic Enlightenment, which was both Spanish and European. These ideas were readily diffused through the American universities by the literary circles that put out the gazettes and journals in the last decades of the colonial period.

It was in this climate of opinion that the academic reformers appeared.[18] The social position of the reformers, of course, was related to their advocacy of change. Among the ecclesiastics, who provided the main contingent of the Catholic Enlightenment, we might identify the following: the *modern Jesuits* of Mexico City, Quito, and the River Plate Basin who were interested, especially in the years just prior to the edict of expulsion, in the new sciences; the *oratoriano* of New Spain, Benito Gamarra; the Franciscan Goicoechea in Guatemala; José Antonio Caballero in Cuba; José Celestino Mutis and the Viceroy Caballero y Góngora in New Granada; Bishop Pérez Calama in Quito (formerly a canon in Puebla whose works inspired Miguel Hidalgo); Toribio Rodríguez de Mendoza and Isidoro de Celis in Lima; Canon Maciel in Buenos Aires; and Deán Gregorio Funes in Córdoba. Among the *modern judges* of the *audiencia* and the men of law we might cite Prosecutor Moreno y Escadón in Bogotá; Judge Ambrosio Cerdán y Pontero in Lima; Judge Villaurrutia in Guatemala; José Baquíjano in Lima, and Juan Egaña in Chile. Among the *modern medical doctors* one would have to include Narciso Esparragosa in Guatemala and Hipólito Unánue in Peru. A special place among these names must be accorded to the successful physician Francisco Javier de Santa Cruz y Espejo, a mestizo, in Quito, who was involved in the religious controversies, the author of a plan of General Studies, and hence known as "Modern Lucian of Quito." Deeply influenced by the Portuguese author Luís Antônio Verney, Espejo was more a manufacturer of plans and schemes than a reformer. Unlike this exceptional product of mestizo society, ambitious as he was to become a member of high society, most of the physicians belonged to the same social and professional groups that had governed the university and the principal institutions of the earlier period. On occasion a physician of high repute would join forces with the reformers.

The Enlightenment in Spanish America was an intellectual movement and not a social transformation. Indeed, this was characteristic of the reforms imposed in countries governed by an enlightened despotism. Whatever changes did take place were not the result of a social revolution, but rather of a change in outlook introduced from above by the state and, to a certain extent, by groups within the church allied with the state.

In the period that began with the so-called enlightened pro-grams, a new objective was sought in the universities—the increase of knowledge in all areas. It was based upon the premise that for Spain and her colonies, the seventeenth century had been a period during which culture in general and education in particular had been grievously separated from European enlightenment and knowledge. More than a desire to shape the appropriate man for the proper post in the right institution, there was now an encyclopedic appetite for knowledge of every kind.

Curriculum Reform

New problems arose immediately following the expulsion of the Jesuits. The resident colleges continued on in one guise or another. As in the case of Córdoba, some of the Jesuit-controlled universities as well as some of their missions were taken over by the Franciscans. The Spanish authorities forbade the teaching of certain doctrines thought to be too Jesuit in content. For example, the doctrine of tyrannicide, developed a century and a half earlier by Juan de Mariana, was suppressed; probabilism in moral theology was condemned as a shelter for laxity, as were the ideas of Suárez in philosophy and theology. Around 1770 there began a movement to adopt plans similar to those initiated in Spain under Cam-pomanes.

In some provinces where only a pontifical university existed, the representatives of the Crown, driven by a mixture of old-fashioned royalism and the new Enlightenment, took advantage of the occasion to ask for the establishment of royal or public universities. In Bogotá, where José Celestino Mutis had led the defense of Copernican cosmography (1774), the attack against the Dominican Colegio-Universidad del Rosario was led by the prosecutor of the *audiencia*, Francisco Antonio Moreno y Escandón. He argued that ecclesiastics were not suited for the teaching of such subjects as physics, jurisprudence, and other worldly sciences. In the 1780s, Archbishop and Viceroy Caballero y Góngora asked for a public university to teach the sciences and vocational disciplines. Even at the Colegio-Universidad del Rosario curriculum changes were

introduced and a *cátedra* in mathematics was created. Nevertheless, the Dominican university was preserved and survived until
Bolívar's time. On the other hand, the Dominicans lost their
monopoly in Quito, where a royal university was founded in 1786.
The university in Córdoba, which had been in Franciscan hands
since the expulsion of the Jesuits, became a state-controlled
institution in 1800. The university in Charcas immediately went
from Jesuit to royal control. New royal universities were created in
Guadalajara (1791), Medellín (1803), and Nicaragua (1812).

As royal colleges were established, episcopal seminaries were
opened or enlarged in many cities with constantly growing
curricula and sometimes offering as many courses as a university,
without ever actually attaining the status of a university. At Mérida
in Yucatán in 1791, besides those studies normally available to
future clerics, law, mathematics, and surgery were taught as a
result of Bishop Estévez's initiative. He was thoroughly persuaded
that "the sciences were the basis of the state's welfare and without
knowledge of them men were of use neither to themselves nor to
their fellow men." In 1803, the bishop of Santiago de Cuba
intended to add to this seminary a *cátedra* in draftsmanship and
instruction in experimental physics and medicine.[19] Now we can
understand in what senses we may speak of a Catholic Enlightenment, especially among the bishops and secular clergy. The regular
clergy, although normally more stubborn in holding on to the
traditional curriculum, were nevertheless, in some convents
anyway, surprisingly receptive to the new currents of thought.

At times the university resisted curriculum reform, but reform
made headway in the colleges or seminaries. In Santiago de Chile,
the old methods and practices were to continue intact until
Independence, while in the Caroline Resident College, the presbyter José Francisco Echaurren taught an eclectic philosophy. As
far as the internal life of the college was concerned, the older ways
of the cloister persisted.

The elimination of dictation was a major educational reform.
The "enlightened" programs, in order to assure that new viewpoints and knowledge were introduced, required that textbooks be
employed, generally the same ones that were being used in Spain.
Without a sizable import of such texts, there would have been
slight possibility for any reform to be effected and the professors
would have continued to rely upon dictation, using the same notes

they had taken as students. This approach to reform reveals the degree to which the Spanish-American Enlightenment was the product of an enlightened despotism, borrowed from abroad and imposed from above, and shows at the same time the Enlightenment's profound limitation, its lack of cultural spontaneity.

The Enlightenment was opposed to the notion that all knowledge begins with the study of Latin and in this respect showed itself in basic disagreement with humanism. The "quarrel between the Ancients and the Moderns" of the seventeenth century had paved the way to victory over humanist erudition. The formation, in the eighteenth century, of national monarchies committed to modernizing the state of all its departments favored the teaching of Spanish as the basic language and as the language of instruction in law, philosophy, the natural sciences, and even theology. The reformers were too imbued with a respect for the classical languages to think of their elimination. Neoclassicism, which flourished at the end of the eighteenth and the beginning of the nineteenth centuries in literature, speech, and art, reinforced the teaching of Latin, while it attempted to prune away the grammatical formalism of the old method and was highly critical of the grammar texts of the Jesuits. The neoclassicists insisted on the reading and translation of the great authors of Latin and Greek antiquity.[20] In 1802 Juan Egaña opened a *cátedra* in rhetoric and the history of literature at the Universidad de San Felipe in Santiago de Chile in which a broad survey of classical and Spanish literature was given.

It was, however, in the *facultades* of philosophy, medicine, and law that the Spanish language gained the greatest currency. Their high regard for the national language was confirmed by the recent decision of Pope Pius VI allowing the Bible to be read by laymen in the vernacular. Shortly thereafter there appeared a Spanish translation by Scio. As far as the scientific disciplines were concerned, all of the reforming projects emphasized the impossibility of studying them in a classical language.[21]

In philosophy (whose scholastic designation, "the arts," was discarded at this time), the predominant trend was toward the elimination of scholasticism and its dialectic forms and the introduction of the new scientific view of the cosmos. The attacks on Aristotelianism grew increasingly strident. The graduates' theses, in the reformed universities, exhibited a familiarity with the post-Cartesian systems. The result of dissolving the bond between the university and scholasticism was to produce a variety of systems in historical order. For example, the program at Lima had the following sequence: history of philosophy and ethics, by Johann Gottlieb Heineccius, a German Scholastic philosopher much in vogue at the time; ontology, by the Portuguese reformer Luís António Verney; mathematics, by Benito Bails; physics, by Peter Van Musschennbroeck and François Jacquier (used also at Alcalá and the Royal Institute of San Isidro). In total, the time required for study was three and a half years. The texts were still in Latin because Spanish ones were lacking, with the exception of the mathematical treatise by Bails.

In the curriculum at the University of Caracas, as it was described in the report of the *visita* of 1815 (when royal troops had won back much of Venezuela from Bolívar's forces), the study of philosophy took three years. In the first year, a student had to take logic, basic mathematics (as prerequisite for physics), astronomy, and geography (employing the most modern atlas); in the second year, physics; and in the third year, psychology, metaphysics, and ethics. The curriculum was still essentially the same as it had been in the former Aristotelian mold, but owing to the work of the reformer Marrero and his disciples, the contents had been significantly altered. From the beginning of the nineteenth century, logic was based upon Condillac and metaphysics on Nicholas Malebranche and Teodoro de Almeida (another of the great popularizers of the new scientific philosophy in Portugal, especially by means of his *Recreación Filosófica*, the Spanish translation of one of his widely read books). In physics and mathematics many of the newly improved or recently invented paraphernalia of science were widely used in classrooms and laboratories: maps, globes, telescopes, thermometers, barometers, and Galvani's battery. In Guatemala, the Franciscan Goicoechea based his teaching of philosophy upon the works of the principal popularizers of Newtonianism: Jean-Antoine Nollet, Brixen, and Jacquier. As this period of adaptation and diffusion developed in this university, as in many others in Spanish America and Spain, the most useful manuals of philosophy were the *Instituciones Filosóficas* by Malvin de Montazet, Archbishop of Lyon, and those written by Jacquier.

In short, reform of the teaching of philosophy involved the diffusion of knowledge about modern science, the introduction of rudimentary experimentation in the small laboratories, and mathematical studies through the writings of such Spanish authors as Tomás Vicente Tosca and Bails. Second, Aristotelian and scholastic logic lost considerable ground, but none of the other philosophic disciplines, such as psychology, metaphysics, and ethics, had any systematic reorientation. All philosophical study, in the strict sense of intellectual formation, was from that time lacking, and it would be this problem that positivism would seek to solve toward the end of the nineteenth century.

The prevalence of Roman law in the professional education of lawyers came under attack by the end of the eighteenth century as the partisans of Spanish law gained in numbers and influence. This development was similar to what was occurring in the teaching of language. The period of the Spanish Enlightenment was also a time of intellectual nationalism, devoted to the recovery of native antiquities and ancient Spanish law, the *Fueros* and the *Partidas*. Beginning with the sixteenth century, there existed an anti-Roman trend whose best-known exponent during the reign of Philip II was Pedro Simón Abril. His works were constantly cited in favor of the usefulness and the teaching of Spanish native law. In Spanish America, the same trend prevailed as seen in such manuals on Spanish law as those written by Ignacio Jordán de Asso y de Río and Miguel de Manuel y Rodríguez.

If we look at Toribio Rodríguez de Mendoza and Mariano Ribero's reform plan of 1788 for the Caroline Resident College of Lima, we find an enthusiastic defense of Spanish as the language of instruction in law as well as an equally ardent advocacy of Hispanic law and precedents over Roman law. All laws, they said, had been given in the language of the people who were to conform to them, just as God had legislated Hebrew for the Hebrews. The *Siete Partidas* were, in their opinion, superior to the Justinian codes. At the end of the colonial regime in 1818, Juan M. Alvarez, a professor at the University of Guatemala, compiled a volume entitled *Instituciones de derecho real de Castilla y de Indias*. When the universities did not reform themselves, instruction in Spanish law and the laws of the Indies was nevertheless conducted at the academies of jurisprudence, institutions bound up with the legal profession. Training in Roman law did not disappear altogether from the reformed universities and colleges, but it was given on a reduced level in manuals (*Institutas*) and in courses on historical background.

The *cátedra* that best embodied the ideology of the Enlightenment in its most rationalist aspect was the *cátedra* of natural and international law, established under Campomanes. It was based upon Johann G. Heineccius' *Elementa Juris Naturae et Gentium* (modified by Joaquín Marín y Mendoza, a *catedrático* at the Royal Institute of San Isidro in Madrid), for use in a Catholic country and published as a manual in 1776, and subsequently reissued. Heineccius followed the legal and political theories of Thomas Hobbes, Samuel von Pufendorf, and Christian Thomasius. The main political doctrine that one finds in Heineccius is Pufendorf's concept of an original social contract and of an absolute but not despotic monarchy. The men of the Spanish Enlightenment saw in the German theories of natural law the most precise formulation of their idea of the Hispanic Monarchy. However, notions of the social contract could just as easily move in the direction of a Rousseauian and revolutionary scheme of things and toward consequences quite different from what the German theorists of the seventeenth and eighteenth centuries had in mind. This *cátedra* was considered to be politically dangerous at the time of the French Revolution and was suppressed in both Spain and the Indies. Its influence on the Creole lawyers of the Independence period, however, appears to have been very great. The Spanish-American delegates in the Cortes at Cádiz appealed for its reinstitution, while it continued to function at home under the control of the local *juntas patrióticas*.

Medieval Hispanic regalism, reinforced in the eighteenth century by Gallicanism, expressed itself fully in the various reforms of Canon Law. Two such reform programs frequently cited the Four Articles of the Gallican Clergy of 1682 and their defense by Bossuet, which implicitly contained theories of the divine right of kings, the supremacy of the councils over the Pope, and the autonomy of the bishops. In the eighteenth century, Gallicanism became, in effect, the official ideology of the Catholic states that wanted to control the clergy or to reform it. *Josefinismo*, an extreme form of Gallicanism suffused with "the convictions of the Enlightenment," sought to maintain the church in subservience to the state, except in matters clearly of religious dogma. In the universities, this trend was reflected in the vogue enjoyed by the anti-Roman canonists Zeger Bernhard Van Espen and Johann

Nikolaus von Hontheim, writing under the name of Justinius Febronius, and in the founding of *cátedras* in church history, conciliar movements, and the teachings of the early church. They had in common an implied critique of ultramontanism, fervently upheld by the Jesuits, showing that this trend was in fact a recent departure from church tradition and opposed to the pristine doctrines and practices of the early church. The Jansenist criticisms of the church, or at least a more moderate form of Gallicanism, influenced a segment of the clergy and determined its attitude during the politico-ecclesiastical crisis in Spanish and Portuguese America from 1810 to 1840.

In theology, the reformist intention was to destroy the heavy weight of scholasticism: first of all, by giving prime importance to the teaching of the sacred Scriptures, much neglected during the colonial period; and second, by a "positive theology" concerned with the teaching of dogma. As a historical and critical introduction to these studies, the *Lugares Teológicos* of Melchor Cano, a famous theologian of the sixteenth century, was recommended. The most widely used text in theology was the *Instituciones Theologicae* by the Archbishop of Lyon, condemned by Rome as being too Jansenist. Moreover, the study of theology became more closely allied with the study of apologetics, being against the "enlightened" ideas, but in a less rigid way than early scholasticism and more in harmony with the literary tastes of the times. The French model was Bergier and the Spanish American was Pablo de Olavide, a Peruvian convert to the suspect philosophical doctrines. Following the 1500s, clerical attitudes passed through various phases from formal scholasticism to positions that were psychological, moral, historical, or polemical in nature. It was not until the end of the nineteenth century that a more embracing philosophy and theology was to be discovered again in Thomism.[22]

The *facultades* of medicine were also beneficiaries of the introduction of modern science and the emphasis on experience in the teaching of philosophy. Medical authorities, from Galen to Hermann Boerhaave, were brought up to date. *Cátedras* in surgery and anatomy appeared here and there. The secularizing of the profession was seen in the fact that the Tribunal del Protomedicato would henceforth control the instruction and licensing of physicians.

The National Period: The Nineteenth and Twentieth Centuries

With the exception of the Independence period and the following decade, 1820–30, the history of the university during the National era is not as well known as for the colonial centuries. This is true for all fields of Latin American history; the nineteenth is probably the least studied of all centuries. From 1830, therefore, our interpretations are necessarily limited. The presence of national boundaries makes it advisable to examine a few of the large universities and hypothesize about what was probably true for most of the others.

1810–20: The Years of the Juntas

The wars of independence were, from the educational and institutional vantage point, a continuation of the "enlightened" reforms and the diffusion of the sort of books adopted since the time of Campomanes. The ideologists of the Independence movement satirized the old principle of authority, developed a philosophical eclecticism, were enthusiastic advocates of science and its social usefulness, restored the *cátedras* in natural law, and strengthened canonical Gallicanism, which was to serve as a theoretical structure for ecclesiastical reforms. If we examine, for example, the university plan of Deán Gregorio Funes for Córdoba (1813), the eighteenth-century image is readily apparent. In philosophy the most obvious change was that the former three years of study were extended to four. The first year traditionally concentrated on logic, the entire second year was devoted to mathematics, and the third to physics. The last year was no longer restricted to psychology and metaphysics, but instead to moral philosophy and constitutional law, a general division of study for all of the *facultades*. The Aristotelian scholastic programs had been pruned for the purpose of developing a more modern ethical and political discipline, although Funes recommended Aristotle's *Ethics* for the course in moral philosophy, finding support for doing so in Feijóo's writings. Another interesting point was the enthusiasm with which the work of the exiled Jesuit Juan Andrés, *Historia Literaria*, was recommended as a text. This book, which was not confined to *belles lettres*, presented a universal panorama of artistic and scientific literature; it was one of the enlightened encyclopedic texts most in vogue. Apart from the University of Mérida in Venezuela (1810), the Independence movement did not produce any new educational institutions. On the contrary, it was rather hostile to them because they were looked upon as bastions of traditionalism. There was much of the disdain seen in the French Revolution in this attitude, for in France the universities had been suppressed in favor of a reordering of the national educational system. The colonial university, however, was less a house of learning than a degree-granting facility whose primary function was to give tests and examinations. The most consistent and systematic teaching and learning took place in the colleges, particularly in the Carolinian resident colleges, which had succeeded those previously operated by the Jesuits. Thus, the national educational plans had to begin at this level rather than on the level of the university.

Chile is a good example of this process at work. Juan Egaña was responsible for elaborating the idea of "public education," which was to become so significant in the intellectual and political history of the nineteenth and twentieth centuries. The ideas related to this concept were not original to Spanish America or to Egaña but were the repercussions of European neoclassicism—the writings of Rousseau; in the case of Egaña, the influence of the Italian philosopher Gaeteno Filangieri; and the revolutionary plans of Condorcet, Lakanal, and Daunou. In his neoclassicist humanism, Egaña went back to the ideal models of Sparta and Plato.

Like so many of the other early national leaders in Spanish America, Egaña sought to bring about republican "virtue" by means of national education—employing the same moral and political sense of the word as Montesquieu had, hoping to instill the "virtues" of patriotism and civic religion. Egaña's ideas on the Instituto Nacional, even though modeled after the Institut de France, made it something different from the conglomerate of academies it was in France. In Chile the intention was to create a national center of general education designed on the broadest possible scale. It was to oversee teaching in the liberal arts and sciences, in the occupational and vocational fields, in gymnastic exercises, and in military and moral drills. The actual conditions of war and the scarcity of personnel and resources during the Independence era severely limited the implementation of this sweeping program and led, more modestly, to a fusion of the colleges and other educational organizations: the Carolinian resident colleges, the Tridentine Seminary, and the Academy of San Luis (founded with the financial support of the Consulado of merchants, which, as in other countries, offered technical training). The merger with the seminary, reflecting a process going on elsewhere in Latin America, brought the secular clerics in contact with education in general and with the new political ideas in particular.

The Instituto's ordinances of 1813, drawn up by its rector, a *catedrático* of philosophy, the presbyter José Francisco Echaurren, adhered closely to Egaña's ideas. Accordingly, the Instituto was to be a truly Catholic organization including rich and poor and the Indians at the missionary college of San Francisco de Chillán. In addition to the standard courses in the traditional curriculum, studies in geography, botany, chemistry, modern languages, history, and certain technical skills such as navigation were offered. Of course, the execution of this plan in 1819 was less perfect than its conception which was typically "enlightened" in inspiration, goals, and content. The Spanish language, which was taught for the first time at the Academy of San Luis, was included along with Latin in general education. Although it was planned to offer both French and English, they were not introduced until two decades later. As far as the university was concerned, its courses were abolished and it existed only as a degree-granting authority.[34]

1820-40: The First Direct Intellectual Influences from Europe

In the middle of the eighteenth century much new thought began to flow from modern Europe to Spanish America. Major ideas came in books by Feijóo and Juan Andrés, in popular translations such as those done by Noël Antoine Pluche and Teodoro de Almeida, and in scholarly publications in Spanish and Latin. About 1820, and for the first time without Spanish intermediaries, two trends of European thought reached the former colonies and were to predominate for some twenty years. One was the school of sensationalist philosophy, particularly as expounded in the works of Destutt de Tracy; the other school was based on Bentham's utilitarianism, which involved a frontal attack on natural law, so long rooted in Latin American soil by the traditions of scholasticism and the Enlightenment. Lafinur and Fernández de Agüero in the *facultad* of philosophy in Buenos Aires and José Joaquín de Mora, Ventura Marín, and J. M. Varas in Santiago de Chile represented the sensationalist school. Someller in Argentina and Azuero in Colombia preached Bentham's utilitarianism. Others could be cited in every country. Both trends, along with Scottish philosophy and empiricism in general, found their best synthesis in Andrés Bello.

Several universities were established during this period. In the 1820s the Universidad de Buenos Aires was founded; in 1826 the law governing the system of higher education in Colombia was passed and the statutes governing the creation of central universities were based on it; and new universities appeared in Bolivia (La Paz and Cochabamba), in Peru (Arequipa), in Mexico (San Luis Potosí and Oaxaca), and Colombia (Cauca). The National University of Uruguay was established in the next decade.

Buenos Aires, in contrast to Córdoba, was an Argentinean city open to trade and ideas. After the establishment of a number of schools and colleges around 1810, the university was founded in 1821. The plan of the first rector, the presbyter Saénz, borrowed the administrative terminology from France: *"prefecturas de los departamentos de estudios."* The major *facultades* were now the sacred sciences (theology and canon law), jurisprudence, medicine, and a new department of exact sciences. The *Academia Práctica de Jurisprudenica* constituted another department. From the organizational point of view, however, the most important of the departments was the *Departmento de Estudios Preparatorios* in which were combined the teaching of Latin, modern languages, logic, metaphysics, rhetoric, physics, mathematics, and the new discipline of political economy. The department's name itself was indicative: by including these subjects under *"estudios preparatorios,"* the distance between them and the rest of the university curriculum anticipated the subsequent separation of secondary education from higher education.

According to the traditional format there were three distinct stages of learning: grammar, which was sometimes the only subject taught in schools with that name; the arts; and the major *facultades.* The university and the colleges, however, included all the levels of students and *catedráticos* in such a way that it was not possible to speak of secondary education. The *estudios preparato-*

rios at Buenos Aires did not completely encompass the former group of the minor *facultades.* Physics and mathematics, modified in form and content, were not a part of the exact sciences. *Estudios preparatorios,* however, included new subjects such as modern languages and political economy, although the latter was shortly to be transferred to the *facultad* of laws, where it was to remain until the era of specialization in the twentieth century. But the organizational separation which we have just described was not at all what Saénz had in mind in 1821. Fifty years were to pass before such restructuring was to take place in Buenos Aires.

In Bogotá around 1824 we see the same new ideas and doctrines rife in the educational world. In the colleges of El Rosario and San Bartolomé, public law was taught on the basis of the writings of the Protestant author Lepage; international law followed Emmerich de Vattel and political economy, J. B. Say; jurisprudence was influenced by Bentham. Spanish gradually replaced Latin owing to the philological books of José Rufino Cuervo. The university plans of 1827 combined the new disciplines and intellectual influences with the legacy of the Spanish Enlightenment. Instruction in the modern languages was promoted and extended to include not only French, but also English by 1828. Studies in the law became the source of political passion, commitment, and controversy, as happened everywhere in Latin America throughout the nineteenth and into the twentieth century. Bolívar had to shut down the courses of public law in 1828, for reasons similar to those that motivated the Spanish Crown to suspend the teaching of natural law in 1793.

In Mexico, the struggle between the Liberals and the Conservatives, and the contest between the liberal forces and the church over who should control education, dominated much of the period after 1830. Both Alamán and Mora, the leaders of the rival parties, came to the same conclusion around 1830: that the university was superfluous and that education could be best organized around separate institutions devoted to the teaching of certain disciplines. This concept was much like the Law Lakanal of the French Revolution, which set up central schools, at once secondary and higher, and failed early in its career. Alamán was in favor of maintaining a continuity with the old colleges; Mora, Quintana Roo, and Lorenzo de Zavala wanted an organization divided into six large new schools, under the control of a Ministry of Public

Education, responsible for assigning professors and developing curricula. Although both parties accepted a reform in the content of education, the Conservatives preferred retaining the existing bases, while the Liberals wanted to erect a totally new bureaucratic structure. The six schools defined in the educational plan of 1833 were: (1) the Preparatoria (where languages, philosophy, mathematics, and philosophy of religion were taught); (2) Humanistic Studies (sensationalist philosophy, history, literature, moral philosophy, political economy, and national statistics); (3) Physical Sciences and Mathematics; (4) Medical Sciences; (5) Jurisprudence; and (6) Ecclesiastical Sciences. In the last school, Biblical and historical studies had greater weight than systematic theology, and a course in the theological foundations of religion was given.

The plan of 1833 may serve as an important example of the liberal goals in Latin America from 1830 to 1860. Without prior sanction by the church, scientific innovations and the new trends in philosophy pervaded the thinking behind the plan. The clergy should be taught under the auspices of the state following the secular, centralist tendencies of Gallicanism. Liberalism in this period did not countenance any separation of church and state, but viewed the relationship between the two from the vantage point of traditional regalism. The suppression of the university and its replacement with an elaborate bureaucratic structure, however, were episodes only in Mexican history.

The Liberal alternative of setting up a Ministry of Public Education did not succeed, and by 1834, the Conservatives, returning to power along with Santa Anna, reopened the university. The colleges of San Juan de Letrán, San Ildefonso, and San Gregorio Magno offered courses in secondary and higher education, while more specialized subjects were given at the two newly founded colleges of medicine and mining. The university was to give courses at a still higher level, rounding out the educational process begun at the colleges. The structure of the *claustro*, the regulations regarding degree-granting, the tests and examinations, and so on, were straight out of medieval Spain and Europe.

By the 1830s, the Latin American states had more or less regularized their relations with Rome. The governments renounced any intention of reforming the ecclesiastical institutions and giving support to a Gallican sectionalism within the clergy. The bishops recaptured the control of their seminaries, which had been merged with the larger colleges during the Independence period. The future priest was educated and shaped by the special nineteenth-century religious spirit and somewhat removed from other intellectual currents of the time. Gallicanism went into a period of decline in Europe and the church reorganized itself around a strengthened Papacy as its surest defense. Ecclesiastical studies developed an antiliberal bias. The first great intellectual countermovement within Catholicism was the traditionalism of Bonald and Joseph de Maistre, whose theological and political philosophy stood against the regnant idea of progress. De Maistre's rich theology of history became intertwined with Bossuet's providentialism, a doctrine of considerable influence in the Hispanic world after the end of the eighteenth century.

One sees these forces at work in the life of Bartolomé de Herrera, rector of the Convictorio de San Carlos in Lima. Brought up under the influence of Rodríguez de Mendoza and the Gallican version of the "Catholic Enlightenment," by 1840 he gradually began to abandon many of these concepts learned as a young man. In canon law, he embraced ultramontanism; in philosophy, he rejected sensationalism in favor of the eclectic spiritualism of Victor Cousin; and in natural law, he found his mentor in the Belgian Catholic liberal Ahrens instead of Heineccius. He forswore the scientific knowledge introduced by Rodríguez de Mendoza. The liberals, however, to combat Bartolomé de Herrera, decided to set up the Colegio de Guadalupe.[24]

1840–1930: The University in Chile and Argentina, Academicism and Professionalism

Chile and Argentina moved away from the medieval university models inherited from Spain to embrace new institutions typically nineteenth-century in nature. The traditional medieval corporate forms slowly disappeared, as evidenced in the elimination of the graduation ceremony and the decline of student participation in university elections. Until the end of the Spanish Empire, traditionalism was a stronger force in Lima and in the universities patterned after it than in Mexico. At least in appearance, the medieval forms were being pushed aside by the new bourgeois civilization imported by the upper classes.

The French educational models were adopted by those countries attempting to modernize the colonial organization of the university. For such a purpose, the French Revolution and the Napoleonic Code provided a number of lasting and useful institutions. For example, the Lycée represented the center of secondary education; the Institut grouped together ,the former academies, although it had no specific educational function; the French university plan of 1808 offered a highly centralized national structure, encompassing all of the *facultades* and professional schools as well as the *facultad de letras y ciencias,* being in effect the upward extension of the Lycée. In short, these were the Grandes Ecoles, monastery or barrackslike in nature, according to the Napoleonic phrase, that were to provide a thorough preparation in various disciplines. One of the institutions of the *ancien régime* that survived the Revolution was the Collège de France, a school of very advanced and refined educational level but unrelated to degree-granting or professional training, and hence in the Latin American setting an unsuitable importation.

If one were to characterize the University of Chile, as its founder Andrés Bello conceived it, it was to resemble the Institut de France, *mutatis mutandis,* but in addition should confer degrees and oversee public education. As a teaching and research institution, its principal function was the transmission and development of literature, historiography, and national statistics. Even though at its establishment in 1842 the doctors of the colonial university were included in the new faculty, in the future it was to include not only the doctors, but also academicians elected because of their professional competence. The doctors of the older institution were too numerous and, in any event, not suited to the new universal context of the university. The university faculty was reorganized and yet never totally abandoned its essence as a learned corporation. The academicians were grouped into five *facultades:* theology; physical sciences and mathematics; medicine; law; and philosophy and the humanities. Although the purely academic impulse produced several works of research, such as chronicles, proceedings, and annals, practical considerations of managing educational affairs and awarding degrees overshadowed research activities.

The educational bodies by the middle of the century were the Instituto Nacional; *liceos* in the provinces devoted to secondary education; the schools of medicine, pharmacy, and obstetrics;

normal schools; the specialized schools for artistic and vocational training (such as architecture, fine arts, music, arts and crafts, and agriculture) that sprang up a few years after the university; and lower down on the scale, the elementary schools. The university directed the whole educational enterprise. At the center of this enterprise, in the Instituto Nacional, secondary or preparatory education was sharply delimited between 1843 and 1852, from the advanced courses in law, the physical sciences, and mathematics. Intermediate education was completely detached from the university. Theology was taught in seminaries and novitiates outside the university, following the general tendency of the nineteenth-century church to separate itself from the university. Until the Instituto Pedagógico was founded in 1889, there was no teaching body related to the *facultad* of philosophy and humanities.

The university's control over the Instituto Nacional and over the vocational and professional schools, in an association in which the university reserved to itself the cultivation of pure knowledge, faithfully reflected Bello's neoclassic humanism. But such pure academicism could not survive long in a society bent on seeing its young made the recipients of professional titles as early as possible. Even in colonial times, anxious fathers were known to pull strings and to put on pressure to see their sons given degrees and quickly admitted to the bar or ordained by the church. *Educación preparatoria,* as Bello himself recognized, did not result in the general formation of character (as had been its original purpose in the minds of the Independence thinkers), but rather became a step leading to entry into the liberal professions. Bello's ideas were modeled on the Institut de France; in reality, however, the University of Chile was more nearly an imitation of the Université de France.

This educational organization is reflected in the *Ley de Instrucción Pública* of 1879. It made a distinction between advanced training for the professions and the "cultivation and promotion of the sciences, letters, and arts," but the machinery of the university was geared to the former. It established the freedom to create new higher and secondary educational institutions that resulted ten years later in the founding of the Universidad Católica. The law replaced the former Council of Deans with a Council of Public Education presided over by the minister of education. The new council was composed of the rector, the deans, the secretary-general, and two members elected by the *claustro*. The council continued to be dominated by the university because the government was represented only by the minister and three counselors picked by the president of the Republic. Control of secondary education was vested in the council so that the curriculum and the educational policies with regard to the *liceos* could be coordinated with those of the university. The five *facultades* remained intact. The main reform of the law was that in each *facultad*, the academicians constituted a small minority, while those with power were *catedráticos*. It was hoped that the professor could be observed and controlled by the doctors and masters, whose unsalaried status lent them an independence of judgment. With the passing of time, however, the *catedráticos* felt themselves to be the repositories of contemporary science and knowledge, and they gained ascendancy.

From this moment on, the Universidad de Chile became a federation of professional schools. The schools of law, medicine, engineering, and the Instituto Pedagógico absorbed all of the purposes and functions of the academic *facultades*. Henceforth, the history of the university was the history of its great schools, some of which—medicine and engineering, for example—were recognized throughout Latin America for their modernity. By this time the concept of the *facultad* had fallen into desuetude; it was only revived in the latter part of the twentieth century when new professional schools were founded and proclaimed their independence by calling themselves a *facultad*. The five *facultades* of the nineteenth century had become thirteen different superstructures by 1968. Furthermore, much the same situation existed regarding academic degrees. Since the requirements for obtaining professional licenses and titles were based upon finishing the licentiate, there was little interest in going on to take the doctorate. It has only been in the 1950s and 1960s that courses have been instituted leading to that degree.

One of the first other than Bello to point a monitory finger at the dangers in the trend to professionalism was the positivist teacher Valentín Letelier. As the *catedrático* in law, he tried to introduce sociology and political science in the law curriculum, but his advice fell on deaf ears. He was able, however, to add a course in the history of law.

The University of Buenos Aires gradually recovered its health after the long dictatorship of Juan Manuel de Rosas. The central figure in its renaissance was Juan María Gutiérrez, who became rector in 1861. He strongly defended the university against governmental encroachments from without and disruption of academic freedom from within. He wanted appointments to be made on the basis of merit and he even went so far as to advocate the freedom of professions from legal restrictions, with the exception of those concerned with public health. The Departamento de Estudios Preparatorios, separated from the university only in 1871, significantly expanded its curriculum owing to Gutiérrez's devoted efforts. He was largely responsible for the introduction of courses in Spanish literature and literary history and, in the upper-level courses, for replacing Latin with history, literature, and mythology. Gutiérrez recommended, without success, that medieval and modern history be taught. History was to take its due place in the curriculum at a much later date and as an innovation to balance the greater emphasis given to the study of languages in secondary education. In 1873, he also initiated an upper level program in the humanities in the university with studies in language, literature, history, and philosophy.

In 1873–74, the university was organized under the authority of the Province of Buenos Aires. As in Chile, it was a university with a faculty of academicians. It had the following *facultades:* humanities and philosophy; medical sciences; law and social sciences; mathematics; and physical and natural sciences (eventually combined with mathematics). The university was basically an academic institution that established standards and held examinations and had the power to grant degrees and professional titles. In 1881, it became a national university, as did Córdoba University, and was governed by the *Ley Avellaneda* of 1885.

Throughout Latin America, the original medieval tradition of the university as an autonomous corporation survived with extraordinary vitality, although there has been a wide variation in the degree of autonomy achieved. The *Ley Avellaneda* entrusted to the national government not only ultimate authority (the *patronato*), as was common practice in Latin America, but also the right to appoint professors. The make-up of the *facultades* was one-third professors and two-thirds academicians. The National Congress was openly hostile to the idea of surrendering power to the *catedráticos* on the grounds that cliques would spring up and create powerful vested interests. The academicians, however, enjoyed lifetime tenure and elected each other from among themselves, which led inevitably to the development of a "academic" atmosphere—in the worst sense of the word. It was only in 1908 that the rector was able to introduce a professional system, along the lines of the regime at the new University of La Plata.

The most serious problem facing the university was that of professionalism. In 1888 Minister of Education Posse complained that the university was solely a means of preparing for a career and that science was being taught primarily for its immediate practical applications. This issue was discussed with greater intensity and fervor in Argentina than it was in Chile. Ten years later, another Minister of Education, Magnasco, endeavored to separate doctoral and research activities from purely professional education. The former was to enjoy wide latitude, the latter was to be strictly regulated. At the same time, Juan Ramón Fernández was advocating complete freedom for academic teaching and research and an examining board to regulate professional training, both within the framework of the university. These ideas never got beyond the project-making stage, and the social and cultural climate that tolerated exaggerated professionalism remained unchanged.

At least a partial corrective to the excesses of professionalism were the newly established research institutes—the Institute of Historical Research (1905), with such men as Ravignani and Levene; and the Institute of Physiology (1919), under Houssay. The imperatives of modernization and specialization led to the creation of new *facultades* such as agronomy and veterinary medicine (1909) and economic sciences (1913). In these respects, the University of Buenos Aires excelled the other universities in Latin America.

In 1918, at the University of Córdoba, the student movement for university reform began that would soon spread to the rest of Argentina and Latin America. The spokesmen of reform were José Batlle y Ordoñez in Uruguay, Hipólito Irigoyen in Argentina, and Arturo Alessandri in Chile.

The Congreso Universitario of 1934 declared that the university was not a training ground for the ruling classes nor a clearinghouse for the moral values and verities of any given time, but rather a laboratory in which all ideas were analyzed. These slogans referred less to research than to the movement of general ideas, the discussion of the great cultural and political themes, and the so-called university extension. The craving for general education was one of the signs of surfeit with the purely professional university at the end of the nineteenth century and the beginning of the twentieth.[25]

Mexico and the Meaning of Positivism

The case of Mexico is significant not only because of the influence of its intellectual leaders, but also because of the conceptual unity they were able to give their doctrines and the zeal they brought to their application.

The ideological extremes of the contest were embodied in Alamán and Mora. Alamán stood for the conservation of traditional society and mores and for continuing the religious and moral indoctrination of the people. Mora favored a teaching that was antidogmatic and antimystical in content and that was oriented toward social uplift.

The liberalism of the revolution of 1857 separated church and state and confiscated the mortmain ecclesiastical properties. The struggle for power then moved from the political to the educational stage. While the liberals advocated doctrinal freedom of instruction, they feared that the clergy would take advantage of their liberalism. Guillermo Prieto, for example, rejected the notion of a dictatorship over the mind and found a solution for the dilemma in having moral education taught in a lay rather than a Catholic school. The concept of freedom of instruction was formally incorporated in the Constitution of 1857. It was at this moment that positivism appeared as an influence, principally through the writings of Gabino Barreda, who thought of the Mexican Revolution of 1857 as a process in which "positivism was pitted against those benighted forces that sought to thwart social progress."

Barreda had a great deal of influence largely because the university had been suppressed by an earlier wave of liberalism at the time of Gómez Farías. A system of advanced schools (escuelas superiores) was established consisting of the preparatoria, the separate schools of jurisprudence; medicine, surgery, and pharmacy; agriculture and veterinary medicine; fine arts; music and rhetoric. The Escuela Nacional Preparatoria, successor to the former facultad of arts, was the matrix of positivism, and all students going on to professional training had to pass through it. Its curriculum was obviously based on the principles of Comtian thought: mathematics, cosmography, astronomy, physics, chemistry, botany, zoology, geography (static sociology), history (dynamic sociology), logic, and sensationalist philosophy. Paralleling this major level of studies, there was a minor level including the classical and modern languages, drawing, and bookbinding. Both levels added up to a full course of five years.

The basic idea running through these schemes and plans was that of giving a scientific outlook to all future professionals, thus assuring an intellectual unity and consensus of opinion among the ruling classes. In this way, as Leopoldo Zea has observed, positivism replaced (or at least gave the hope that it would replace) the old Catholic and scholastic education. In Mexico more than in any Latin American country except Brazil, it was the prevailing system of thought for the nonecclesiastical reformers of society. Positivism has had the greatest impact on the university next to scholasticism and shared with it the emphasis on intellectualism.

As other critics have noticed, the Mexican and Latin American brand of positivism, because of its extreme antichurch bias, lacked the internal ideological coherence and constructive emphasis found in Comte, and was based more upon Littré and Spencer. The result was that in Mexico, positivism took the guise of a systematic scientism, a fanatical attack upon everything "metaphysical," and naturally assaulted anything that appeared to be "theological." Besides being caught in the quarrels of the church-state issue, positivism was linked with equal fanaticism to the doctrine of universal education, which could only weaken the liberating spirit of true education, with its individualism and the free play of the intellect.

Positivism for the followers of Barreda became a nationalizing ideology for the newly rich and the functionaries on the rise that undergirded the regime of Porfirio Díaz. The eventual outcome was the disintegration of Mexican society in the Revolution of 1910.

One of the important moderate figures of liberalism and positivism in Mexico was Justo Sierra. He was affectionately known as *"el maestro."* His conception of the *"universidad libre"* counterbalanced the stultifying imposition of an intellectual orthodoxy within the university. He accepted positivism, but not its intellectual exclusiveness or its arid naturalist scientism. When the new

Universidad Nacional opened its doors in 1910 under his leadership, with its school of advanced studies (later to be the Facultad de Filosofía), Mexico had a house of intellect clearly opposed to the narrow orthodoxy of positivism. In his later years, Justo Sierra moved away from what he viewed as the intellectual barrenness of positivism to embrace an open "spiritualism" of the mind that would encourage studies in universal history and Mexican archaeology. Pedro Henríquez Ureña contributed to the movement started by Sierra with his research in literary history. In subsequent years, Mexico was refreshed intellectually by the philosophies and ideologies of Europe. Antonio Caso's work strongly reflects the ideas of Boutroux and Bergson; vitalism and voluntarism, derived from classicist sources, show their influences in the voluminous writings of José Vasconcelos.[26]

The importance of positivism in Mexico lies in the fact that, although it fell into a sort of cloying intellectual orthodoxy marked by a narrow scientism, it stood for an attempt to give a supraprofessional training, a true "public education"—in the civic sense in which the term was understood at the time of the Independence—and to produce a new intellectual elite that would replace the clergy.

The university always had an intricate alliance with the state because the state sanctioned and licensed the professionals. The royal and national universities were supported by the state; the pontifical universities could be considered equally allied with the state because of the global structure in which both powers were married. Only the recently founded Catholic universities, which appeared between 1880 and 1951, owing to the ideological schism between church and state, can be considered "private" institutions. Even this assertion must be hedged, especially in looking toward the future. The alliance of the university and the state has not in general prevented the internal autonomy of teaching and research. Despite the widespread politicalization and the politics that university power groups are given to, there is still an atmosphere of restraint and respect that impedes the suppression of internal freedoms for long periods of time.

On reviewing the history of the nineteenth and twentieth centuries, we have been struck with the problem of professionalism and culture. The debate over this somewhat artificial dichotomy began at the end of the last century, and even today there are no really satisfactory solutions to it. The tendency has been to confuse the necessary practical training to produce professionals with the professions themselves which play important cultural and social roles.

NOTES

1. For a good general survey, see Stephen d'Irsay, *Histoire des universités françaises et étrangères* (Paris, 1933). For Spain, see Vicente de la Fuente's standard *Historia de las universidades, colegios y demás establecimientos de enseñanza en España*, 4 vols. (Madrid, 1884–89), and the more recent study by C. María Ajo González y Saínz de Zúñiga, *Historia de las universidades hispánicas: orígenes y desarrollo desde su aparición hasta nuestros días*, 3 vols. (Madrid, 1957–). For Alcalá, see Chapter 2 in Marcel Bataillon, *Erasmo y España: estudios sobre la historia espiritual del siglo xvi* (Mexico City, 1967).

2. Ajo González y Saínz, *Universidades hispánicas*, 2:133ff.

3. Marcel Bataillon, "Une université dans le Nouveau Monde," *Annales* (1952).

4. Ajo González y Saínz, *Universidades hispánicas*, 2:159ff. See also Alberto M. Carreño, *La fundación de la real y pontificia Universidad de México* (Mexico City, 1958) and F. Esteva Barba, *Cultura virreinal* (Barcelona, 1965).

5. Ajo González y Saínz, *Universidades hispánicas*, 2:145ff.

6. Luis A. Eguiguren, *Diccionario histórico-cronológico de la Universidad Real y Pontificia de San Marcos y sus colegios: crónica e investigación*, 5 vols. (Lima, 1940–50).

7. Ibid, 1:182ff.

8. Francisco Cervantes de Salazar, the first professor of rhetoric at the University of Mexico, was a student of Vives.

9. J. M. Gallegos Rocafull, *El pensamiento mexicano en los siglos xvi y xvii* (Mexico City, 1951).

10. John Tate Lanning, *The University in the Kingdom of Guatemala* (Ithaca, N.Y., 1955), cites 1697 legislation permitting the admission of noble Indians; later, in 1772, this legislation was extended to permit them to graduate *"sin pompa ni costas."* See Ajo González y Saínz, *Universidades hispánicas*, 2:155ff.

11. José Toribio Medina, *La instrucción pública en Chile desde sus orígenes hasta la fundación de la Universidad de San Felipe*, 2 vols. (Santiago, 1905), and *Historia de la Real Universidad de San Felipe de Santiago de Chile*, 2 vols. (Santiago, 1928). See also I. Leal, *Historia de la Universidad de Caracas, 1721–1827* (Caracas, 1963).

12. Mantilla's letter, Archivo General de Indias, Quito, leg. 97. See G. Hernández de Alba, *Crónica del muy ilustre Colegio Mayor de Nuestra Señora de Rosario en Santa Fé de Bogotá* (Bogotá, 1939) and *Aspectos de la cultura en Colombia* (Bogotá, 1947).

13. Achivo General de Indias, Santo Domingo, leg. 490.

14. Medina, *Historia de la Real Universidad de San Felipe*, vol 2.

15. José Manuel Rivas Sacconi, *El latín en Colombia* (Bogotá, 1949).

16. Achivo General de Indias, Lima, leg. 337.

17. Eguiguren, *Diccionario histórico-cronológico*, 2:83ff.

18. I have dealt with these matters at greater length in "Estudios sobre el Galicanismo y la 'Ilustración Católica' en América Española," Revista Chilena de Historia y Geografía (1957).

19. Achivo General de Indias, México, leg. 3101, and Santo Domingo, leg. 2214.

20. See the proposals of Rodríguez de Mendoza discussed in Eguiguren, *Diccionario histórico-cronológico*.

21. Ibid.

22. For a discussion of the religious mentality of the period, see my article cited in note 18 supra and my "El pensamiento de Juan Egaña sobre la reforma eclesiástica: avance y repliegue de una ideología de la época de la Independencia," *Boletín de la Academia Chilena de la Historia* 68 (1963).

23. Mario Góngora, "El rasgo utópico en el pensamiento de Juan Egaña," *Anales de la Universidad de Chile* 129 (1964); Domingo Amunátegui Solar, *Los primeros años del Instituto Nacional* (Santiago, 1889); G. Hernández del Alba, *Vida y escritos del doctor José Felix Restrepo* (Bogotá, 1935); Biblioteca Nacional de Buenos Aires, ed., *Papeles de Gregorio Funes* (Buenos Aires, 1940); Roberto Peña, *El pensamiento político del Deán Funes* (n.p., n.d.).

24. Ricardo Levene, *La fundación de la Universidad de Buenos Aires* (Buenos Aires, 1940); Solar, *Los primeros años;* G. Hernández de Alba, *Aspectos de la cultura;* Juan de Díos Méndez y Mendoza *Historia de la Universidad Central de Venezuela* (Caracas, 1924) and *Suplemento a las constituciones de la Nacional y Pontificia Universidad de México* (Mexico City, 1839); for a discussion of Herrera, see Jorge Basadre, *Chile, Perú, y Bolivia independientes* (Barcelona, 1948) and Jorge Guillermo Leguía, *Estudios históricos* (Santiago, 1939).

25. Luis Galdames, *La Universidad de Chile* (Santiago, 1937); and *Valentín Letelier y su obra, 1852–1919* (Santiago, 1937); Tulio Halperin Donghi, *Historia de la Universidad de Buenos Aires* (Buenos Aires, 1962); Julio V. González, *La universidad: teoría y acción de la reforma* (Buenos Aires, 1957).

26. In Daniel Cosío Villegas's edited *Historia moderna de México* (Mexico City, 1955–65), see the volumes and appropriate sections in L. González y González, *La república restaurada; la vida social* and M. González Navarro, *El Porfiriato: la vida social;* Luis Villor, "La cultura mexicana de 1910 a 1960," *Historia Mexicana,* No. 38; Manual González Ramírez, *La revolución social de México,* 2 vols. (Mexico City, 1960–66), vol. 1; Víctor Alba, *Las ideas sociales contemporáneas en México* (Mexico City, 1960); and José Bravo Ugarte, *México independiente* (Mexico City, 1956).

3

Origin and Philosophy
of the Brazilian University

Anisio Teixeira

During the fifteenth and sixteenth centuries Portugal was a tiny kingdom with a long history. Following the days when Ibero-Celts inhabited the Iberian Peninsula, Lusitania was visited by Phoenicians, then occupied by Carthaginians, and later conquered by the Romans. The Goths and Visigoths were succeeded by the Moors. By the thirteenth century the Lusitanians emerged in the Iberian world as an independent people, endowed with their own social character and occupying their present territory. The struggles to maintain independence continued, however, with Castile and later with Spain, and the vicissitudes of occupation and independence provided a constant theme until the Napoleonic invasions at the beginning of the nineteenth century.

The Atlantic seaboard of the Iberian Peninsula was thus a crossroads of extended and complex cultural experience, and this must have contributed to the fusion of a human group of singular energy, heir to the Roman tradition of government and conquest. Once a central power was established on a definite territory, the Portuguese turned toward the sea. Propelled by advances in navigation, the discovery of America, and the opening of the searoads to the east, Portugal extended the influence of Europe throughout the world.

Portugal identified itself with the forces and interests that had produced, in the course of centuries, Catholic power. It re-created the missionary devotion to propagating the faith that had prevailed during the first centuries of the Middle Ages. During the 1400s and 1500s, Catholic power was going through a period of crisis that was to culminate in the Reformation, the division of the Christian world, and a gradual decline of the Pope's temporal power. Succeeding years were to usher in what is designated historically as the beginning of "modern" times—the absolute power of kings, the birth of nationalism, the Enlightenment of the eighteenth century, and, finally, the secularization of human life and the transfer of power to the populace. With rising material prosperity in this era of social change, the Portuguese saw themselves as being in a position to defend, and then to restore, the great Age of Faith.

The civilization that was to cast its shadow over the American colony arrived at a Catholic synthesis of medieval thought, thanks to the work of its universities, particularly in Paris. Portugal became an heir to this culture, and the University of Coimbra a center of Thomistic philosophy, the conciliation of Aristotelian Hellenism with Catholic theology, which was to become a systematic classical culture for the training of a lay elite and an ecclesiastical personnel.

Aristotle and Thomas Aquinas both were creators of a rational and deductive type of knowledge, used for purposes of government and power that bore fruit in devices of argument, reason, and rule rather than in contemplation and meditation. The university was a body destined to the pursuit and study of this knowledge, which was first theological in nature and later juridical, philosophical, and professional. The result was the codification of an essentially aristocratic culture founded on a closed and dogmatic world view.

In Italy, the European reencounter with classical antiquity was to produce the Renaissance man, but in Spain and Portugal it produced the man of the Inquisition, who set out to persecute heretics and Jews and to restore the stability of the faith upset by the Reformation. He was dogmatic, intolerant, and antagonistic to the developing secularization of human life even though Portugal's power and commerce now embraced four continents. As a vassal of papal power, Portugal was granted possession of its new territories and cast in the role of restorer of Catholic orthodoxy and propagator of the faith. In this mission the Portuguese empire, heavily armed and centralized, was served by the Catholic Church and the Society of Jesus, a new body within the church imbued with the militant spirit of the Counter-Reformation.

The mercantile spirit, originally limited to trade in slaves and oriental spices, led to exploration of the New World. Here the Portuguese found only vegetable products at first; later they introduced new agricultural products; and eventually they discovered gold and diamonds. The wealth this discovery bestowed on them was exceeded only by the wealth of Spain.

World exploration and conquest brought with them power and riches based on slave labor. The Portuguese built an empire that in certain ways suggests the empires of antiquity rather than the states of the modern world. The newly found opulence, placed in the hands of the aristocratic class of warriors, administrators, and merchants, made possible a life of pomp and grandeur, and for prodigal royalty, a sumptuous life at court. These habits and attitudes spread to the colonies. The religious syncretism of the Catholic cult fostered a splendor rivaling that of the temples and monuments of antiquity.

The Portuguese empire in Brazil was not an experience characterized by poverty and primitive living conditions. It is this aspect that needs to be considered if we are to understand the success of Portugal in its colonial enterprise, the surprising continuity of culture between Portugal and Brazil, the absence of resentment and hostility between colonizer and colonized in the respective ruling classes, and the fact that, paradoxically, like Portugal itself, Brazil is an aged and in a certain sense unchanging nation, nostalgic for departed glories, rather than a young nation seeking out its destiny. A feeling for the future appears only now in the twentieth century, and this explains the resistance it encounters from the long-established social structures of Brazil.

Lusitanian Education in Medieval and Colonial Times

Brazil was to Portugal what England had been to the Catholic Church in the sixth century, when Pope Gregory I sent Augustine to Christianize it with the Bible in one hand and a Latin grammar in the other. No less was required of priests like Manuel de Nobrega, José de Anchieta, and other Jesuits in their "enterprise" of winning the native population for the faith. The conquistadors and colonizers from the mother country represented the enterprise of the sword, re-creating in Brazil an ecclesiastical state complete with clergy, nobility, and slaves. Commercial exploitation and the Christian crusade of the Jesuits ran parallel to one another, with sporadic conflicts, until finally the Jesuits were expelled. The result of this double effort was the large-scale extinction of the Indians and the conversion of the people to Catholicism. The Portuguese language spread throughout the vast territory; the three races (white, black, and Indian) learned to live together in tolerance thanks to miscegenation; and a fairly solid authoritarian order was created.

As commercial enterprise in Brazil assumed a private form with extensive lands to be occupied and administered, the government of the colony became an elaborate project. It represented a substantial work of organization, defense, and education, and with its bureaucracy of functionaries, Portuguese soldiers, and educators, this government established an empire so vigorous that it lasted until the end of the nineteenth century. Portugal did everything it could do to prevent any autonomous development in Brazil. It closed the frontiers and insisted that all civil servants should be Portuguese; it monopolized trade and denied its new lands the right to have factories, print shops, or universities. Slavery provided a labor force, annihilation of the native population removed all obstacles to complete occupation, and miscegenation served the growth of population. The offspring of white men and Negro and Indian women came to enjoy the privileges of the dominant white race. The racial melting pot provided the demographic composition of the nascent elite of a reborn archaic empire.

If the Jesuit enterprise had survived, with its native settlements speaking Tupí-Guaraní (language articulated and systemized by the Jesuit priests in their effort to Christianize the Indians), the new country would have contained an indigenous nation alongside the dominant white elite. With the expulsion of the Jesuits, however, the two nonwhite races were shaped by the three cultures of the Brazilian complex—Luso-Catholic, Negro, and Indian.

It was not long before the Brazilian-born community of "whites" in the colony began to demand racial discrimination in the Jesuit colleges and opposed the emancipation of Indian slaves. The outcome of these attitudes was a social structure different from that of Europe, where the main estates were clergy, nobility, and commons. In Brazil there were only two strata: whites, in the Brazilian sense described above; and slaves, meaning Negros and segregated or enslaved Indians. Here was a new type of ecclesiastical state with a white elite of clergy and nobility. There was no participation of the people, as the concept was understood in Europe. By virtue of their education, the clergy sometimes escaped the rigorous test of heredity although, generally speaking, the criterion of "clean blood" and noble birth was strictly applied in the selection of candidates for an ecclesiastical career.

Having passed the test, however, the clergy—whether monastic monks, cloistered nuns, or local parish priests—all held the social and economic privileges of the nobility, including that of holding public office. This was practically the only career available: even in the realm of justice, canon law was more important than civil law. Medicine was subject to the same restrictions as law, and instruction in medicine did nothing to change the spirit of teaching, since medical lore was bound by Aristotelian concepts of nature.

All education was conducted in Latin—church Latin—and did nothing to encourage any interest in the study of those new problems that the real situation of the colony might raise. It was an eminently intellectual and conservative education, identical to that offered in the mother country.

Up to and following independence, the education that opened the doors to the privileges of a closed and rigid social order was a literary one with emphasis on the dissertation, exegesis, scholastic reasoning, and rhetoric. The school system was designed to train clergymen and jurists, as canonists, in the manner conceived by the *Ratio Studiorum* of the Jesuits, drawn up in the sixteenth century and representing the culture of the late Middle Ages. It taught classical culture, not as a means to creative understanding, but as a formal instrument to guarantee the strict orthodoxy of the Counter-Reformation and to reinforce a rigid organization of the state. The nineteen Jesuit schools disseminated a formal Christian culture, suggesting St. Gregory; subjects were taught through patristic writings, the New Testament Scriptures, and all that was most dogmatic in the teachings of Aristotle.

In the Jesuit schools, Portuguese could be spoken only during recess and on holidays. The course in classical letters included the

Roman writers from Ovid to Horace, and the Greeks from Homer to Demosthenes. Cicero and Virgil were considered the masters of style. After the course in letters came arts and sciences, embracing logic, physics, metaphysics, ethics, and mathematics. The second course took three years and was followed by a course in dialectics and moral (case studies) and speculative theology. Moral theology and speculative theology had become regular subjects by 1565 and 1572, respectively.

As early as the sixteenth century, consequently, Brazil was preparing two categories of clergy, the lettered clergy (teachers and preachers) and the evangelizers (dedicated to the conversion of the Indians). The awarding of academic degrees began in 1575, when a Bachelor of Arts was conferred at a celebration that excited the whole city of Bahía. The Jesuit father who wrote the colony's Annual Report noted that "Throughout the centuries no one in Brazil had risen so high." There was full consciousness of the significance of the transplantation of the epoch's culture to the distant lands of Portuguese America. In 1578 the first Master of Arts degrees were conferred, and by 1581 Anchieta was able to write:

> The number of students has reached 100. . . . In these regions, where no one cultivates letters and all devote themselves to business, this is the maximum. . . . Certain students were raised to the dignity of Masters. The ceremony was carried out with the greatest solemnity, with the pomp and circumstance customary in the Academies of Europe, such as never had been done here. Nothing was lacking, neither the ring, nor the book, nor the horse, nor the birettaed page, nor the silk mortarboard.

The impressiveness of the procession and the solemn bestowal of insignia in the "doctoral" celebrations marked the apogee of Brazilian studies in the sixteenth century. There was some discussion later as to the legitimacy of the degrees, since Brazil had no university; in 1597, however, the Jesuits were granted the right to confer them. In 1605 the provincial Pedro Rodrigues could write that in the "college" of Bahía "there are public studies . . . which graduate Masters of Arts and of Moral and Speculative Theology, from which emerge many good philosophers, artists and preachers."

As a strictly vocational training course for priests and jurists, education had no other concern than conserving and safeguarding the status quo. The tranquil acceptance of this state of things began to break down only in the second half of the eighteenth century. Although scholastic education continued to be in Latin, there were symptoms of unrest in Portugal in opposition to the excessively formal mode of instruction. A broad movement took shape to reform Latin grammar and introduce the vernacular as an intermediary in the study of Latin culture. This movement marks the beginning of the modern period, when attention turns to the national culture as a variant of the great common culture of Europe. Latin now comes to be studied, strictly speaking, as a foreign language, although the discipline of its grammar and rhetoric was still considered essential for training the mind and forming the intellect. It was through Latin authors that ancient culture, as developed by the philosophers of the Middle Ages, was transmitted; and this transferral of culture was continued by the post-Renaissance philosophers and writers.

As if to demonstrate how impervious the Jesuit system was to modern ideas, as late as 1746 the rector of the Colégio de Artes could still issue instruction that

> in examinations, Lessons, public and private Theses, new concepts or opinions shall not be taught, those little accepted or useless for study of the Major Sciences (Theology, Law, Canon Law, Medicine and Mathematics) such as the works of René Descartes, Gassendi, Newton and others, and specifically any science that defends the Atoms of Epicurus, or denies the reality of the Eucharistic accidents, or any conclusions opposed to the system of Aristotle, which in these schools must be followed, as has been recommended many times in the regulations of this Colégio de Artes.

It was against such resistance to modern European thought that reform of instruction in the kingdom developed.

The first criticisms of the existing school system came from the academic world itself but something deeper was at issue—the transition from an ecclesiastic to a secular state, requiring the Portuguese government to adapt itself to the new eighteenth-century concepts and conditions already prevailing in the more advanced countries of Europe. These ideas gave rise to a new intellectual and political elite. This elite came to be called the "foreignized elite," and its leading exponent was the Marques de Pombal, a *fidalgo* who had lived for many years abroad, particularly in England. Dom José I appointed him prime minister for the purpose of carrying out a radical reform of the kingdom, not only economically but also educationally and culturally.

> If many of Pombal's reforms proved abortive, shortlived, or downright harmful, certain outstanding achievements survived his fall and the clerical reaction which followed. He abolished slavery in Portugal in 1761–73, although not so much from humanitarian motives as to prevent Negroes from being employed as household servants in Portugal instead of as fieldhands and goldminers in Brazil. Not only did he abolish the colourbar in the Asian colonies by ordaining—and enforcing—the principle that 'His Majesty does not distinguish between his vassals by their colour but by their merits', but he went to absurd lengths in trying to encourage intermarriage between the white settlers in Brazil and the stone-age Amerindians. He drastically reformed the antiquated curriculum of the Coimbra University, modernizing the teaching of law, mathematics and medicine. He tried to foster the growth of a better-educated middle class by such methods as the establishment of a Commercial College at Lisbon, and by the creation of government-subsidized schools in Portugal, Brazil, and Goa. He swept away the iniquitous legal and social distinction between the 'Old' Christians and the 'New', enacting the most stringent laws against anti-semitism, thus purging Portuguese society of an evil which had poisoned it for centuries.[1]

In the early part of the nineteenth century, the process of Brazilian national emancipation was facilitated by graduates of Coimbra who, reflecting the *Reforma Pombalina*, had already made their first contacts with science and with the new ideas of Europe and particularly France. Gilberto Freyre has called the reign of Pedro II "the reign of the college graduates."[2]

The University of Coimbra and Brazilian Resistance to the University Idea

Coimbra served as the university of both the mother country and its colony. It was in no sense inferior to other universities of the epoch. In the sixteenth century, it had come under the control of the Jesuits and change only appeared with Pombal's reforms. His educational reforms were interpreted in Brazil as tantamount to the destruction of the existing educational system. Resistance was perhaps greater than in Portugal; the isolation and segregation of Brazil had made its social and cultural conditions backward even compared to Portugal's.

Until the nineteenth century Brazilians went to Coimbra to study after finishing their courses in the royal Jesuit "colleges" (secondary schools) at home. In the eighteenth century these students were required to do only one year in the Colégio de Artes of Coimbra before entering the advanced courses in theology, canon law, civil law, medicine, and philosophy. After the reform of 1772, the physical and natural sciences were also included. During the first three colonial centuries, more than 2,500 Brazilian-born youths were graduated from Coimbra.

A Brazilian at Coimbra was not a foreigner but rather a Portuguese born in Brazil. Francisco de Lemos de Faria Pereira Coutinho, born near Rio de Janeiro, was a member of the Junta de Providência Literária (set up to study the radical university reform of Pombal) and went on to become the executor of the reform and rector of the university for some thirty years. José Bonifácio de Andrade, the "Patriarch of Brazilian Independence," was at one time a professor at the University at Coimbra. Various other Brazilians were also professors there.

Inasmuch as independence took the form of a separation of thrones, a cultural identification continued for the duration of the empire (1822–89). It was only after the founding of the republic that a clear and formal distinction could eventually be made between the two national cultures.

In the five years preceding the *Reforma Pombalina* (1764–68), the University of Coimbra had an enrollment of 20,453 students from the whole Portuguese Empire, distributed among theology (566), medicine (996), law (2,493), and canon law (16,398).

Shortly after King John VI and his court, taking refuge in Brazil from his French-occupied Portuguese kingdom, arrived in Bahía in January 1808, the local business community asked him to found a "literary university" there, offering a substantial sum of money to build the royal palace and support the university. The request went unheeded. Instead of a university, the Prince Regent decided, in February 1808, to provide instruction in surgery, anatomy, and obstetrics. The gesture was in response to a request by the Surgeon General of the Kingdom, José Carreia Picanço, a former professor at Coimbra, who was a Brazilian.

Following the transfer of the court to Rio de Janeiro, there was a modest expansion of (1) primary education along with the establishment of vocational schools; (2) a selective system of training the elite through a limited number of secondary schools; and (3) higher education, exclusively for the liberal professions, which was offered in a half-dozen separate national institutions on a part-time basis.

In addition to the schools of surgery and anatomy in Bahía and Rio, and the Naval Academy—all begun in 1808—in 1810 King John VI created the Military Academy. In 1814 he set up the course in agriculture, and in 1816 the Royal Academy of Painting, Sculpture, and Architecture. After independence, Emperor Dom Pedro I, on August 11, 1827, created the law courses in São Paulo and Olinda. During the regency of Dom Pedro II, the School of Mines and Metallurgy was founded in Ouro Preto, in 1832; the School of Pharmacy, also in Ouro Preto, was founded in 1839; and in Rio de Janeiro, in 1830, the Colégio Imperial Pedro II. The only such act of Emperor Dom Pedro II himself was to officiate at the opening of the School of Mines, thirty-four years after its formal creation.

These were the sole institutions of higher learning in Brazil up to 1889, the year of the proclamation of the republic. During the almost fifty-year reign of Dom Pedro II, not a single new school was created. It was only in his last speech from the throne, eighty years after the first school of higher education was founded, that the Emperor finally acknowledged the need for universities for the north and the south. The last years of the empire were taken up with other problems—the abolition of slavery, a military crisis, and tensions within the church; the tardy and vague recommendation was not acted upon even by the Republic.

In 1830, the Colégio Imperial Pedro II was founded, which,

together with similar institutions in the provinces, took over the
tasks of secondary education. The curriculum was of a classical-
scientific type, faintly suggesting that of the French *lycée*. Because
it offered studies in Latin and Greek, the course could be loosely
termed humanistic. Strictly speaking, however, Latin and Greek
courses, like French and English, were taught only as languages,
and did not include the respective literatures.

From the time of the flight of the Portuguese royal family to
Brazil in 1808 until the founding of the republic in 1889, there
were numerous and repeated appeals for the establishment of a
university, but all were met by direct refusal, silence, indifference,
or arguments such as those of Almeida de Oliveira and the
positivists, which identified universities with obsolete forms of
medieval culture. No less than twenty-four bills on the university
alone were put forward between 1808 and 1882. The last two were
drafted by Ruy Barbosa in 1882, but in his own words, "They slept
the sleep of the Chamber of Deputies, where they succumbed to
the mold and moths of the archives."

The constitutional monarch permitted himself to be persuaded
that the new learning would be better served by specialized
university-level schools, in keeping with the spirit of the scientific
diversification of knowledge. He overlooked the fact that the
fundamental function of modern higher education was to promote
the common national culture and not to perpetuate the universal
culture of the Middle Ages. The new national culture could not be
built with applied sciences alone, but needed a study of the
national language and literature, and of the human and physical
sciences in the basic fields of academic knowledge.

Education at the higher level of professional schools after
independence was a part-time occupation, with part-time teachers.
The professors had active professional lives outside school, and the
few hours per week they devoted to the students were occupied
with full-scale master lectures. The part-time school, absurd as it
may seem, nurtured a secret ambition to imitate the full-time
university, in the sense of training "scholars" and as seen in the cult
and the admiration of intellectual success gained by one or another
student. The espoused system of values was in sharp contrast to the
actual practice of the schools, their organization, their methods of
work, the space and time devoted to teaching, and the merely

symbolic payment of teachers. But when a student, in spite of all this, proved himself a *scholar*, the way in which he was applauded and celebrated went far beyond the practice in countries where such values were solidly established.

Higher Education in Brazil in the Nineteenth Century

With regard to both social structure and education, the colonial period reached into the nineteenth century, and held back for a hundred years Brazil's social and economic development. Educational opportunities were kept within strict limits, so that the small Brazilian elite, trained during the colonial era, could take over the reins of government, replacing the old Portuguese elite. The transition to independence was less violent than in most of the other Latin American countries, and the replacement of the group of Portuguese born in Portugal by Portuguese born in Brazil took place smoothly. Monarchy, King, aristocracy, and slavery were all preserved; the same system of administration and taxing remained, as did the same power structure, and the same education for the elite. The existence of an elite with a secondhand education, proud to prefer Latin and later French to their own Portuguese, and having a certain undeniable intellectual refinement, permitted Brazilians to harbor the illusion that the appalling backwardness of the nineteenth century, thanks to which even slavery could be retained, represented some rare kind of stability, political wisdom, and national good sense, compared with the political tumult of much of Latin America.

Whereas modern Europe, without any great historical exactitude, conceived the stereotype of a "medieval night" for its own long period of stagnation, the Brazilian intellectual classes came to consider the colony and the empire that was its continuation practically roseate periods, the "cultured" and prosperous times of the nation's development. On this foundation they built a structure of rationalizations that lasted throughout the century, and from which Brazilians have never freed themselves. Even today it is reflected in a national conservatism that fails to take seriously the aspirations of the prosperous, nationalist middle class that arose during the first half of the twentieth century. Underlying this conservatism is a persistent sense of dependence—as though the nation must never hope to do more than reflect Western European trends and developments. A corollary of that conservatism is the notion that Brazil's structure of social inequality must be maintained in order to preserve the nation.

After completing the secondary course, the postindependence Brazilian had no opportunity to go on to advanced studies in the humanities, letters, or sciences as academic disciplines. This made it extremely difficult to train teachers for the secondary schools, for which the Colégio Imperial Pedro II was the model.

Public competitive examinations for teaching appointments became the incentive for the training of teachers through self-study. Tradition (as John Dewey wrote in *Culture and Freedom*) can generate sufficient energy to maintain the conditions that created it, but habits can result that obstruct a view of what is really going on; there is a mirage in which the tradition appears to be in full vigor when, in fact, it is in decline. The empire represented a period of decline which continued through the years of the Republic until 1930, when the first Faculty of Philosophy, Sciences, and Letters was set up. A certain number of teachers succeeded in getting such training, particularly in philology, the Portuguese language, and occasionally Latin; but since the historians, scholars, essayists, and men of letters were all self-taught, the competitive examinations for positions in the secondary and advanced schools functioned like a kind of competitive examination for the *agrégés* in France. France, however, provided advanced academic studies within the university. Humanistic culture became a sort of hobby for *aficionados*, dedicated self-taught amateurs who studied in rich and well-stocked private libraries. The bureaucratic tradition lived on in the minds of these elites. By the nineteenth century, it was no longer the custom to go to Coimbra; but to go to the Sorbonne was a purely individual *tour de force*, appropriate not so much for potential high school teachers as for doctors and candidates for chairs in the medical schools.

Ignoring any possible confusion or contradictions in this situation, the national intelligentsia continued to live in a dream world. Here, they proclaimed, was another France, with tastes predominantly literary, erudite, and scholastic. And certainly Brazil had her "scholars," if not profound and original, at least in many cases learned and brilliant. There was no shortage of writers either, although Brazilian literature was lacking in the creativity that only immersion in a real and not an imagined culture can produce. Brazil attempted to produce a national culture merely on the basis of the study of applied sciences.

When the university was finally established, however, it was more symbolic than real, since all it did was bring together the schools of law, medicine, and engineering under the common administration of a rector. The tradition of isolated and independent colleges, which had ruled since the beginning of the monarchy, continued without essential change. It was necessary that the nation, now independent, should become aware of the need of a *Brazilian* university, a university that could serve as a center for the elaboration of a new national culture, a university that would really be sensitive to the country's problems, crises, and growth. The consciousness of a national culture was developed by the activity of private learned societies and the work of Brazilian authors and literary critics.

Afranio Coutinho in his *A Tradicão Afortunada* (1968) studied Brazilian literature in the nineteenth century and has shown how through literary criticism developed at that time by the individual action of writers and scholars, the consciousness of a national literature was aroused—a task that should have been performed by a university.

This lag between the national school system and a developing national culture in Brazil constitutes a permanent feature of postindependence education, reflected by the hesitant and uncertain character of government leadership during the empire. With his obsessive spirit of modernization, the Emperor acted as a guardian of the status quo rather than as a forward-looking guide for the young nation. To cite Freyre again, "There was no greater academician in our country than Pedro II. Nor anyone less native and more European."[3]

The Scholar and the Rise of the University

The origins of the cult of the intellectual may be found in the educated man's identification with the clergy and the nobility, and in the notion that intellectual pursuits brought the greatest honors. The careers of a priest, a monk, or, later, a liberal professional all led to titles, degrees, and privileges conferred by the university. The tradition carried over to the independent institutions of higher learning of the empire, which preserved the customs of the University of Coimbra. These customs may be seen in the procedures followed for winning the *cátedra*—a public competition among the various candidates in the style of the grand disputes of the medieval university. In preparation for such competition the candidate would spend years of laborious effort. In order merely to qualify he had to submit an original printed thesis, and then had to prepare himself to be examined on any item of the chair's encyclopedic program. The examination consisted of a written essay, a lecture-class test, and a practical test (when the chair so required) on any point in the subject drawn at random. In addition, the candidate had to defend his written thesis in public, where he was questioned for hours by professors. This was done before an audience that followed the battle with passion and curiosity.

These examinations covered such a vast field of knowledge that it was not unusual for a candidate to suffer embarrassing failure. On the other hand, success reflected exceptional ability or incredible luck and in either case warranted applause from a public anxiously following the contest. When the competition ended, the new professor's studies ended too; now all he had to do was rest on his laurels.

The historical roots of this system of choosing professors may be found in the disputes of medieval schooling, which were widely diffused during the colonial period. As early as the sixteenth century, the courses opened with the *Grandes Disputas*. Culture became confused with intellectual feats of memory and shrewdness in speculative exegesis, just as one might display dexterity and skill in games.

The Jesuit colleges, the University of Coimbra, and the ways of Portuguese culture bequeathed to Brazilians a taste for grammar and philology, historical and literary studies, and arts and letters. Brazilians have made notable contributions in the field of jurisprudence. In literature, along with poetry and fiction, criticism has been especially noteworthy. There have been few works in philosophy, and the same is true for science and mathematics. In technology, aside from civil engineering, there has been no outstanding work. Medical studies have been of importance, not only in the way of scientific achievement, but also in what might be called medical humanities. Allied with studies in jurisprudence, there has been some concern with the social and political sciences.

The Brazilian scholar was largely self-taught; he depended mostly on his own resources and was generally subject to the dominant influence of some foreign culture—Portuguese, French, English, or German. Each measured his own value by the degree to which he achieved the standards of his chosen culture, standards that had not been transmitted to him by his native schooling. More recently there have been scholars heavily influenced by American culture, particularly in the social sciences. Until the twentieth century, typical Brazilian scholarship lacked the balance between the autochthonous and the alien that only the experience of intellectual intercourse can develop. Hence, to the scholar, Brazilian culture appeared primarily as superficial erudition; everything he said was customarily substantiated with copious quotations from foreign sources. Today this situation is considerably altered, and there are many scholars who are original in their concepts and take an interest in strictly Brazilian affairs.

There is no exact correspondence between the university professor and the Brazilian scholar. Generally speaking, the scholars and writers stand outside rather than inside the schools. Let us not forget, however, that Brazilian university-level schools were professional or vocational, and that during the nineteenth century and the first two decades of the twentieth, they were small and very exclusive. This was due to the limited number of *catedráticos* and the tradition of life tenure. Because the institutions of higher education did not operate on a full-time basis and did not pay satisfactory salaries, they did not attract scholars who wished to devote themselves exclusively to their studies. It was common, rather, for these scholars to seek certain higher-paying jobs (as diplomatic representatives, for instance), which, unlike the schools, did not hold them to regular work and spared them the travail of public competitive examinations. Not everyone followed this course; their literary works did not grow out of their teaching activity but rather out of their individual studies, sometimes in fields quite distinct from the chairs over which they presided. The duties of their professorships were often trimmed in recognition of their high prestige. Such was the homage paid by the school to the cult of scholarship that sometimes the scholars were excused from holding any classes at all.

Until 1930 the law schools were largely responsible for training the leaders of Brazil. It was these schools that preserved the distinctively Brazilian habits of thought and feeling, the liking for argument and deductive reasoning, for discourse and oratory, jurisprudence, history, the political and social essay, as well as for the predominantly generalizing, literary, and esthetic cast of the national mentality. The medical schools developed Brazil's appreciation for science, while the engineering schools, based on the Paris Polytechnical, taught it the utility of mathematics.

Although Brazil had no historical and geographical studies at the higher level until the 1930s, it developed a broad interest in these subjects with the stimulus and support of private institutions (such as the Geographical and Historical Institutes, which anticipated by many years the faculties of philosophy of future universities). These institutes, set up in many states under the aegis of the National Historical Institute, were a significant development in Brazil. In addition, scientific studies were fostered by the Brazilian Society for the Advancement of Science.

The study of the vernacular became general in the nineteenth century, and Portuguese became a subject that was taken seriously. Such studies, combined with an emphasis on medieval classicism, later on the Renaissance, and then on the cult of the "intellect" as it was conceived in scholastic education, molded the basic character of the Brazilian mind.

It has been this ornamental culture, perhaps more than any other factor, that has impeded Latin America's democratic and industrial development, which depends essentially on the utilitarian and scientific culture that could not be transferred by Portugal and Spain.

Liberal republican thought, informed by the idea that education was the province of society and the individual rather than of the state, restricted the public function in the field of culture to the regulation and promotion of private initiative, thus reinforcing the private school tradition dating from the days of the empire. In turn, this policy led to private schools of higher learning and to schools maintained by state governments, both of whose diplomas were accepted throughout the country so long as the school was federally authorized and inspected. Between 1889 and 1918, fifty-six new establishments of higher education, most of them private, were added to the fourteen that existed at the end of the empire.

The idea of a university surfaced again in 1915 in the Carlos Maximiliano Law for the reform of higher education. This law authorized the government, "when it thought opportune," to merge the polytechnical school and the School of Medicine of Rio de Janeiro into a university, incorporating also one of the free private law schools. Five years later, in 1920, the University of Rio de Janeiro was created on this basis, and in 1927, the University of Minas Gerais in Belo Horizonte. The tradition of higher professional schools persisted, however, and the university was conceived merely as a device to bring the three schools together under a common administration. Meanwhile, the university idea continued to brew in the form of academic studies in "philosophy, science and letters," and in the widely discussed educational surveys conducted by the newspaper *Estado de São Paulo* (1926) and by the *Associacão Brasileira de Educação* (1928).

One year after the revolution of 1930, a new law permitted a school of "letters, sciences, and education" to replace one of the three traditional schools in the make-up of a university. The University of São Paulo was opened in 1934, bringing together, in addition to the traditional schools, the Faculty of Philosophy, Science, and Letters, and the Institute of Education. The University of the Federal District opened at almost the same time, combining the Schools of Economics and Law, Sciences, Letters, and Education, and the Art Institute. The University of Rio de Janeiro was reorganized in 1937 as the University of Brazil, including the Faculty of Philosophy and the School of Economics.

When these schools were founded, missions of European teachers were imported in order to launch the new enterprise. They set themselves the goal, particularly in São Paulo, of becoming the central core of the university. Their propaedeutic courses would be preparatory for the professional schools, and later for specialization in literature, science, and philosophy. The old tradition of separate institutions of higher professional education died hard. Rebuffed, the Faculty of Philosophy, Sciences, and Letters was to develop primarily as a new professional school, a normal school for the training of secondary school teachers, with an isolated and independent existence like other professional schools. This, however, did not prevent the better and richer of the normal schools, especially when integrated into universities, from becoming schools for the preparation of specialists in the fields of letters and the sciences, social as well as natural, physical, and mathematical.

The real change that took place in higher education during the first decades of the twentieth century was marked by the introduction of experimental science into the university. Owing to the peculiar confederative structure of the Brazilian university, this change was not felt throughout the university, but only in some of its schools. The first to join the new trend were the schools of medicine. They were the great modern schools of the Brazilian university in formation, and it was these institutions that would effect the transition from a traditional and relatively static type of learning to the experimental and scientific type. They altered their methods in order to teach the new subjects; they started laboratories and bred animals for scientific experiments; and they developed pure and applied research. In addition, the medical schools trained a body of scientists and professionals who were the peers of scientists and professionals in the advanced countries, and they developed, in public health and in the hospitals, medical standards of high quality. In engineering, also, particularly in civil engineering, there was notable progress. Jurisprudence made significant strides forward in the schools of São Paulo and Recife.

Despite these long-needed reforms, the remaining shortcomings of higher education became increasingly noticeable after World War II, when Brazil's economic development required a more consistent and emphatic inclusion of science and research in higher education and the university. The need for a graduate school was apparent. The university ceased to be simply a vehicle for the transmission of existing knowledge; it had to be the discoverer or creator of new knowledge. The reform of higher education thus could not rest with the faculty of philosophy, sciences, and letters created in the 1930s. With its three- or four-year courses, it could not go much beyond the ancient Colégio de Artes of Coimbra, or the liberal arts college of Anglo-American education.

By creating this new faculty, Brazilians did not come any closer to Humboldt's model of the German university, with its emphasis on research and high-level teaching. The training of teachers at secondary schools and, on rare occasions, liberal arts colleges, has expanded so that there are now more than one hundred such programs. This rapid growth was paralleled by a similar expansion in schools of economics and administration. Higher education today offers more than fifty different programs at the undergraduate level in more than seven hundred schools, three hundred of them still outside the almost fifty universities.

The most pressing task has been to integrate these multiple special schools, now isolated from each other and involving unjustifiable duplication of teaching staff and equipment, into broader groupings so that efficient use may be made of human and material resources. The need to rationalize the teaching services, which, because of rapid growth, had become somewhat haphazard, was addressed in 1966–67 by decree and by laws for restructuring the university.

The second task is more intractable—reforming the university so that it can fulfill its mission as an institution of advanced teaching and research, capable of building a national culture and expanding the bounds of human knowledge. This has been a mission that was not and could not be assigned to part-time schools and part-time, self-taught instructors. The only exception to this has been the school of medicine. The graduate school cannot be a simple extension of present schools, but should be a new school that would extend the courses offered by the present faculties of philosophy and economics and the schools for professional training.

The University of Brasilia, founded in 1962, was designed as a new structure embracing the four great purposes of a university: the teaching and development of general culture; the refinement of special disciplines; the provision for broad and varied professional training; and the conduct of research. Furthermore, as an integral part of Brazilian society and indeed as one of its central institutions, the University of Brasilia was conceived as a house of intellect to serve the country as a center of studies, planning, and technical assistance to government, industry, agriculture, and the whole of national life. It is the modern university of Abraham Flexner in all of its amplitude, linked with the spirit of service, that shaped the American land-grant college.

The University of Brasilia was intended as a prototype for the coming reform of all Brazilian universities. It is a new university designed to promote, accompany, and serve national development. Although a hundred years late, it offers hope of emulating, in the last quarter of the twentieth century, what the university has accomplished in the United States. The creation of a graduate school can provide the instrument for restoring the true standards of higher education.

NOTES

1. For a good description of Pombal's dictatorship and the reforms he attempted, see Chapter VIII in Charles R. Boxer. *The Portuguese Seaborne Empire: 1415–1825* (New York, 1969). The quote is to be found on pp. 191–92.

2. Gilberto Freyre, *The Mansions and the Shanties* (New York, 1963). p. 356.

3. Ibid.

4

The European Background

Hanns-Albert Steger

By the end of the eighteenth century, the European "commonwealth of universities" had gone through a crisis that threatened its very existence. The crisis pervaded all of the "ecumenical" institutions of the medieval world—the Catholic Church, the Holy Roman Empire, and the expanding kingdoms of Spain and Portugal.[1] These seemingly eternal realms were being subverted by an unrelenting process of secularization: the skeptical bent of mind characteristic of the Enlightenment, scientific curiosity, the new economics of mercantilism, utilitarianism, and the belief in progress. Such were the corrosive agents, epitomized in the great French *Encyclopédie*, that undid the *ancien régime*.

With the French Revolution, the struggle between the sacred and the secular was resolved in favor of the secular. The abolition in 1793 of the French universities by Robespierre's Committee of Public Safety temporarily ruptured the medieval tradition of the university. When French troops seized Pope Pius VI in 1798, papal claims to temporal powers were rudely challenged, as was the separate existence of the Vatican City. The Holy Roman Emperor was shorn of his imperial glory, and in 1804 his ecumenical authority was restricted to the single state of Austria. The three hundred-year-old Spanish Empire began to disintegrate when Spain itself was occupied by Napoleon's troops and the viceroyalties of the Americas were replaced by the successor states. When the Braganzas and their court fled Lisbon for Rio de Janeiro in fear of their lives, the Kingdom of Brazil was elevated to the seat of empire and Portugal was momentarily reduced to the status of an occupied territory.

Today we know that the decline of medieval ecumenical institutions was but the beginning of a vast transformation in world politics. Louis Auguste Blanqui was later (in 1837) to label this phenomenon *"la révolution industrielle,"* interpreting it in anarcho-syndicalist terms. Blanqui felt that the forces thus released were the result of man's reflections about himself and his temporal destiny, its immanent foundation in this world, and its emancipation from all transcendentalism.[2] The *Déclaration des droits de l'homme et du citoyen* of 1791 refers to rights posited by man himself and justified by him alone and not by God. The divinely human element of man's essence was henceforth, as Ernst Bloch has said, "to be processed out of the progress of history"—in short, to be understood as part of man's efforts to make himself. Man's history had no transcendental vectors; it was purely immanent or, as Alfred Weber would have it, "immanently transcendental."

The French Revolution marked the beginning of a hundred-year war between the world of the "ecumenical communities" and the "modern" system of nation-state legitimacies. The victory of the latter over the former was incomplete. Insulated remnants of ecumenical communities that managed to survive were to become the bases for counterattacks.

Three of these survivals are of special importance in the present context. There is, first, the Latin American university system. Seen from Europe, it appears to be isomorphous, "a sort of academic greenhouse reproducing the cultural climate of the Iberian peninsula," in the words of Sir Eric Ashby.[3] Viewed from Latin America, however, one is struck by its heteromorphism.[4] Spanish Enlightenment under the Bourbons, Pombal's reforms in Portugal, and the general disorientation resulting from the Napoleonic wars combined to silence the command centers of that system: Salamanca and Alcalá in Spain, Coimbra and Évora in Portugal. In Latin America, on the other hand, without comparable institutional moorings, the university was cast adrift. Spared the crucible of the French Revolution, it carried on, much as the Coptic Church of Ethiopia managed to remain Christian behind the walls of Islam. Latin America's opportunity for a similar autochthonous development—the alliance of Creoles and Indians as demanded by Tupac Amarú in 1790—was not realized. Instead, the Creoles, pursuing their independence from Spain in a two-front war against *gachupines* and Indians, rejected the option for revolutionary reforms. The university became a plaything for an elite alienated on its own continent. Initially institutions of thoroughgoing paternalism, they became city-oriented agencies for the management of the dubious business interests of merchants and traders and their British (and later French) consigners. They changed from colonial haciendas of education into urban headquarters of "conservative" or "liberal" purveyors of European views, whether of the Holy Alliance or of the unholy "religion of reason" taught by Auguste Comte's *sociologie*.

Among the other great survivals of the Middle Ages that withstood the onslaught of the French Revolution, there were the English college federations in Oxford and Cambridge. Close replicas of the monasteries on Mount Athos—the model for Thomas More's *Utopia*—they were at the same time the bastions of the Anglican Church.[5] Like the Anglican Church itself, the college federations, undisturbed by the Reformation of the Council of Trent, managed to preserve their tradition from the Middle Ages through the French Revolution and beyond. The changes and revolutionary reforms brought on by the Industrial Revolution in the mid-nineteenth century did not affect the essential core: "Oxbridge" was never to fall prey to the type of nationalism that characterized continental Europe. It remained "ecumenical," a realm defined in terms not of "frontiers" but of "horizons." Here was one of the reasons for the uniqueness of Cambridge in the second half of the eighteenth century. It was the only medieval-type university that could boast not only of a scientific achievement of worldwide significance, but also of one of the most important accomplishments of the Enlightenment itself: Sir Isaac Newton's mathematics had, from the end of the seventeenth century, become a major and then a mandatory subject in the university. The discovery of the laws of gravitation and college politics were not unrelated to one another.

There was among the noteworthy medieval survivals, finally, the university system of the German language realm. Although, despite its "modern" or enlightened beginnings in Halle and Göttingen, it crumbled under the impact of the French Revolution, one important sector of the system—that of the organized student body—managed to endure and escape the winds of revolution, much to the chagrin of later reformers.[6]

Ernst Moritz Arndt, in his 1815 analysis of the German university system, was to advocate the *Studentenstaat*. The counterblow against the French forces of occupation was, indeed, first struck by the organized students. The Wars of Liberation were, from the students' point of view, nothing but a two-front battle against the *ancien régime* and against the Revolution, the ideology of a foreign military presence.

The German university system was a conglomerate of both university archetypes: the "master" university of Paris and the "student" university of Bologna. It never succeeded in integrating them, as did Oxford and Cambridge, to produce another type: the university in which the "fellow" rules. The German university remained a house divided; *Studentenstaat* and *Professorenstaat* were linked in a peculiar symbiosis whose nature allowed the student participants in the Wartburg Festival of 1817 to become the frustrated professorial representatives of parliament who met in Frankfurt's St. Paul's Cathedral in 1848.

Wilhelm von Humboldt's blueprint for the University of Berlin was predicated on the assumption of a German "fellow"—who did not exist, lest one mistake the person of his brother Alexander as a valid substitute. Instead, the new university was inhabited by *Professoren* and *Burschen* living worlds apart under the same roof.

The lineup in the struggle between the "commonwealth of universities" and the French Revolution at the turn of the century may be described in the following way. On one side the Anglo-American camp with Oxford, Cambridge, Harvard, William and Mary, Yale, and Princeton; the Latin American camp of fourteen insulated Hispanic universities, with Brazil having no universities whatever and continuing to be oriented toward Coimbra; and the university remnants in the cultural sphere of influence of the old Roman Empire of the German nation. Facing them on the other side was the vast domain of the French Revolution. In seizing the University of Paris, the revolution had deprived the "commonwealth" of its old capital, from which pronouncements of worldwide importance had been issued.

The French attempted to develop a radically new system of education claiming universal validity. The educational objectives of the revolution were set forth in the program for the *écoles centrales*—in effect only from 1795, when they were opened by the Convention, until 1802, when they were closed by Napoleon.[7] The revolution's educational goals included: (1) the elimination of Latin and the related ideology of the *ancien régime*, and their replacement by a thoroughly revised curriculum relevant to the problems of present-day society; (2) the abolition of faculty control by the church, and its replacement by lay control informed by the spirit of the *Encyclopédie* and the Enlightenment; (3) the abandonment of the methods of collective indoctrination and the rigid class division of pupils associated with it, and their replacement by the freely structured curriculum of the student electing his courses in accordance with his particular interests and abilities (a scheme, incidentally, that has much in common with today's U.S. high schools).

The education system was to adjust the student to the present, not to the past. The norms of education were no longer thought to dwell in a transcendental heaven of eternal verities, but were assumed to be immanent in the nature of man and posited by man himself. The teacher-student relationship of old was to be put on its head; instead of the teacher determining what the student should learn, the student would decide what he wanted the teacher to teach him.

It was the will of the revolutionaries that the call to *liberté, égalité,* and *fraternité* was to be no mere ideological battle cry; it was to serve as the organizing principle for a new system of education and culture. With this kind of foundation, however, the educational system would fail as a pillar of Napoleon's empire and of his desire to create a new social order. Napoleon's reform of education commenced in 1802 and reached its acme with the founding of the *Université Impériale* in 1808.[8]

The educational system, reflecting the change from the revolutionary war to the "great patriotic war," no longer responded to the *Être suprême*, but to a *Grand Maître* who, like the commander of an army of occupation, controls the movements of everyone under his command. Universal military training and universal compulsory education were cut from the same cloth. Henceforth, the professors would resume their traditional positions of dominance, becoming the real beneficiaries of the French Revolution and the guarantors of its institutionalized permanence.

Every aspect of education was considered part of the *Université*. The regional prefects of education, usurping the "liberated" title of rector, called themselves *Recteur d'Académie* (rector of a given academic district), but the new system turned out to be not so new after all. Thinly disguised with the rhetoric of laicism and secularism, the *Université* was a rather precise replica of the Jesuit educational system. It was, and in essence still is, the secular version of a system anathematized by every enlightened revolutionary.

It was now that the peculiar dichotomy characterizing French education made itself felt. That which was truly modern and revolutionary—all the paraphernalia of industrial technology—was kept outside the monstrous structure of the *Université*. To Napoleon, all polytechnical education and training (on which the *Encyclopédie* and the philosophy of the Enlightenment had placed so much emphasis, and with which the *Convention* had concerned itself) were auxiliary sciences of warfare, designed principally for the training of pioneers and sappers. The whole complex of the *Grandes Écoles* was in effect nothing but the defunct medieval university. In the research institutes, on the other hand, as with the Institut de France and the *grand corps savants* generally, the ideas and programs of the revolutionary pre-Napoleonic tribunals remained relatively intact.

The French bourgeoisie of the Enlightenment, once it was firmly entrenched in the *Directoire*, insisted upon its price of victory: the reintroduction of the very educational structures by which it had been nourished. The university system was thus frozen in the state of development reached during the era of mercantilism, reflecting the controversies surrounding Voltaire and the *Encyclopédie*. Napoleon's university reform simply ratified a prerevolutionary phase of bourgeois self-consciousness, a phase that had been reached in Germany at the same time, without a revolution, by the University of Halle. Ironically, it was Napoleon who in 1807 closed the University of Halle, thereby providing the final impetus for the creation of the University of Berlin.

By canceling the educational reforms of the French Revolution, Napoleon made a political decision of far-reaching consequences. He sought to coordinate, wholly in the style of an Imperial-Catholic catechism defining divine and imperial order, the imperial educational system, as a lay variant, with the closed *orbis catholicus*—an arrangement still in existence today.

In the wake of the bourgeois revolution of 1830, the French educational system extended its sweep to the entire Hispanic, Mediterranean, and Latin American world. To this day, it has determined the style by which all structural problems of education are formulated. This has been true even when the structural substratum was unrelated to the French model, as occurred when the Latin American *escuelas normales* of the nineteenth and twentieth centuries were made into de facto universities for the talented poor. The French influence prevails in Mexico, with its Escuela Nacional Preparatoria, an institution of paramount importance from the standpoint of educational policy; and in La Plata, Argentina, with its Colegio Nacional de la Plata. To the extent that the French teaching model was merged with the Hispanic research tradition of the *colegios mayores,* here were, potentially, the elements of a second university system. Some of the most distinguished Latin American scholars of our century, such as Alfonso Reyes, Antonio Caso, and Pedro Enrique Ureña, have been closely associated with these *escuelas normales.*

The adoption of the French educational system in Latin America applied primarily to the French ways of teaching, not to their research techniques. As far as teaching was concerned, the reforms held out by the *Convention* as models for the whole of "civilized" mankind were completely subordinated to the idea of the nation state. In relation to research, the new revolutionary reality, in which the *arts et métiers* and, finally, Auguste Comte's *philosophie positive* set the tone, was permitted to grow; it was a world characterized by the cult of reason, by increased specialization, and by the Paris World Fairs of 1855 and 1867 (counterparts to the London World Fairs of 1851 and 1862). The research activities organized under the Institut de France or the other great creation of the *Convention,* the *Musée National d'Histoire Naturelle,* became scientific research enterprises of international repute. Most of the research associates at these institutes received their appointments during the periods of the Directoire or Consulat, when they were rather young men, little more than twenty years old.

The progressive impulse of the revolution created a new atmosphere different from that of the *facultés,* which denied their hospitality to the new sciences. The year 1868 saw the establishment, just after the second Paris World Fair, of the *École Pratique des Hautes Études* outside the *facultés*. Ever since, it has been extremely difficult in France for the results of scientific research, not to say the very spirit of research, to exercise any tangible influence on the structure of teaching. With the growth of industrialization and of the natural science research associated with it, the gulf separating the researchers from the teachers would continue to widen during the nineteenth century.

The new scientific atmosphere could not be thought of as separate from the world metropolis that was Paris. It was mandatory for the members of the Institut to reside in Paris. Whatever there was outside, culturally speaking, was provincial and had meaning and purpose only as a potential resource for Paris. The Napoleonic system functioned like a gigantic pump sucking all available brain power to Paris—"the capital of the nineteenth century," as Walter Benjamin called it—thereby causing an intellectual impoverishment of the provinces more severe than under the *ancien régime*. Organized scientific research thus represented a huge system of exploitation enabling the metropolis to hold the province in perpetual subjection and dependency.

The Latin American universities of the nineteenth century may be said to have been a "province" of the French educational system (without its own metropolis, to be sure, for its metropolis was Paris). There was no reason for transplanting to Latin America the other part of the French educational enterprise, its organization of modern natural science research. The failure to do so had developed from the experience of several decades. In Spain, owing to Charles III, and in Portugal, to the Marquis of Pombal, the Enlightenment had not been subversive of the *ancien régime*. Rather, the Enlightenment had been prescribed and imposed from above, just as it had been in Prussia by Frederick II. The Spanish *afrancesados* under Charles III began to look to Paris as their real capital. The French Revolution, and especially the Napoleonic occupation of the Iberian Peninsula, had the effect of interrupting rather than facilitating the process of Gallicanization that would resume under the aegis of the Holy Alliance.

It could be said that Latin America adopted only one side of the French educational coin. Its own beginnings in organized scientific research, as they existed in some of the *colegios mayores*, were neglected or permitted to die out. Other than Mexico, which remained without a central university, the well-nigh complete transplantation of the French model was but a momentary possibility in the Lusitanian realm. In 1823, Emperor Pedro I weighed the possibility of founding an Universidade do Brasil, analogous to the Université de France, for the purpose of overseeing the entire education of the country. In the early nineteenth century, Rio de Janeiro might well have exercised the monopoly necessary for a successful operation of the system, but debate over a national education law was to last a whole century; it was only in 1962 that the *Lei de diretrizes e bases da educacão nacional* was passed.[9]

The educational system suffered the same inversion of function as other imports of European culture to Latin America. Isolated from its sociocultural moorings, the transplanted French educational system supported rather than undermined colonial immobilism.

Latin American Variations on the French Model

The modifications of the French university model in Latin America had been long under way by the middle of the nineteenth century. In the main, these changes must be understood in terms of the social agents, whose role was not paralleled by anything in the French situation, responsible for the university in Latin America. Ever since the time of Charles III, the *criollos* had viewed themselves with French eyes.

In 1779, Charles III aligned Spain with France in the war against England, thereby giving aid to the North American rebels in their struggle against the mother country. As a consequence of this alliance, the Creole rebels did not ally themselves with the North American revolutionaries. Marcano, Alvisto, and Juan José Godoy opened their rebel headquarters in London. In Latin America it was the French version of the rights of man that was debated, and the French-Spanish rather than the English rituals were observed by the Free Masons.

The ideas of the Enlightenment made their entry into the Latin American universities long before the outbreak of the French Revolution. John Tate Lanning has illustrated this point in his writings about Guatemala, and Julian Marías has discussed the promise of a reformed society in his *La España posible de Carlos III*. The French Revolution was counterproductive; it inhibited the spread of the Enlightenment and tended to strengthen rather than weaken the forces of the *ancien régime*. The bold rhetoric of the revolution served these forces well in the struggle for independence and in the establishment of a Creole version of the *ancien régime*.

Saint-Simon was one of the very few ideologues to believe the French Revolution would be meaningless if it did not encourage the creation of a technological, scientific, and industrial civilization. It was this negative potentiality that became a reality in Latin America. Throughout the nineteenth century, the *criollo* elite of big landholders, merchants, and mine owners used the rhetoric of the French Revolution to arrest and obstruct the structural changes set in motion by the revolution itself.

The University of Chile which was founded in Santiago, was of Napoleonic design, a form used by Bello in his prolonged attempt to return to the pristine forms of the *Siete Partidas* of Alfonso X. The effect of this procedure was twofold. On the one hand, it permitted the new model to become a striking success throughout the continent precisely because people thought they "knew and understood" what it "really" meant. On the other hand, it permitted some of Bello's less sophisticated followers to mistake his Aesopian language for his real intentions, with the result that the reform failed to reach its objectives.

As in France, the university in Latin America was forced to fit itself into the framework of nationalism—an artificial nationalism bereft of any solid social basis, for in Latin America, unlike Europe, the political forms of the nation state antedated the existence of national societies. Beneath the political surface, the old encompassing, ecumenical way of life persisted unscathed. It is chiefly for this reason that, despite all the national differences—*mexicanidad, brasilianidade, peruanidad, argentinidad,* and so forth—one is struck by the basic unity, if not uniformity, of higher education in Latin America.

In contrast to the French system, the curriculum in the universities of Latin America showed little sensitivity to the needs of society. The professional training program was artificially superimposed on the colonial university. There was no concomitant process of industrialization to inspire professional education and to encourage vigorous scientific research to maintain and enhance its impetus. Lacking this corrective, the negative aspects of the professionalizing university could flourish.

The professors were alumni who practiced their professions, to be sure, but they had little if any contact with ongoing scientific research and for the most part relied on the wisdom and knowledge imparted to them by their elders. Professional education thus became a kind of standstill operation that, until the beginning of the twentieth century, helped to widen rather than diminish the gulf between modern scientific research and what was actually being dispensed in courses carrying the label of science. What made things worse was that Latin American society, unlike the French, had no highly specialized national civil service to include the professors; instead, because of the low role-prestige accruing to university incumbents, its social value as an institution was marginal.

The Latin American university of the postmedieval period looked upon training in the science of law as general preparation and conditioning for responsible participation and leadership in public affairs. As significant social types, the Spanish-speaking *abogado* and the Portuguese-speaking *bacharel* symbolized the continuity of Latin American society because the Independence movement left the basic social structure unaltered and heralded a change only in the top political leadership positions. Even in France, the professional university would have been unthinkable without a solid civil service apparatus lending stability to the French ship of state. Because this prerequisite was lacking in Latin America, the universities looked to the liberal or conservative party rather than to the formal state for support in building and maintaining the new lay institutions. This reality was not only one of the main roots of the politicalization of the university, it was also a constitutive element of the entire system of higher education in Latin America. The non-lay-oriented, conservative groups established a university system of their own, known as the "Catholic universities."

By the end of the nineteenth century, the Latin American university was wholly incapable of bridging the gap between modern science and what passed under that name in its lecture halls. This was true especially where, in faithful imitation of the professional model, it rejected as superfluous every kind of general, or not immediately profession-oriented, basic science education.

For example, it was, and by and large still is, the rule to offer not chemistry, but "Chemistry for Physicians" in *Escuela A;* "Chemistry for Pharmacists" in *Escuela B;* and "Chemistry for Engineers" in *Escuela C.* "Chemistry for Chemists" could not be offered, according to this logic, until there was a corresponding career for chemists. This could not happen unless there were independent research institutions capable of training chemists. In France—the persistence of the traditional university notwithstanding—the corrective was always provided by truly impressive research efforts. They gave to the professional university its proper social underpinning. The Latin American university at the beginning of the twentieth century, on the other hand, was but a status-symbol-purveying institution functioning in the relatively static sociocultural context of a preindustrial era. Although it used the "language" of the French university, the Latin American university was not part of a functionally oriented, mobile system of education.

Teaching and Research in the English and Hispanic Systems

The purpose of Napoleon's blockade was to isolate England from the continent, but it also had the effect of insulating the country against the French Revolution. Even the publication in 1792 of Tom Paine's *The Rights of Man* could not change that. The tone had first been set by the appearance in 1790 of Edmund Burke's *Reflections on the French Revolution.* As John Stuart Mill was to emphasize clearly in 1867 in his inaugural lecture at the Scottish University of St. Andrew's: "There is a tolerably general agreement about what a University is not. It is not a place of professional education. Universities are not intended to teach the knowledge required to fit men for some special mode of gaining their livelihood."[10]

As Sheldon Rothblatt has noted, Mill's statement was true for the college federations, but not for the universities of Oxford and Cambridge. The last two had undergone an organizational change since the beginning of the Industrial Revolution. Toward the end of the eighteenth century, the university at Oxford and Cambridge had merely been a joint secretariat to handle matters concerning the federation as a whole. Courses of study and methods of instruction remained the preserve of the individual colleges. They had their own ideas about the aims and purposes of education, which were accurately expressed in the inaugural address of John Stuart Mill.

A distinguishing feature of the educational philosophy of Oxford and Cambridge was a humanism strongly influenced by the ideas of Greek antiquity. In Cambridge, thanks to Isaac Newton, special importance came to be attached to mathematics. Students had to sit for a university—not college—examination in mathematics as part of the famous (and infamous) "tripos"—honors examination for the degree of Bachelor of Arts. Only King's College, regarded as a sort of extension of Eton, steadfastly refused to include mathematics in its curriculum. Nor was Eton itself to offer any course in mathematics until 1840. Despite the great mathematics tradition at Cambridge, one of its most important and prestigious colleges offered no mathematics at all until the middle of the nineteenth century. As in France, the new mathematically oriented natural sciences first developed outside academe. Applied science and technology were especially dependent for their development on the new urban middle classes and the Industrial Revolution.

Eventually the English university was able to incorporate the new disciplines by using the functional possibilities of the central secretariat: the university. There arose in the first half of the nineteenth century something new: a double-purpose kind of education and training within one institution. While the colleges, with their emphasis on the liberal arts, continued to impart the kind of moral education essential for men of character who would be leaders and custodians of the cultural heritage, the university and the faculties assumed the burden of teaching and training students for the professions in line with the requirements of a modern age. Two kinds of education, each with a distinct philosophy, were increasingly provided by the same persons. The two educational philosophies, the liberal and the utilitarian, began to overlap without merging.

The professor was not, as in France, the traditional university lecturer, but rather, as in Germany, the teacher-scientist. To the Oxford reformers in the middle of the nineteenth century, the German teacher-scientist (or scientist-teacher) was primarily a specialist—which, in the German view of things, was but an incidental aspect of the professor's role. Benjamin Jowett, for example, expressed the Oxford point of view in 1847: "We are so far below the level of the German Ocean that I fear one day we shall be utterly deluged."[11]

These two influences from abroad enabled Oxford and Cambridge, after the Reform Bills of the middle of the nineteenth century, to pursue a unique objective. They succeeded in reconciling the educational ideals of the English university with its medieval roots, and the French, with its orientation toward modern science. The figure mediating this union of seeming opposites was that of the teacher-scientist of Germany. The English professor was not the product of German educational philosophy—a philosophy which held that true education was not so much the result of deliberate pedagogical effort as it was a religious experience within the person, brought on by participation or ritual involvement in the scholarly enterprise. The English scientist-teacher, especially in his capacity as tutor, was assigned pedagogical duties completely alien to the German *Herr Professor.*

The English solution remained unique. With the college federation as its starting point, it was practicable only where a liberal arts education continued to be functional—to a social elite for whom, in the words, recorded in 1858, of a contemporary observer, Johan Grote, "The importance of a classical education lay in its use as a common denominator, a means of communication among educated men."[12]

As the oldest survival of the ecumenical university tradition of the Middle Ages, Oxbridge proved to be an institution of extraordinary flexibility. As such it was more capable of adjusting to modern conditions than those institutions on the European continent subjected to the changes of violent revolution. Although the English educational system did not break under the impact of the new sciences, it could not cope with another problem facing it. The bureaucratic organization of the state and the economy in modern society demanded interstitial specialists in such large numbers that neither the training capacities of the two old universities nor the social layers that contributed the personnel were sufficient to meet the demands. Nor could this social elite be motivated to perform functions that they felt were properly middle-class. Hence, the establishment of universities in the new industrial centers, such as Owens College, Manchester, in 1851. These "redbrick universities" were almost exclusively geared to the middle sectors in regard to both recruitment of students and their training in the requisite skills and knowledges.

The crucial social agents of the first phase of the Industrial Revolution were the relatively small minority of industrial workers able to read and write, seeking, in typically British fashion, to help themselves without waiting for the state to come to their rescue. They founded the Mechanics' Institutions that were the embryonic stage of a system represented in France by the *écoles des arts et métiers*. If the British government had been guided by ideas similar to the French in advancing the national education of its people, the initiative of the Mechanics' Institutions would undoubtedly have led to the creation of an elaborate network of polytechnical schools, which would have linked the applied sciences to the industrial needs of the nation.[13]

In 1850 the most advanced industrial nation in the world could boast of only two poorly paying chairs in engineering. The London World Fair of 1851 was regarded as a high point of crafts and industry. By 1867, however, industrial leadership had passed into the hands of the *polytechniciens* trained in the French *écoles*. The lesson learned in England from this development led not to the establishment of a system of polytechnical schools independent of the university (such as the *École Polytechnique* in Paris and the technical colleges in Berlin-Charlottenburg, Zurich, and Delft), but rather to the gradual opening of the universities to the teaching of science and technology. To this day, however, engineers and technicians have not been fully integrated into the British university system. As Eric Ashby has said, "They are tolerated, but not assimilated." The elite system of Oxford and Cambridge was able to maintain its dominant position against the new competition. It could do so because it had split in two and set standards of excellence even in the new sciences.

In the clearinghouse type of organization of the University of London, the English system developed an export model whose influence may be observed all over the world. The transplantation of that model has been one of the most remarkable events in the history of the modern European university. Two ingeniously simple devices aided in securing world renown for the London model: (1) the cooperative-secretariat (which had been quite impotent *vis-à-vis* the colleges) was transformed into an autonomous examining authority that would grant a London degree to anyone who passed the examinations—whether or not he were fully matriculated in one of the "schools" of the university "external degree examinations"; (2) the special relationship, which gave the newly formed colleges throughout the empire maximum opportunities for initiative and adaptation within the framework of London degrees in subjects in the London syllabus. It became possible, for the first time, to transplant a European university model to non-Christian societies, such as India. To paraphrase Ashby, the free-trade principle was extended to the distribution and acquisition of university certficates.

The colleges and institutes incorporated in the University of London, referred to as "schools," offer a whole variety of study courses. In this sense, they resemble structurally the *colegios mayores*. Under the organizational pressures of the professional university, however, the "schools," originally geared to no particular profession, soon became professional schools for physicians, teachers, engineers, chemists, and so forth. The idea of providing independent basic courses of study, as in the multidisciplinary "schools" of the University of London, never came into its own. Instead the tendency to splinter continued unabated, ending in the demise of the idea of basic science courses. Today the *escuelas* are, with few exceptions, bastions of structural immobility in the Latin American university. They managed to rob themselves of their scientific foundations.

The changes in the social function of examinations had their origin in the need and desire to make the university more "efficient," to operate it—borrowing a phrase from the educational debates of the Enlightenment—like an "academic coal mine," producing competent experts according to standardized norms.[14]

The achievement test has been a hallmark of the professional university. Its use was in frank opposition to the educational ideals of ecumenicism, a philosophy concerned with the wholeness of the world and man's relation to it, not with fitting men for any particular profession. The success of a classical education was measured by imponderable and qualitative, rather than quantitative, criteria. It revealed itself in public disputations, where, at least in principle, the student was expected to demonstrate, not the mastery of an encyclopedic body of knowledge, but his thorough understanding of the "realist" or "nominalist" order of the universe as expounded in classical doctrine.[15]

The modern test, on the other hand, was related to the life-and-death struggle of economic survival; the impersonal gauge of objective, "positive" knowledge represented the final, impartial arbiter. Teachers and students were no longer expected to commit themselves to certain "theses," but were to be processed anonymously by the knowledge machine of the *Encyclopédie*. Like every other thing produced in the new commodity economy, knowledge became a commodity—something external, alien to the person producing it, and subject to manipulation by those in control of the university as a knowledge factory. It was they who decided what norms were to govern what careers, tests being an objective, impersonal, and reliable means of reinforcing and legitimizing their control of the academic production plants.

Notwithstanding the innovations in examination customs and techniques, the medieval disputation has not entirely disappeared from the university in Spanish-speaking America. In Spain, it had its golden age in the fourteenth and fifteenth centuries. It was an expression of the living relationship between the student and his scholarly "raw material," including the writings of Aristotle. Through the *examen*, the *doctores* sought to ascertain the student's competence in handling the craft tools used by the "guild," even as in the *vejamen* the candidate was taunted by the biting wit and irony of his *conmilitones*—a solemn ritual which bound one to an increasingly precarious social system.

By the nineteenth century, these examination forms had rigidified into routines. They survive in the thesis defense at Spanish and Latin American university graduations and in the *Habilitation* —the solemn treatise presentation—at German universities on the occasion of formal admission of a university lecturer. They are reminders of the educational ideas of a preindustrial order, where a university education was valued not so much as an instrument of upward social mobility but as a symbol by which a person could prove his membership in a divinely ordained estate. Social mobility was not something to be achieved by the individual himself, as in the French *concours*, but something helped along by a superordinate until the candidate was considered worthy of admission to the elevated station of his sponsors. Such is still the logic underlying the

German university system with its doctoral and *Habilitation* "fathers."

The founding in 1876 of the Institución Libre de Enseñanza in Madrid combined the tradition of the English colleges with the high-level academic standards of the new German university and the traditions of the old Hispanic *colegios mayores*. As the first school in Spain that was independent of the state and the church, it was to produce men of well-rounded, liberal education and competence who would lead their nation.[16] It was the reaction against state intervention that led to the founding of the Institución Libre, and to the revival in Spain of a tradition, never to die again, of strong and sincere resistance against outside interference in academic teaching and research.

The Institución Libre was inspired by the philosophy of Krausismo in the 1860s and 1870s, which represented the idea of Karl Christian Friedrich Krause, a German philosopher and disciple of Schelling whose treatise on the origin of man, *Urbild der Menschheit*, was published in 1811. This work provided a rationale for a professor-scientist answerable to no one but his own scholarly conscience. The expulsion of the Krausist professors from the University of Madrid in 1867 was directly related to the publication of Krause's lectures on the basic truths of science, *Vorlesungen über die Grundwahrheiten der Wissenschaft*, in 1829.

In the case of Spain, which was to become so crucial for the Latin American university, the first contact with the new world of industrialism and the impersonal method and scientific discipline associated with it had come about as a result of Julián Sanz del Rio's accidental encounter with Krause's philosophy during a visit to Austria in 1843. The application of Krausismo, however, was soon to be modified by something wholly foreign to the German idea of education: the educational ideals of the English college. The second director of the Institución Libre was the art historian Manuel Bartolomé Cossío, who had once paid an extensive visit to Benjamin Jowett in Oxford. He obtained rather detailed information about the Oxford reform plans that sought to effect a marriage between the encouragement of science and research and the continued emphasis on the classical tradition.

There were not even the beginnings of industrialization in Spain when the left-liberal group of men around the Institución Libre was stirred by modern thoughts of reform. It was not until José

Ortega y Gasset, with his severe critique of the university and his emphasis on the necessity of Europeanizing Spain, that there was an apparent but shortlived change. The importance of this towering figure for the Spanish-speaking world cannot be exaggerated. It was through exposure to his ideas, followed by their interpretation and reinterpretation, that was born the distinctive Hispanic version of what is scientific and modern that maintained its currency alongside the German, Anglo-Saxon, and French versions of modernity.

A whole generation of promising young Spaniards who were sent to England and Germany in the 1920s and early 1930s for advanced education and *ampliación* came back to their country with a deep-seated admiration for Europe. Whether in acceptance of or in rejection of the spirit of modern Europe, such was the atmosphere that nurtured Salvador de Madariaga and Ortega y Gasset on the one hand, and Miguel de Unamuno on the other.

In 1939, the Casa de España in Mexico, later the Colegio de México, was to absorb a goodly number of scholars and scientists who fled their homeland after the fall of the Spanish Republic. The Casa de España, modeled after the Collège de France, diffused the spirit of modern Europe to the Latin American university and reignited the latent educational potential of the ecumenical order.

Another aspect of the growing movement of intellectuals asserting their independence of both state and church was the founding in Madrid of the Residencia Universitaria, where English college traditions were made to merge with the homegrown ways of the *colegios mayores*. A successful program of studies abroad had its origin in these initiatives, with a special Junta para la Ampliación de Estudios eventually encouraging a large number of young scholars and scientists to go abroad, mainly to Germany and England, for advanced study.

German and American Influences

The idea of *Wissenschaftlichkeit*—science, learning, order, organization, modernity—was the result of a European debate about the aims and purposes of higher education inspired by classical German philosophy and expounded in German universities. The social basis of education has only in recent years become a subject for scrutiny, as part of a more general critique of modern society by such German scholars as Friedrich Tenbruck, Helmut Schelsky, and Joachim Heydorn.[17] From 1794 to 1804, three distinct groups of thinkers pointed the way to modernity: (1) the philosophers of the prerevolutionary Enlightenment—above all, Immanuel Kant, whose *Religion Within the Boundaries of Pure Reason* appeared in 1793; (2) the thinkers and poets profoundly influenced by the French Revolution—men like Hegel, Schelling, and Hölderlin, who lived through the year 1789 as students in Tübingen; and (3) the patriotic youths, like Heinrich von Kleist, prominent in the resistance against the French.

The representatives of modernity all belonged to the second classification, among whose members were the two brothers Humboldt. It was this group that, in founding the University of Berlin in 1810, sought to build up an institution that would nurture a new spirit, rather than stand as a model or an instrument for the reform of existing institutions. In 1789, Schiller delivered his inaugural lecture at the University of Jena, and in 1812, Fichte resigned his position as rector at the University of Berlin. These dates delimit the span of events that determined the course of higher education in Western Europe down to our own days. The end of this period, particularly in regard to the university, was signaled by the Karlsbad Decrees of September 1819, which nipped in the bud every movement for autonomy in German higher education.

Tenbruck has pointed out that during the short period of "open possibilities," the "social matrix" (that is, the actual social conditions of change and growth) had expanded. Gone were the appeal and the viability of the petty principalities, and moving into the foreground were the activist groups insisting on a new national form of existence. The new national form, however, was something other than the *grande nation* of the French under Napoleon. In German-speaking lands, the idea of *Nation* belonged to the store of ecumenical traditions from the bankrupt estate of the Holy Roman Empire. As Tenbruck says, German culture has had no educational tradition independent from the university, and German national consciousness was from the beginning an academic, university-related matter. It remained so even when that consciousness, and the ideals of education that were part of it, became at one with the mind of the German people.

"Modernity," as a sociological concept,[18] was for the Germans of that period first of all "an imaginative anticipation and exploration of existence," not a revolutionary transformation of social conditions and relations, such as those enforced by the *Code Napoleon*. Any changes in the real world would only be the result of "imaginative anticipation," the goal of unifying the nation. Higher education became the monopoly of the university professors. The universities transformed themselves into a network of institutions exercising an effective monopoly control of higher education. Here was also the source of the characteristically German barriers that prevented the growing working class from entering the institutions of higher learning. Schelsky has called attention to the fact that the economy-based class conflict described by Karl Marx was considered by and exacerbated, reaffirmed, and rationalized in these key institutions of society.

To the forces of ecumenicism in both the European and the non-European universities, the German philosophy of education provided a congenial rationale. The German idea of "imaginative anticipation and exploration of existence" seemed tailor-made for a lagging social reality; it was "above" it and valuable as an instrument that was "profound" and "theoretical," although not immediately practical and political.

It is at the High Table of the English colleges, the time and place of the common meal, that from the early Middle Ages to this day such education for character has been most visibly practiced. Anselm's teacher, Lanfranc of Pavia (1005–89), had first taught at Bec in Normandy. Later William the Conquerer, whom Lanfranc assisted in reforming and reorganizing the English church, appointed him Archbishop of Canterbury. His scholarly fame had already spread all over Europe. During the common meal he would read and comment on the texts of Latin authors. One day, the story goes, an obvious ignoramus presided at High Table. He interrupted Lanfranc and bade him to correct his pronunciation—to say *"docēre"* instead of *"dŏcēre"*; thereupon Lanfranc yielded and simply committed the error he had been requested to make.[19]

The subtle irony of this gesture revealed the sovereignty of the truly educated person. It signified, indeed, that it was part of a world vastly different from the crude and humorless educational life-style in Germany during the eighteenth and nineteenth centuries. It suggested that importance, not of the abstract authority of a superordinate fool to enforce compliance with a silly request, but the strength of the underlying assent to a binding code of behavior, a tacit understanding of the practical usefulness and, at the same time, veniality, of that code. It was the common denominator, the means of communication among educated men, the cement that bound the members of this group to one another.

From the English point of view, the utter lack of such a bond between teacher and student, tutor and pupil, so characteristic for German universities to this day, was something simply inhuman. To E. B. Pusey, writing in Oxford in 1854, such a university was but a "forcing house for intellect."[20] How right he was in this allusion to the possible dangers inherent in the German system! The wretchedly supine attitude of the German university toward the inhuman regime of the Nazis is the product of history.

For these failures one must not, however, blame the educational philosophy of Wilhelm von Humboldt. The culprits were the officials and beneficiaries of the Prussian Empire. Their property-oriented, middle-class psychology, their pecuniary canons of taste and valuation led them to misinterpret Humboldt's ideas. It is the same misinterpretation that informs the appeals to the so-called spirit of Wilhelm von Humboldt voiced in our own day. Heydorn has shown how, at the turn of the century, Humboldt's philosophy of education was distorted into a political instrument to further the interests of the Prussian-German bourgeoisie. Heydorn has demonstrated in a challenging reinterpretation of Humboldt's *Lithuanian School Plan and Constitution for the Jews,* that his overriding concern was with the realm where man would be an end, not a means, with institutions that would educate the youth of Germany in an atmosphere of freedom, enabling them to resist becoming the mere tools, however efficient, and the victims of the "production idiocy" of an industrial system. Only in this way could man fulfill himself, make the most of the chance consciously to shape his own history. Wilhelm von Humboldt's educational ideas did not merely "imaginatively anticipate"; they were immediately practical and political. His *Constitution for the Jews* contained statements that flatly contradict the late-bourgeois Humboldt stereotype, including the following: "The serf that becomes a lord has made a leap; for lords and serfs are uncommon phenomena. But he whose hands are freed from the fetters that held them only gets where all men ought to start." This, says Heydorn, was a clarion call for the true liberation of man, for a state that knows neither lords nor serfs, where men obey no other master but their reason. The link was thus established to the famous chapter on the lord and the serf in Hegel's *Phenomenology of the Spirit* and to the later economic reinterpretation of that chapter by Karl Marx.[21]

The revolutionary implications of the educational ideals of the German classics held continuing ideological appeal and attractiveness, and the ability to inspire political action, if not immediately, at least indirectly as delayed-action devices that were sure to go off time and again. Erich Fromm's *Marx's Concept of Man,* an analysis of Marx's economic and philosophical manuscripts of 1844, has done much to show, especially to Latin Americans, the extent to which the philosophy of Karl Marx was inspired by the ideas and ideals of the German classics whose philosophy was conservative and revolutionary at the same time.

Humboldt, Hegel, and Marx offered three different interpretations of the problem of modern man, considered by each a matter of the greatest urgency. In Heydorn's interpretation of Humboldt, the problem was the liberation of man from the chains of economic determinism. Although industrial society has dehumanized man, transforming him into an automaton, it is in society that he must find the conditions of reconstituting himself in his human wholeness—indeed, his freedom and ascent are possible only on this basis of his decline.

The power of these German ideas was such that by the end of the nineteenth century even the French educational system was compelled to restore the principle of the institutional unity of the university. In 1896 the basic law of the French universities—drafted under Education Minister Raymond Poincaré and the permanent Ministerial Counselor Louis Liard—was promulgated. That law, which contains an explicit reference to the German model, has with few changes remained in effect to this day. The *facultés* separated by Napoleon were reunited administratively, but the oneness of teaching and research symbolized in the person of the teacher-scientist that was the pride of the new German university, could not be achieved by administrative devices of this sort. In effect the research activities of the Institut de France and other institutions remained as isolated from the university as before.

The only case of successful transplantation onto foreign soil of the German university model—both structurally and substantively —was that of The Johns Hopkins University, founded in 1876. The graduate school of the American university as an institution for advanced study and research was strongly influenced by the theory and practice of the German university. The differences should not be overlooked, however, for education in the United States has always meant a response to the challenges of a growing and expanding society, a society that knew no Middle Ages and acted like a practical "community." The revolutionary impulse of the German idea of education, therefore, merely assumed the form of an abstract demand for upgrading academic standards. As a high-level enterprise, the German university sustained a strong claim to international repute.

The philosophy of the classical American university did not originate as an "imaginative anticipation" of social reality. It sought no revolutionary transformation of state and society by abolishing the exploitation of man by man. Rather, it had its roots in the "Great Awakening," in William Tennent's "log college," where "new lights" were being spread. The democratic ideas of the busiest agents of American education, the Methodists, clearly derived from the Anglican church and German pietism. They stand in the same relationship to the radicalism of classical German philosophy as the reformist beliefs of the British working-class sects, John Trevor's "Labour Church," and even the Fabian Society relate to the revolutionary humanism of continental Marxism. In Britain, as Eric Hobsbawm has demonstrated, the bourgeoisie had won its revolution long before the masses and the middle sectors were imbued with an agnostic ideology. "The declaration of the rights of man," he says, "revealed itself among the English people not in the Roman toga and the enlightened prose of the late eighteenth century, but in the guise of the Old Testament prophets and in the biblical language of Bunyan: The Bible, *Pilgrim's Progress*, and Fox's *Book of Martyrs* were the texts from which the British working-class learned to read their ABC's of politics."[22]

Having experienced neither the continental European nor the Anglo-Saxon kinds of Enlightenment and industrialization, the American example—a third alternative—became increasingly more important, even dominant in Latin America. Unique situations tended to make certain developments more exemplary than they might have been otherwise. The zeal of the domestic missionary movement that made the United States a land of colleges led to the development of the land-grant college, with its emphasis on scientific agriculture and technology. There were, of course, conservative educators who spoke with unconcealed condescension of those "cow colleges" and tried to belittle their efforts at agricultural education and scientific agriculture as "seed corn gospel trains." The land-grant colleges, however, represented a most promising extension of the European, especially the English, university system. Because they were an incentive to achieve technical competence, they have since become generally the most respected and imitated university model in the Third World. As against the early English college model, the changes wrought under the pressure of a moving frontier were above all in the direction of a fundamental democratization of the curriculum, of blurring the distinction between professional and vocational education, and of vesting institutional control of the university, not in the hands of a faculty-administrator or a state official, but in an extrauniversity board of trustees and president.

In the field of higher education, Catholic traditionalism reasserted itself with the establishment in 1834 of the University of Louvain, Belgium, as the Université Catholique, and with the founding of Notre Dame University in the United States in 1842. The official *facultés de théologie,* vegetating within the framework of the *Université de France,* were first "overhauled" and, in 1886, by the simple device of canceling all budget allocations, put out of existence altogether. In 1876 the first Catholic university was established in Paris. With this move, the counterposition achieved high visibility in the very capital of the revolution. In its structure, however, the new university did not differ from the secular *facultés.* This was the price it had to pay for publicly recognized graduations. The first Catholic university in Latin America was established in Santiago de Chile in 1888 in the same city that had seen Andrés Bello's university become the model for all of Spanish America.[23]

In Germany, the traditionalist countermovement made use of Humboldt's university model of 1810, which pointed the way to modernity in the language of idealistic philosophy. The equality of men demanded by Humboldt was to be achieved by means of an otherworldly revolution of spirit. In this way the thousand-year rule of humanism was to be realized.

Karl Marx "concretized" these ideas by turning them right side up. In this sense, he was the heir and executor of the last will and testament of classical German philosophy. The German universities owed their initial revival to this impulse. Soon enough, however, all their energies were turned inward, and a prerevolutionary Enlightenment philosophy in the guise of modern neo-Kantianism came to prevail. Higher education no longer signaled the revolutionary transformation of society and the equality of men, but the rigorous ethics of duty, albeit with the accents of Prussian militarism and categorical imperatives. This was, indeed, the version of the German university that was to gain the greatest currency abroad.

The Catholic counterposition of the period had actually accepted the Napoleonic reforms of the university. It merely changed again the ideological prefixes, and thereby reaffirmed the fundamental structural affinity of the universities. The German notion of *Wissenschaftlichkeit*, however, implied universal standards of university performance. Predicated upon the interdependence of teaching and research, this German concept categorically rejected the suggestion that there could be scholarly teaching without research. There was a difference between German *Wissenchaftlichkeit* and French science, with the Germans primarily concerned with standards of the social sciences and humanities, the *Geisteswissenschaften*, rather than with those of the natural sciences.

Herbert Lionel Elvin has called attention to some important terminological distinctions in the levels and purposes of higher education in England.[24] Benjamin Jowett of Oxford, for example, considered "research" as investigations in the natural sciences, while "learning" and "scholarship" were sought in the social sciences and humanities, the traditional province of the liberal arts college. In France, *recherches scientifiques* referred to the natural sciences, but it was not a different concept of science that distinguished them from the *méthode raisonée* of the social sciences and humanities, for both were based on the *Reasoned Dictionary of the Sciences, Arts and Trades*, as read the subtitle of the *Encyclopédie*.

At the beginning of the twentieth century, then, there were three basic forms of university education: (1) education as a common denominator, a means of communication among liberally educated men of character and courteous bearing—the education of the English liberal arts college; (2) the education of scientific personnel—in the "academic mining company" of the French

Enlightenment; and (3) education for the advancement of knowledge—with *Wissenschaftlichkeit* defined in neo-Kantian terms as the ideal of the German university.

Newly added as a fourth form was that of the American university, with its focus on the practical (especially as it developed in the land-grant institutions), and one of the great forces for economic and social mobility. Only in France had the ground been prepared by a pervasive spirit of agnostic Enlightenment, and only there did an explicit counterposition arise—in the form of *Universités Catholiques*. Yet even this counter form, in order to give voice at all to its antirevolutionary conservatism, had to employ the language of the lay *méthode raisonée*. Herein lies the Catholic university's peculiar strength and weaknesses in the French and French-oriented systems of higher education.

The Attempt to Modernize the Latin American University

By the end of the nineteenth century, the gulf separating the traditionalist university in Latin America from the institutions of higher learning in Europe and the United States was wide. Auguste Comte's *Positive Philosophy* had made its entry into Latin America by the middle of the nineteenth century, but for all its appeal to the sciences and emphasis on material development, it did not lead to modernization.

The book was interpreted by the urbane, well-spoken group as an invitation to rearrange their society to attune it to Comte's law of progress discovered in an entirely different social climate. In Brazil, positivism promoted republicanism and played an important role in the overthrow of the empire and the establishment of the republic in 1889. In neither case, however, did Comte's positivism contribute anything to the growth of the scientific spirit, to the idea that knowledge be sought, tested, and retested according to universally recognized standards of judgment, and never accepted on the ground that it was the revelation of any authority, human or divine. On the contrary, Comte's positivism became an effective shield for the Latin American university against all external influences of modern science.

By the end of the nineteenth century, strong voices of dissatisfaction with the politics and philosophy of positivism were raised, voices that reaffirmed the human personality and insisted that the sciences in which personality played a part be treated differently from those where it was absent. The reaction was especially strong in Mexico, where Alfonso Reyes's *Visión de Anáhuac* (written in Madrid in 1917) was viewed as the virtual manifesto of the opposition; in Uruguay, where José Enrique Rodó issued a ringing appeal for Latin American self-affirmation and spirituality; and in Argentina, where Coriolano Alberini and Alejandro Korn offered a philosophy of personality, freedom, and values that showed an affinity with contemporary French and German philosophy of life and culture.

The Comtian tradition has since reasserted itself in the form of a more sophisticated neopositivism that had its origin in the different social molds of Europe and the United States. Continuing to express itself in the Comtian style, neopositivism has functioned as a working philosophy and social science for special application in Latin America. As pointed out by Juan Carlos Agulla, its influence has been seen even, and perhaps especially, in the work of Ortega y Gasset, particularly his *El hombre y la gente.*[25]

The problem of modernization continues to confront the entire block of national universities in Latin America—those *universités impériales* without an empire and without institutes of scientific research to set universal standards and norms. By the turn of the century, Andrés Bello's model had been imitated in all the capitals of the continent, as Humboldt's model had been all over Germany. It was not until the reopening by Justo Sierra of the National University of Mexico on the centennial of the *grito de Dolores* in 1910, during the last days of the Porfiriato, that this phase of university development can be said to have ended.

Much more difficult and complex was the situation in Portuguese America. For a whole century it had been impossible to enact a basic education law, even though the Congress debated and rejected thirty-two different proposals. It was not until 1915 that the Universidad do Brasil was finally established, based on the French model of 1896.

The Catholic private universities came into existence in Latin America about fifty years after the national universities. As part of the great wave of Jesuit institution founding, this phase of the Catholic university movement may also be said to have come to an end. Of the twenty-one Jesuit universities in Latin America in

1968, twenty were founded between 1940 and 1967—the sole exception being Bogota's Universidad Javeriana, founded in 1930.

The development of two parallel university systems has contributed to the ideological polarization of higher education in Latin America. The struggle for the separation of church and state was fierce. Most prominent among the liberal lay leaders were men like José Victorino Lastarria (1817–88) in Chile, Gabino Barreda (1818–81) in Mexico, Manuel González Prada (1848–1918) in Peru, and Enrique José Varona (1849–1933) in Cuba. The controversies eventually froze into positional warfare between the two systems, with the *Kulturkampf* finally turning into a ritual exercise for the person who decided to identify himself with one or the other system. The decision as to which type of university one should matriculate in has since become for the student an existential act.

This bifurcation has extended to Latin American society generally, whether one thinks of *colorados* and *blancos* in Uruguay, or *liberales* and *conservadores* in Colombia. In these circumstances, even the debates about the modernization of higher education have become highly politicized. Two examples may serve to illustrate this point. In the first place, academic freedom should be considered one of the most important prerequisites for the advancement of knowledge. It is the freedom of the scholar in the academy, a freedom that has in almost all Latin American states been constitutionally guaranteed under the title of *libertad de enseñanza*. Rafael Gutiérrez Girardot, in an analysis of the controversies surrounding this constitutional provision, has pointed out that the opponents of secular constitutional theory have tried to turn this freedom to teach into a subjective license to teach. *Libertad de enseñanza*, as originally conceived, says Gutiérrez, "is not at all a subjective freedom, but an essential, objective element of thought and intelligence; it is, thus, a kind of freedom that first comes into being in the scholar's activity as teacher and scholar and is grounded in the very structure of the disinterested pursuit of truth."

Once *libertad de enseñanza* is interpreted as an absolute license to teach what and as one sees fit, a problem arises concerning the freedom of particular social groups to spread the light in accordance with their own commitment to a more or less clearly articulated and authoritatively interpreted ideology. "The subject of that freedom," continues Gutiérrez, "is the abstract personality of the parents; they must be granted this freedom to teach and learn as a matter of natural law. The founding of private educational institutions thus becomes an inalienable right of individuals. As a matter of natural law, it stands over and above any positive law, the politics of law, and the educational requirements and objectives of state and society."[26]

In the second place, *libertad de enseñanza* was one of the principal issues of the 1918 student rebellion of Córdoba, a crucial event not only in the history of the modern Latin American university, but of immediate political importance in most, if not all, Latin American countries. In his astute analysis of the reform movement, Ernesto Garzón Valdés has pointed out that it was in its demand for modernization, especially in its insistence on autonomy as a condition for modernization, that the Córdoba Reform restored the link with the European tradition of the Latin American university.[27] To be sure, the reform led to a revival of ecumenical traditions, but it never succeeded in its objective of modernization.

The autonomy movement that began with the Córdoba Reform came to an end with the enactment of the new law of the University of Mexico (making it both "national" and "autonomous") in March 1945. Under the impact of the Cuban Revolution, however, entirely new viewpoints about university autonomy and reform have appeared.

The Latin American university has been strong enough to resist the pressures of modernization. The peculiar pattern of urban settlement may have contributed to this. The city was, after all, the native soil of the university. In the colonial period, the Latin American universities, except for those institutions under the direct control of the religious orders, were all firmly planted in the center of the city. University building was one of the indicators that all authority derived, ultimately, from the Crown. Thus, the university took its place alongside the other principal institutions of the colonial regime—the church, the government, the municipality, the judiciary—on the *Plaza Mayor*. This typical scene is perhaps still most clearly preserved in Antigua, Guatemala. In the absence of any independent patriciate to produce a particular urban consciousness, the mentality of the professors and students of the Latin American university turned instead toward the special agencies of power existing in the colonial period. It was a mentality that bore the clear imprint of the colonial city-state.

In the course of the nineteenth century, some vital changes affected the urban power structure. Referring especially to the northeast of Brazil, Gilberto Freyre speaks of a re-Europeanization of the colonial city in connection with the decline of the colonial plantation economy, and the movement of upper-class families from the *casa grande* of the sugar plantation to the *sobrado* in the city. Although the growing urbanization of the country intensified the contrasts between city and country, the urban population did not develop a peculiar urban mentality. Roger Vekemans, following Toynbee, has described city dwellers as a "Herodianized" population; even as Herod had once continued to reside physically in Palestine while spiritually remaining a citizen of Rome, city dwellers continued physically to reside in Latin America, while mentally and spiritually they lived in Europe or North America.[28] This re-Europeanization was promoted further by returning students, the sons of the plantation owners or even of the new bourgeoisie of the cities. These students, who had gone to Europe to study, brought back new ideas from Paris or Montpellier and, in the case of Brazil, were subsequently to play a decisive role in the transformation of the empire. Moreover, there was a gradual shifting of the seats of power either to new commercial and industrial centers, such as Bogotá or Mexico City, or through the imposition of new centers on old structures, as in Caracas and Quito.

It was inevitable that such changes would affect the relationship between the university and the city, and the role that each believed it ought to play. Architecturally, the "introverted" house, so confining and forbidding in appearance, made room for the "extroverted," open façade facing the street. Socially, the *abogado* became the hero of the day. Symbol of a society that had entered a phase of bourgeois urbanization without dethroning the land-owning class, the *abogado's* rise in the field of politics was rapid. He represented the political triumph of a new element of Latin American life, the new aristocracy of the city residences, the refined city man—as the *Herr Professor* represented the aristocracy of cap and gown in charge of bourgeois education in Germany.

In the city, the firm grip of government rule was somewhat

loosened, becoming more flexible and less visible, yet never merely marginal. Flexibility, which permitted the strengthening of the economic infrastructure, seemed more important than high visibility and location of particular governmental offices around the Plaza Mayor. Toward the end of the eighteenth century, it already was possible to observe (for instance in Recife, Brazil) a process not unlike that which marked the transition from the dominance of medieval towns to the modern states emerging in the Renaissance: the proliferation of the city mansions of the plantation owners. There was one important difference, however, between the Brazilian city and the European town around 1900: the former had no solid working class.

The power structure of the Latin American city in the nineteenth century may explain why, from a European viewpoint, such a Renaissancelike aura surrounded the figure of the *abogado*. Given the particular relationship between town and gown, *abogado* and *hacendado*, there was not much chance for the forces of modernization coming from the ecumenical frame of Europe to affect the foundations of the Latin American university. On the contrary, as long as the basic social structures remained the same, the university would be strong enough to withstand the winds of change.

The Córdoba Reform marked the beginning of the end of the university of Andrés Bello. This movement altered the university from an oligarchically controlled Napoleonic institution to a school somewhat representative of the middle sectors. In his book *El estudiante de la mesa redonda* (1933), Germán Arciniegas presents a summation of the effects of the reform that is still valid today. Its success made possible the rise of a new center of resistance against modernization. The institutional freedom of the Anglo-American university, and—in the area of academic competence, at least—of the German university as well, produced opposite results in Latin America. Nonacademic activities became more important than academic matters. The principles of the reform have not improved the quality of higher education but have led to the downgrading of academic standards. Such was the consequence of transplanting European ideas and institutions into the wholly different social and cultural climate of Latin America.

In his *Géographie de l'énergie,* Pierre George has drawn a comparative picture of world development in terms of the distribution of units of energy.[29] Thus, in 1950 Latin America had about 240, Africa 150, prerevolutionary China 150, and India and Indonesia less than 100 units. The United States, Britain, and Germany, on the other hand, each had more than 5,000 units of energy. For Latin America to bridge this gap in a short period of time would require some magical or divine intervention.

Autonomy as an institutional safeguard of a university not geared to the free and independent pursuit of knowledge tends not only to protect it against interference by the state, but also to insulate it against change and progress in social consciousness. The university's activities may actually be detrimental to the long-term interests of society, thus making it a bulwark of immobilization rather than an agent of change. It must, on the contrary, educate its students to resist the pressures of organized interests and groups, training them, as S. M. Lipset says, "to be constructively critical, to be able to initiate changes while appreciating what they have inherited," although in the developing countries the role of the university will be more "transgressive" than traditional.[30] The place of the *señorito*—educated abroad, with *savoir-vivre* as proof of his membership in the "Herodianized" class—is taken by the planned scholarship and exchange programs for the training of the young men and women who will become members of the elites of their societies to exercise skills in science and technology, management and administration. Aiming at nothing less than the creation of agents of modernization in the Latin American university, these programs have begun to work against themselves precisely where they seemed to be most successful. They have encouraged an ever more acute "brain drain" and thus contributed to frustrating their own designs.[31]

In their attempt to redefine the concept of modernization, contemporary German scholars have begun to reexamine the role of the university. One of the first to do so was Helmut Schelsky.[32] He believes the onward march of technological and scientific civilization is irrepressible. It now encompasses the entire globe and has produced something new: an *"actual* world citizenry." It has made the preindustrial production form of scientific knowledge, the pure household production of knowledge as it were, wholly obsolete. Beginning with the natural sciences, the research institute has become an autonomous production plant within and outside the university. Max Weber was among the first to reflect upon this process in his 1919 lecture "Science as a Vocation." Structurally, there has since been no fundamental difference between a scientific institute for the production of knowledge and a capitalist plant for the production of goods.

The artificial world of science and technology as it affects our immediate relation with and knowledge of nature; the globalization of our existence; and the increasing dubiousness of national boundaries—these are among the symptoms of change demanding an altered idea of modernization as the condition of progress. In the European and American university, science has come into its own and knowledge is identified with scientific discovery to such an extent that the two have become, as Husserl said, constitutive elements of the immediate "world of life." Education must, if it is to do any good at all, henceforth start from this new base of scientific thought and action. It must no longer be thought of as that which is likely to be the result of a classical German schooling. In Schelsky's words, "It is only the lesson of practical life—and today this means mainly the full experience of scientific thought and action—that will permit man to reach the threshold from which the problem of education may be properly raised. The attainment of a superior spiritual and moral quality of life as the aim of education is possible only on the basis of the prior scientific experience of the world."[33]

The aim of education may now be defined as the achievement of "spiritual and moral sovereignty vis-à-vis the challenges of life and the world, as they arise in the course of our practical experience in a universe governed by modern science." Educating the person today "implies enabling him to examine, judge, and control the consequences of science, more especially in its applied and technological aspects that are the bases of our scientific civilization."

As against history and the humanities, special importance, grounded in the very idea of education, has thus come to be attached to both the behavioral sciences and the natural sciences. It was primarily from these latter two provinces that the impulse to create the "artificial world" had come. Humboldt's revolutionary call for equality has found its modern equivalent in Ernst Bloch's appeal to "synthesize" into one global *humanum* federation all the economic, technological, social, political, and cultural achievements of man—a "synthesis" capable of accomplishment only on the basis of the spiritual and moral sovereignty of the individual judging and controlling the objective necessities that allegedly govern all scientific and technological thought and action. The distinctive function of the university in this phase of scientific and technological civilization has been extended so as to produce men of authoritative judgment in such matters.

Notes

1. The term ecumenical is used here to refer to structures of governance and the Christian views upon which they were based. Both aimed at creating and maintaining a sacred world order, and both ought to be considered "horizons" rather than "limits." See Alois Dempf, *Sacrum Imperium: Geschichte und Staatsphilosophie des Mittelalters und der politischen Renaissance* (Darmstadt, 1967) and Karl Löwith, *Weltgeschichte und Heilsgeschehen* (Stuttgart, 1967).

2. See Alfred Weber, *Kulturgeschichte also Kultursoziologie* (Heidelberg, 1950); Ernst Bloch, *Tübinger Einleitung in die Philosophie* (Frankfurt, 1963); Hans Freyer, *Theorie des gegenwärtigen Zeitalters* (Stuttgart, 1955); and Hanno Kesting, *Geschichtsphilosophie und Weltbürgerkrieg* (Heidelberg, 1959).

3. Sir Eric Ashby, *Technology and the Academics* (London, 1958), and *Universities: British, Indian, African* (London, 1966).

4. Hanns-Albert Steger, *Die Universitäten in der gesellschaftlichen Entwicklung Lateinamerikas*, 2 vols. (Gütersloh, 1967), vol. 1.

5. See John Ziman, "The College System at Oxford and Cambridge," *Minerva* 1 (1963); Sheldon Rothblatt, *The Revolution of the Dons: Cambridge and Society in Victorian England* (New York, 1968).

6. See Helmut Schelsky, *Einsamkeit und Freiheit: Idee und Gestalt der deutschen Universität und ihrer Reformen* (Hamburg, 1963); Wolfgang Kalischer, ed., *Die Universität und ihre Studentenschaften: Universitas magistrorum et scholarium—Versuch einer Dokumentation aus Gesetzen, Erlassen, Beschlüssen, Reden, Schriften und Briefen* (Essen-Bredeney, 1966–67), and in the same volume E. M. Arndt, "Über den deutschen Studentenstaat" (1815).

7. See the special issue of *Esprit* (Paris, 1964): "Faire l'Université. Dossier pour la réforme de l'enseignement supérieur"; and Gerald Antoine and Jean-Claude Passeron, *La réforme de l'université* (Paris, 1966); Michel Vermot-Gauchy, *L'éducation naaionale dans la France de demain* (Monaco, 1965).

8. Marcel Buchard, "Les universitiés françaises," *Revue de l'Enseignement Supérieure* (1960); Heinz Forsteneichner, *Das wissenschaftliche Leben in Frankreich* (Essen-Bredeney, 1963).

9. A. Alonso, S. J., *L'Expansion de l'enseignement supérieur* (Paris, 1960).

10. Rothblatt, *Revolution of the Dons*, p. 248.

11. Ashby, *Universities*, p. 21.

12. Rothblatt, *Revolution of the Dons,* p. 258.

13. Ashby, *Technology,* passim.

14. Schelsky, *Einsamkeit,* pp. 36ff.

15. For the different meanings of "realist" and "nominalist" in medieval and modern usage, see Paul Honigsheim, "Zur Soziologie der mittelalterlichen Scholastik: Die soziologische Bedeutung der nominalistischen Philosophie." In *Erinnerungsgabe für Max Weber,* 2 vols. (München, 1923), 2:173–218.

16. Vicente Cacho Viu, *La institución libre de enseñanza* (Madrid, 1964); Juan López Morillas, *El Krausismo español* (Mexico City, 1954); Pierre Jobit, *Les éducateurs del l'Espagne contemporaine* (Paris, 1939); Raymond Carr, *Spain 1808–1939* (Oxford, 1966).

17. Friedrich K. Tenbruck, "Bildung, Gesellschaft, Wissenschaft." In *Wissenschaftliche Politik,* edited by D. Oberndörfer (Freiburg/brsg., 1962); Schelsky, *Einsamkeit;* Heinz-Joachim Heydorn, "Wilhelm von Humboldt: Abstand und Nähe," *Der evangelische Erzieher: Ztschr. f. Pädagogik und Theologie* (1968):41–56.

18. I use the term in the sense of Ralf Dahrendorf, *Gesellschaft und Demokratie in Deutschland* (München, 1965).

19. Eugenio Garin, *Geschichte und Dokumente der abendländischen Pädagogik,* 2 vols. (Hamburg, 1964), 1:17, 46ff.

20. Ashby, *Universities,* p. 22.

21. Erich Fromm, *Marx's Concept of Man* (New York, 1961).

22. Eric J. Hobsbawm, *Primitive Rebels: Studies in Archaic Forms of Social Movement in the 19th and 20th Centuries* (Manchester, 1959).

23. René Aigrain, *Les universités catholiques* (Paris, 1935).

24. Herbert Lionel Elvin, "Stellung und Ziele der englischen Universitäten." In *Universtät und moderne Welt,* edited by Richard Schwarz, pp. 368f. (Berlin, 1962).

25. Juan Carlos Agulla, *La contribución de Ortega a la teoría sociológica* (Córdoba, 1962).

26. Rafael Gutiérrez Girardot, "Zehn Thesen zum Thema Privat-Universität und Unterentwicklung," In *Grundzüge des lateinamerikanischen Hochschulwesens: Eine Einführung in sein Problem,* edited by H. A. Steger (Baden-Baden, 1965).

27. Ernesto Garzón Valdés, "Die Universitätsreform von Córdoba/Argentinien (1918)." In *Grundzüge,* edited by H. A. Steger. See especially pp. 163–218.

28. Roger Vekemans, "Análisis psico-social de la situación pre-revolucionaria de América Latina," *Mensaje* 115 (1963).

29. Pierre George, *Géographie de l'énergie* (Paris, 1950).

30. Seymour Martin Lipset, ed., "Student Politics," *Comparative Education Review* (Special Issue) 10 (1966); idem., "Students and Politics," *Daedalus* (1968); also, Hanns-Albert Steger, "El movimiento estudiantil revolucionario latino americano," *Eco* 80 (1966).

31. Enrique Oteiza, *Emigration of Highly Qualified Personnel from Argentina: A Latin American "Brain-Drain" Case* (Buenos Aires, 1967).

32. Helmut Schelsky, "Der Mensch in der Wissenschaftlichen Zivilisation." In *Auf der Suche nach Wirklichkeit,* pp. 439–80 (Düsseldorf-Köln, 1965). See also idem., *Einsamkeit,* pp. 178–305 (n.p., n.d.).

33. Schelsky, *Einsamkeit,* p. 297.

5

Models of the Latin American University

Orlando Albornoz

At the beginning of the century, the River Plate Basin was the most conspicuous zone of dynamic economic expansion and stable political development in Latin America. Mexico began its civil war and revolution, while the other Latin American countries, struggling to find some way of creating viable nation states, were frequently falling under dictatorial governments. It is not surprising, then, that the intellectual epicenter of the university reform movement was located in Uruguay and Argentina. The *reforma* was successful insofar as the concept of university autonomy was embraced and members of the university community won the right to govern themselves and to select those who would govern them without governmental interference. Democratization of the university, in the sense of opening its doors to all classes and extending educational opportunities to all citizens, remains an ideal. Only in the more advanced nations, however, does a relatively high degree of opportunity exist. In the more traditional societies the university is still an institution open only to the elite, in somewhat the same manner as the colonial university (not being equipped philosophically or materially to accept the masses).

In these societies, there had not been a middle class large enough to make sufficiently insistent demands for higher education as a form of public service. One of the major factors in university reform in Argentina was the increase in the size of the student population and the emergence of student organizations. At the University of Buenos Aires, the students in the faculties of medicine, engineering, and law set up their own organizations between 1900 and 1905. These soon became instruments through which students could voice their opinions, exert pressure, formulate demands, oppose administrative policies, and hamper university operations. In 1903, the students in the Faculty of Law organized a strike because the university authorities ignored their petition for relatively mild reforms. As the strike progressed, the students became more adamant and increased the items on their list of reforms; before the imbroglio was over, the National Congress and even the president were involved in trying to return the university to its normal operations. By 1905, the students in the Faculty of Medicine were organizing a series of demonstrations to protest the procedure for granting a *cátedra*.[1]

World War I and the influence of positivist and evolutionary ideas had eroded the traditional attitudes toward the sciences. Centers of scientific research were founded, opening new perspectives on teaching and training. Intellectual life took on a new vitality because of the increased production and circulation of books and because of visits from distinguished intellectuals who traveled to Buenos Aires to lecture. The nation's population had swelled enormously (especially because of immigration from Italy), the economy was rapidly expanding, and the political scene had been remade by the entry of newly organized special interest groups, labor unions, and political parties representative of the urban middle classes. Much the same process was happening elsewhere in Latin America, but only where the political game had been opened to the new claimants and where the economy was a productive engine for social change could the reform movement have a lasting effect on higher education. Even today one finds countries where the reform has not been fully introduced.

Alfredo Palacios, Alejandro Korn, and José Ingenieros, the intellectual luminaries who had done so much by their writings to bring Argentina to the front rank of the Hispanic literary world, enthusiastically supported the movement. Argentina's claim to leadership was based also upon a good system of communications with Europe and the United States, an active printing industry, and two of the most prestigious and influential newspapers in the Spanish-speaking world.

Although more than five hundred miles inland and surrounded by mountains, Córdoba nevertheless felt the reverberations of intellectual activity in Buenos Aires—something the conservative leaders of Córdoba disliked and feared. By 1917, Córdoba was a city divided; liberal, socialist, and anarchistic ideas had filtered into Córdoba and quickly found advocates.

The University of Córdoba was a typical university of its time, with 1,500 students and the three traditional faculties of law, medicine, and engineering. At the end of 1917, the students of medicine had begun to protest a decision by the university authorities to close a student dormitory. It was but a short step to make demands for changes in the university's administration. On March 14, 1918, the students of medicine formed what they called the Committee in Favor of Reform in cooperation with students from the other faculties. The committee then called a strike on June 21 and took the position that the strike would remain in effect until the students' demands were satisfied. On the same day the *Córdoba Manifiesto* was issued; it has become the Declaration of Independence for all Latin American students. From this moment, the university situation in the provincial town was a national problem of international significance.

> Men of a free republic, we have just shaken off the last chains which shackled us to a monarchic and monastic domination —and this situation in the twentieth century! We are determined to speak the truth frankly and boldly. Córdoba has been redeemed. We have given our country one more freedom and we have removed a point of dishonor. The pain which yet endures is the freedom yet to come. We have not erred, our hearts tell us so. We are on the eve of revolution, the tocsin for all America has sounded!

This opening paragraph of the *Manifiesto de la Juventud Argentina de Córdoba a los Hombres Libres de Sud-América* sets the tone of the entire message to "all our comrades [*compañeros*] in Latin America."[2] The *Manifiesto* goes on to say that

> The university has been until now a refuge for the mediocre, a sinecure for the ignorant, an asylum for the invalid, and, even worse, a place in which every form of tyranny could be

preached and practised. The university is thus the exact image of a decadent society, a senile man who will neither retire nor die.

The students were determined to remove what they called "the archaic and barbarous" exercise of authority within the university. They felt that authority was used to uphold a sham dignity and a false competence and that it had turned the house of study into a stronghold of tyranny. The Córdoba rebels demanded "a genuine democracy and a form of government where sovereignty is vested primarily in the students," because

> The dominant characteristic of youth is its heroism. It is disinterested and pure. It is not yet contaminated with the errors of age. The young can make no mistake in choosing their teachers. Adulation and self-seeking find no response among the young. The young must be allowed to select their teachers and superiors for, certainly, their choice will meet with success. Henceforth, the republic of the university will have as its teachers only those who are makers of souls, creators of truth, beauty, and goodness.

Throughout the reform movement there runs a strong antireligious bias, concentrated upon the Jesuits, whom the students accused of opposing the *reforma* because they knew that when it triumphed, it would spell the end of "the menace of clerical control of education."

The reform movement awakened public opinion to the anachronistic mechanisms and procedures of the traditional colonial university. The labor movement looked sympathetically upon the students' demands and it was no mere romantic assumption at the time to see the students, the intellectuals, and the workers joining forces in one common interest—democratizing society. This ideal remains alive, but only intermittently has it been translated into reality.

The immediate impact of the reform movement was felt first of all in those countries near Argentina—Uruguay, Chile, Bolivia, and Peru. Alfredo Palacios visited Bolivia and Peru in 1919. Students in Argentina and Chile pledged themselves to a common course of action in 1920. In the same year, Argentinian students, led by Gabriel del Mazo, and Peruvian students, headed by Víctor Raúl

Haya de la Torre, signed agreements that had the purpose of internationalizing the Córdoba demands. In 1921, Haya de la Torre went to Argentina specifically to study the implications of the *Córdoba Manifiesto* and to meet with the student leaders. Of greater significance in the long run was the International Student Congress, held in Mexico City in the same year. Students from the United States, Europe, Asia, and many parts of Latin America attended. The Congress urged the adoption of fundamental reforms, such as student participation in the government of a university, academic freedom, and free tuition. They proclaimed themselves in favor of developing closer and more fraternal bonds with the proletariat by means of university extension. They called for an effective internationalism that would unite all peoples in an "international community" and expressed their strong opposition to militarism, dictatorship, and imperialism.

In Medellín in 1922 and in Bogotá in 1924, Colombian students proclaimed their allegiance to the *Córdoba Manifiesto;* in 1923 Cuban students did so in a national meeting. In Venezuela, university students led the opposition to the Gómez dictatorship waving as their banner the principles of the reform movement.

The international organizations developed by the students did not have enough force or following to affect the structure of the university. Governmental intervention in university affairs is so frequent that the pattern seems to be more repressive than libertarian. The struggle for students' rights—the basis of the *Córdoba Manifiesto*—has occupied the center of the stage on which the university controversy has been acted out, and its impact has been greatest in the national universities. The private university has been relatively unaffected.

The Córdoba reform did not bring about any immediate changes in the structure of the Latin American university. It remained oriented toward the traditional studies of medicine, law, and engineering, incorporating humanities and philosophy, which reflected a strong French influence. Until 1945 the university continued to function in the buildings erected in the colonial period, which sometimes, as in the case of Mexico City and Buenos Aires, were scattered inconveniently about the city. An old concept of university life newly applied, the *cité universitaire,* was to create a new university ecology and spawn the new urban complex known as *la ciudad universitaria.* The selection of a piece of city land for the location of a university, the principal national university, was perhaps the first measure taken by Latin American governments to promote the growth of higher education, committing heretofore untapped resources to the university. After 1945 the demographic pressure of students who had received primary and secondary schooling on a massive scale could no longer be ignored. New social groups, previously denied the opportunity of higher education, were now waiting restively at the threshold of the university. With no junior colleges, trade schools, or technical training centers, the university was obliged to accept the newcomers who had no other place to go.

The construction of a *ciudad universitaria* sought to fulfill the traditional concept of a university community in which professors and students living together in the same place would achieve—by means of dialogue, conviviality, and a degree of isolation from the outside—the ideal of the full growth of the individual's intellectual capacities. The *ciudad universitaria* was thus generally located at a site somewhat distant from the center of the city.

By 1950, the idea of the *ciudad universitaria* had come into its own. The most impressive example was the Universidad Nacional Autónoma in Mexico City, a striking architectural expression of Mexican art through which the nation intended to show its pride in indigenous creativity. The Universidad Central de Venezuela in Caracas was conceived along the same lines, although in this case the inspiration was found in contemporary France and not in national art. Bógota, Quito, São Paulo, and Brasilia followed the same pattern. In the 1960s the Central American countries had undertaken the construction of a new university, partly inspired by Mexico City's *ciudad universitaria.* In Argentina and Chile, however, the national universities continue to operate in the more traditional separate quarters.

The university city, as the site for a republic of the intellect, would have had undeniable success if the human resources and the process for recruiting talent in a national and democratic manner had been given as much attention as the physical facilities. The growing number of students has come close to cancelling out the effort to reduce the student-classroom ratio. The huge buildings planned as libraries remain unused as such for want of books to fill the shelves. At its present stage of development, the *ciudad universitaria* has dramatized the contrast between the possibilities of the physical plant and the potentialities of its inhabitants. In many countries the concentration of university buildings in one spot seems to have caused more problems than it has solved. Although conflicting class schedules and the isolation of the separate faculties have to some extent been overcome, the *ciudad universitaria* has also made possible an increase of student political activity stirred up by political parties and other pressure groups.

As new trends have appeared in the private sector, there have emerged two types of the private model of the university: the Catholic university and the technologically oriented university modeled after its North American counterpart. The latter has also grown as an offshoot of the national model, with the possible intention of offering itself as an alternative to the national university. Two significant examples of the technological university are to be found in the Tecnológico de Monterrey (Mexico), a private organization, and in the Universidad de Oriente (Venezuela), a governmental organization.

The North American research-oriented university is to the Latin American university what the German university was to U.S. colleges around 1900. The spread of industrialization, the influence of the United States, and the needs of the more progressive sectors of society, both private and public, required trained personnel equipped to carry out the plans of social and economic development. Thus, the U.S. model has had almost no competition and has become, like the Soviet university, a new model of higher education. The research-oriented university in Latin America gets aid from the industrial sector in each country and from the United States and international organizations to a greater extent than the national universities. The latter often receive less financial help because their students and professors, sometimes in large numbers, constitute a political opposition that appears threatening to those who might otherwise be willing to lend support to them.

Although Catholic universities were weakened by the liberal and positivist crusade from the late eighteenth through the last part of the nineteenth century, the greatest assault upon them came with the expulsion of the Jesuits in the eighteenth century.[3] A recent resurgence of the Jesuits, however, has coincided with the establishment of numerous Catholic universities, most of which are run by them.

Catholic universities began to appear in significant numbers with the opening of the Pontificia Boliviana in Medellín in 1936 and the Universidad Javeriana in Bogotá in 1937. These two, along with the Pontificia Universidad Católica in Chile founded in 1888, are among the most prestigious Catholic universities in Latin America. The Universidad Pontificia of Peru was created in 1949 as a national university enjoying the same legal status as other national universities. By the end of the 1950s some fifty Catholic universities had been opened in Argentina, as well as one in Caracas in 1953 and one in Paraguay in 1959. Even in Mexico, a Catholic university began functioning in 1963. The academic structure of the Catholic universities is oriented toward traditional matters and less concerned with research than are the national universities; there is less social awareness on their campuses than in the universities financed by public funds.

The Universidad Católica de Nuestra Señora de Ascunción, which may serve as an example, consists of a community of professors, students, and graduates under the authority, tutelage, and protection of the Church. It is an institution of higher education whose purposes are: (1) to preserve, transmit, and deepen the spiritual inheritance of humanity in its three dimensions—moral, scientific, and technical; (2) to provide religious instruction that conforms with the doctrines and precepts of the Catholic Church; (3) to provide proper training in the liberal and technical professions; and (4) to contribute to the study and dissemination of the sciences and the arts and to stimulate an inquiring spirit of mind among its members in the pursuit of knowledge in all areas.

Generally speaking, more than half of all Latin American students are in the national universities. The significance of students in the private institutions cannot be judged by numbers alone, however; the quality of private education and the later influence of their graduates in society have brought a significant increase in the role of the private sector vis-à-vis the public sector.

One has the general impression that all students attend a country's largest university, such as UNAM in Mexico City or the Universidad de Buenos Aires. These are, indeed, two very large institutions, each with over 80,000 students in some kind of attendance (twenty-five percent in each are part-time students or are pursuing some form of preuniversity studies). It should be remembered, however, that the small provincial university with a few thousand students and very limited resources is the typical university.

To elaborate on these generalizations, it may be helpful to describe a real university situation in Colombia. The National University, set in the national capital, is the oldest and biggest of all Colombian universities. Located in the heart of the downtown area and set within the limits of the *ciudad universitaria*, it is nationally and internationally the most important of Colombia's universities. Because of the diversity of its student body, it represents a microcosm of Colombian society, drawing students from all the social strata and geographical areas of the country. The Javeriana, which represents the typical private denominational university, recruits its students mainly from families that have a strong identification with the Catholic church. These students are more politically conservative and come from the upper classes. The Universidad Libre is a small school dedicated to teaching and careers in the law and education; it has a strong working-class or labor-elite orientation and is regarded as a center of radical politics. The Universidad de los Andes is an example of the newer private university, with a small enrollment of mostly upper-class students, academically oriented toward the modern professions, with an emphasis on economic development and urban planning. The university in Popayán, in the south of Colombia, is a small and traditional institution reflecting the life of the provincial capital and devoted to the teaching of such conventional subjects as medicine, law, and civil engineering.

Colombia's student population is younger in the private universities than in the public ones: at the Universidad de los Andes sixty-five percent are under twenty; at the National forty-seven percent are between nineteen and twenty-one; and at the Universidad Libre, some seventy-five percent are between the ages of twenty-two and thirty. Forty percent of the students at the Javeriana are women, while in Popayán only nine percent are women. In the other universities the proportion of men to women is four to one. The ratio reflects the position and participation of women in Latin American society—women still have little effect on public affairs except through family ties or church affiliation.

In general, students attending private universities have experienced a longer period of residence in a large city and have a better acquaintance with city life-styles than students at public universities. The newer arrivals to the city tend to go to the national universities, whether located in the national capital or in the provinces. For example, eighty-six percent of the students at the Javeriana come from cities with populations greater than 100,000, as do thirty-six percent at the National University, and fifty-eight percent at the Universidad Libre. Those coming from places with less than 20,000 inhabitants account for thirty-five percent of the students at the Universidad Libre, fifteen at the Nacional, eight percent at the Javeriana, and three percent at Los Andes. Thus, private universities tend to have more urbanized students than public universities except for those like the Libre, which recruit their students from the working classes.

In addition, we find that there is a greater proportion of part-time students in the public universities. Only ten percent of the students at Los Andes are engaged in any type of gainful employment, compared with sixty percent at the Libre and twenty percent at the Nacional. The Javeriana is much like Los Andes and the University at Popayán is closer to the Nacional in this sense. In other words, more students from the working classes go to the public national or provincial universities than to the privately organized universities, and working students obviously have less time for their studies than do full-time students.

There is a correlation between the size of the student's family and the type of university he attends. Smaller families tend to send their sons to private schools. In some families the older brother will enter the labor market directly, without any higher education, having in mind the support of his younger brother or brothers in their studies. The younger son or sons are thus seen as the main hope of the family for ascending the social scale, higher education being thought of as one of the best means for achieving upward social mobility.

A student's outlook and conduct are affected by whether or not he lives with his family. Students attending private universities are typically under family control or influence. In Bogotá only ten percent of those who attend private institutions live on their own, in contrast with thirty-five percent at the public universities.

The public universities located in the larger urban centers become sites of greater political controversy and student participation than do the provincial and private universities, even when these are in populous urban areas. Thus, approximately fifty-five percent of the students at the Nacional, seventy-five percent at the Libre, and fifty-two percent of those at Popayán had joined in a strike or a demonstration in the late 1960s and early 1970s, while the corresponding percentage at private universities stood at about five percent. Much the same situation prevails with the influence of political parties in the universities. The public universities are more politicized and more ideologically oriented than are the private or technically oriented schools such as Los Andes. Fourteen percent of the students at Los Andes admit to participating actively in political party affairs, compared with forty-five percent at both the Nacional and the Javeriana—the former leaning leftward and to nonreligious stances and the latter rightward and to more religious justifications of political opinions and activities.

The religious universities, almost all Catholic institutions, possess a doctrinal body of ideas that gives them ethical and philosophical criteria enabling them to validate and legitimize any situation. The matter of academic freedom does not arise because the ideological codes of the church have already prescribed what is permissible to teach in the classrooms. While the religious universities have some secular concerns, such as the training of professionals, they are ruled by an idea that is essentially extraacademic—the preservation and diffusion of the faith. These universities ordinarily do not experience crises that demand a definition or redefinition of fundamental principles or of the direction and purpose of the university.

In the national and public universities ideological controversy and partisan conflict are frequent. The students bring an ideological heterogeneity and speak more often in terms of Latin America and of national matters than at private universities. Academic freedom is a more likely subject of dispute.

The private universities manage to retain a greater amount of autonomy and self-governance than the national universities. The aims of the national university may be at odds with those of the state—the Latin American university is an integral part of the political scene—while the private universities are more in accord with the goals of society and lack a direct political role. National universities frequently identify with, or join the ranks of, opposition groups against the government in power. The instances of cooperation between national universities and the government are usually rare and short-lived, except during the brief euphoria following the fall of a dictator.

The private universities have no effective system of *cogobierno*. They are operated like private enterprises; decisions are made at the top, and while students and faculty may influence decisions, they do not participate in the decision-making process. On the other hand, the system of governance at the national universities does provide for the joint participation of the administration, professors, and students in decision making—at least in theory. *Cogobierno* affects administrative and academic matters equally, and the failure to differentiate between technical and academic functions embroils the university in conflicts and tensions.

The characteristics of the Latin American university are such that no university, no matter how much it differs from the general pattern, can escape the structural limitations inherent in a developing area. The role of the university is more distinct, as an element of development, to the extent that the area is able to agree upon common social and political goals, principally in the matters of economic and social development.

NOTES

1. See Tulio Halperin Donghi, *Historia de la Universidad de Buenos Aires* (Buenos Aires, 1962).

2. The Córdoba Manifiesto is easily available in Spanish. For an English translation, see *University Reform in Latin America: Analyses and Documents*, edited by International Student Conference (Leyden, 1961).

3. See Magnus Mörner, ed., *The Expulsion of the Jesuits from Latin America* (New York, 1965).

6

University Reform

José Luis Romero

At the beginning of the reform movement, emphasis on professionalization and disdain for general theorizing in the traditional vein characterized the Latin American university. The Argentine Hector Ripa Alberdi summarized its objectives:

> Our country has been governed both in politics and in education by men of the past century, modeled by the rough hand of positive philosophy. Old ideas and old theories were the tasteless bread passed on to the new generation. Young men left their universities narrowly trained and ill-equipped for the life tasks ahead of them. The tyranny of those who had not gone further than the Comtian catechism had enchained the Argentine mind and left it without desires to excel, without noble hopes, or without a flicker of idealism.[1]

For the most part, study at Latin American universities failed to be exacting, competitive, or research-oriented. Although there were excellently trained professors—some of great distinction in their fields—they had no influence on the tone of university life, which was controlled by an exclusive social group.

The Peruvian historian Luis Alberto Sánchez characterized the faculty of his university as follows:

> The professors had come to their posts as if by divine right. There were no heretics and the academic community was

ever vigilant of all promotions. Sons inherited the chairs of
their fathers, and brothers were frequently alternate occupants. At one time some twelve chairs at the University of San
Marcos in Lima were controlled by two families. The title
was inalienable although competition for it might precede or
follow its actual possession. A professor held his post for life;
no one trifled with his rights and prerogatives or even dared to
object to his repeating his texts from memory year after year.[2]

Teachers such as these must be blamed for what the university
had become by 1918. The Argentine philosopher Alejandro Korn's
diagnosis was in these terms:

> A crisis of culture had descended on the university. On the
> one hand, the persistence of the past and the grip of
> corruption, rampant mediocrity, the routine and torpor of
> teaching techniques, and on the other hand, the mildly
> utilitarian and professional orientation of teaching, the lack of
> any transcendent interests, the neglect of the educational
> ideal, and finally the cruel authoritarianism and the absence
> of moral authority gave rise to this reaction which was born
> with the new generation.[3]

An analysis of the documents the reform produced reveals a
coherent set of ideas concerning what the university should not be
and somewhat less precise notions about what it should be. The
university was not to be a rigid institution limiting itself to the
transmission of practical skills and knowledge to successive generations of candidates for the professions; neither was it to content
itself with serving the interests and privileges of those in power. In
the early stages of the reform movement, it seemed enough to
substitute certain professors for others. Later on, the new generation realized that more sweeping changes in teaching methods and
university organization were needed. Finally, they thought that it
was necessary to reorient its spirit, to open the university to all the
social and scientific concerns of a changing world, and to modify its
general functions while still permitting it to keep some of its
traditional ones.

Because the new generation was not sufficiently homogeneous,
either socially or intellectually, some groups placed emphasis on
the functional transformation of the university; others stressed the

cultural mission of the university; and still others focused on what they began to call its "social function." The influence of the antipositivist philosophies was extremely strong, appealing to Plato and making use of Bergson. The scientific method was condemned as an accomplice of the utilitarian view of life, and an idealism was proclaimed that was a mixture of philosophical jargon and popular speech. Societies founded on privilege were denounced, and while the new generation looked forward to a bourgeois liberal democracy—a form of government and society that even today is almost nonexistent in Latin America—others, with a vague desire for profound transformation of the social structure, anticipated the Russian Revolution of 1917.

At Córdoba, in 1918, the battle lines were already clearly drawn. Not only many professors but also many students and even a good part of the old families of Córdoba agreed to ride with the waves of revolutionary change—whether abroad or at home in the recent triumph of the Radical party—rather than be engulfed in a futile struggle against it. In the vanguard of this movement was the Corda Fratres, a Catholic organization whose leaders were drawn from the hierarchy of the Catholic Church and which was headed by the bishop of the city. The student strike, with evident popular support and unmistakable sympathy from the government, brought the progressive elements together in their demand to abolish the monopoly of university governance then vested in a clique of fifteen academicians. The challenge to constituted authority, the specific statements about university problems, and the more general ones about social and cultural matters transcended the limited objectives of the movement, with the result that the federal government was obliged to involve itself in the affairs of the university and to take a hand in the modification of university government. President Hipólito Irigoyen acceded to the request to intervene almost immediately. Nevertheless, traditional provincial society managed to thwart the implementation of the student reform plan, and the assembly made up of all the professors (who under the new regime were to elect the rector) succumbed to pressure designating a man notoriously opposed to any reform. The assembly, convened on June 15, 1918, was denounced by the students, who then occupied the university, disowned the new rector, and proclaimed a general strike. Six days later one of the student leaders, Deodoro Roca, wrote the *Manifiesto Liminar*, an appeal from the university youth of Córdoba to "all free men of South America." Adopted by the newly founded University Federation of Córdoba, it sought to explain the several purposes for which the movement had been launched:

> The University Federation of Córdoba believes that it must make known to the country and to America the moral and legal circumstances which invalidate the electoral act of 15 June. While proclaiming the ideals and principles which inspire the youth of Argentina at this moment, we wish to identify the local problems and conflicts and also to incite others to continue the attack on the bastions of clerical oppression. There have been in fact no serious disruptions either in the National University of Córdoba or in the city. We have seen the birth of a true revolution which will take under its banner all the free men of the continent. We will retell the events so that all may see the justice of our actions as well as our shame at the cowardice and perfidy of the reactionaries. The acts of violence for which we take full responsibility were carried out in the pursuit of pure ideas. We stood against and disavowed an anachronistic uprising. Those acts represented also the extent of our indignation in the face of moral turpitude, pretense, and artful deceit in the guise of legality. The morality of the ruling classes was atrophied by a traditional Pharisaism and by a dreadful dearth of ideals.[4]

The direct results of the movement were short-lived attempts at self-government in the university—the firing of many professors; the appointment of new ones, some very young; and, finally, the election of a new rector who satisfied the students. But the indirect results were many and far-reaching. It was clear from the beginning that several different tendencies were at work in the student movement and that each had effects other than those originally intended. The more flexibly organized University of Buenos Aires tried to cope with the restlessness before actual fighting broke out. While upholding the existing legal principles, it approved in 1918 a statute that incorporated some of the goals of the Córdoba movement. The various faculties and schools were to be governed by a council of tenured and nontenured professors, some of whom were to be elected by the students. The principles of open enrollment and academic freedom were accepted—considered by the students as reforms essential in arresting the deterioration of teaching. At the University of La Plata, where shortly before there had been an attempt to modernize along the lines of the North American universities, serious conflicts created an extremely tense climate. Eventually, however, the statutes at La Plata were modified along the lines of those adopted at Córdoba and Buenos Aires. Ultimately, it was the sympathy for the student movement demonstrated by the national government under President Irigoyen that allowed it to develop and realize its principal objectives.

During the same years, somewhat similar social conditions prevailed in other parts of Latin America, sometimes producing analogous reform movements having the same effects. Uruguay had enjoyed an early flowering of democracy. Its university, founded in 1849, had the hallmarks of the Napoleonic model. From 1908 on it had a democratic organization, with student participation in the councils of the *facultades*. The university's long-hallowed autonomy was publicly recognized and sanctioned by the Constitution of 1917. Nevertheless, student agitation continued after 1918, aimed at the modernization of teaching and greater participation of students in the governance of the university. Given the political and social climate of Uruguay, where *Batllismo* as a doctrine and policy had introduced many forward-looking social changes, there were fewer occasions for violent student action than in those countries burdened with a colonial university tradition and an oligarchic structure of society.

In Peru, even more than in Argentina, the old-line families controlled most of the wealth and looked upon the university as their feudal property. A long battle was joined between these entrenched interests and the so-called progressive vanguard—including such men as Manuel González Prada, Abraham Valdelomar, and Clorinda Matto de Turner—who had bitterly denounced the social evils afflicting their country. In 1919, the students demanded the right to dismiss incompetent professors, traditionally appointed from among the ruling groups of Peruvian society. Violence was rife, and as time passed it became apparent that there was a close link between the demands for university reform and reform of the total social structure. These two themes, along with others, were perceptively analyzed by José Carlos Mariátegui as he explored

what he called *"la realidad peruana."* As in Argentina, the
university demands were incorporated into some of the policies of a
new government, that of Augusto Leguía, which had come to
power by challenging and dividing the oligarchy and promising a
more liberal regime. In 1920 an educational bill of rights was
proclaimed setting forth the most democratic and modern of
principles: the right to hire and fire professors, student representation, academic freedom, open enrollment, and upgrading of
teaching practices. But the most important result of the student
movement was the creation of *universidades populares* subsequently identified with the name of González Prada. These schools
developed university extension education, not through the activities of the official university itself, but rather through the efforts of
the students who took on what they considered to be a social duty
to the disinherited classes.

By 1923 student movements had also made their appearance in
Cuba, with calls to fire incompetent teachers and to reform the
system of government by means of student representation in the
university councils. Here also, the new government (of Gerardo
Machado y Morales), seeking allies against the traditional social
groups, looked with sympathy upon the student movement and
gave it its support. During these same years, there were other
equally strong movements in Venezuela, Guatemala, and Brazil.
Elsewhere, student unrest, originating in part from an ideological
commitment or a sense of outrage at political and social injustice,
eventually produced an analysis of social and university problems,
thus exposing, perhaps for the first time, the root causes heretofore
not noticed or not included in the contemporary political controversies. Such, for example, was the case in Chile, where the First
Student Congress of 1920 hammered out a broad critique of
national problems, and in Mexico, a hostile political climate
notwithstanding, where the first Latin American Congress of
University Reform was held in 1921 for the purpose of careful and
critical discussion of the institutional problems of Latin America.

It was not long before there was a reversal in official policy,
moving abruptly from tolerance to repression, as a reaction to the
students' extreme political and social demands. Statutes created to
institute reform were revised or revoked, and by the end of the
1920s there was a recrudescence of student unrest. In many of the
leading universities in Latin America—in Argentina under José F.

Uriburu, in Brazil under Getulio Vargas, in Venezuela under Juan Vicente Gómez, in Mexico under Plutarco Elías Calles, in Chile under Carlos Ibáñez, and in Uruguay under Gabriel Terra—dictatorial regimes in various guises locally attacked the student movements as their prime political opposition and took steps to repress them severely. A similar policy toward student agitation was assumed by the Perón government in 1946.

In the 1930s and 1940s students took part in the struggle against fascism and nazism, supported the Spanish Republic, and generally condemned the policies of the United States. Within the student movement there were, however, minority groups of the right, some with an openly fascist leaning and others that were antileftist to start with and opposed to the trend toward anti-Americanism.

The reform movement embraced the principle of autonomy, but tried to make the university community—the *"demos,"* as the youth of 1918 liked to say—sufficiently independent to challenge the conservative society of which it was a part. University autonomy facilitated the reorientation and modernization of the university—a basic goal of the reform movement—and specific fields, such as administration, finance, science, and politics. Political and ideological autonomy would permit the university to define its own complex of problems as perceived by the students, who were most committed to structural change.

The reform movement proposed that university government be in the hands of tripartite councils with equal representation of professors, students, and graduates. This objective was never achieved. In theory this goal rested on the principle enunciated by José Ortega y Gasset that the "university must be the institutional projection of the student." His message was that higher education depended on the student rather than on any given organization of knowledge or the professor. As understood by the reform movement, Ortega's message meant increased student action: it was the students, not the professors, who were free of special group interests and not beholden to the status quo.

The social distance between professors and students derived from a rigid concept of authority, but it also served to mask the professor's ignorance and to shield him from the probings of dialogue. At first, the reform movement aimed at eliminating professors who were notoriously incompetent, ignorant of their discipline, or wedded to outworn ideas. Subsequently, it tried to impose new conditions for the appointment of professors by subjecting them to public contests designed to frustrate ruling-class schemes to avoid the perils of routinization and bureaucratization. Appointments were to be for a limited time and subject to periodic contests to determine the competence of those who held the chair in question.

The reform went further by establishing the principle of the parallel professorship, which provided an opportunity to hear different views on a subject. It established noncompulsory attendance: students would not be obliged to listen to those who did not teach anything. These two principles undermined the authoritarian approach of university teaching and challenged the ivory-tower attitude of the *catedrático*. The reform viewed the student as a pupil or learner, not as a mere apprentice passing through the university and picking up on the way a bag of skills and formulas for the more or less successful exercise of a lucrative profession. There were calls for research institutes, seminars, and workshops, but beyond these specific requests, what the reform aspired to was renewed contact between the professor and the student.

Of the two models on which the Latin American University was based—the colonial and the Napoleonic—it was the former, with its emphasis on forming character (as opposed to the latter's emphasis on producing a professional) that the reform embraced in its emphasis on the significance of general education. The image of the university became ambiguous and controversial: on the one hand, it was concerned with the problems of real life and, on the other, it had a "specific mission," to train professionals and to engage in scientific research uncontaminated by politics. The university committed to the training of professionals had been born in an intellectual atmosphere of utilitarianism and in a society that felt assured of its own stability. In fact, however, social instability had increased dramatically during the nineteenth century and worsened after the shock of World War I, while the tenets of utilitarian philosophy underwent a similarly profound crisis. The reform had taken up from the beginning the defense of a nonutilitarian idea of man, such as had been formulated by Alejandro Korn in 1918 in his memorable essay *Incipit Vita Nova*. The basic duty of the nonutilitarian man was to strive toward the realization of those ethical principles that human reason, untrammeled by any form of servitude, could fashion in the face of the demands of reality.

Reality, for the reform movement, meant social reality. Utilitarian professionalism, which deliberately ignored immediate social problems, seemed plainly immoral. Rather, it was the express purpose of the reform to amplify the professionalizing role of the university must not shy away from social problems. Rather it should the measure of things—so that he could accept his obligation to solve problems without compromising his reason.

By advocating that the university systematically study the paramount national problems, such as the state of the economy, public health, and education, and that it take positions on the thorny questions of freedom of conscience and thought, abuses of power, and social welfare, the reform moved the university in one way or another toward militancy. Adversaries of the reform claimed that this implied a politicization of the university, but the reform retorted that although it was against party politics the university must not shy away from social problems. Rather it should be a positive agent of change. Militancy in the service of social change was implicit in the university's mission, but a militancy without dogmatism and with complete respect for the free flow of ideas.

Not everywhere did the political climate favor university reform. In Mexico, for example, the revolution that had broken out in 1910 had since pitted generations against each other on matters other than university reform. This issue, while of major importance in public forums in other parts of Latin America, remained for a long time in Mexico a secondary concern. Outside Mexico, however, the university was the most vulnerable institution of the old order and easily the most likely to be besieged by the new generation, with the result that it became a bastion from which to mount forays into the social and political life of the nation. The conflicting partisanships on the matter of university reform revealed that political and social problems had superimposed themselves on the university and that it, as an institution, had permanently lost its character as an inviolate house of learning.

The study of the social, economic, and political situation of Latin America led to an appreciation of the decisive influence exerted by the great powers upon the economic life of the various countries. In criticizing the policies of Great Britain and the United States in Latin America, the reform proclaimed the universal application of the principle of self-determination. Protesting U.S. intervention in

Santo Domingo in 1916, President Irigoyen of Argentina voiced this sentiment thus: *"los pueblos son sagrados para los pueblos."* José Vasconcelos in Mexico, Manuel Ugarte, José Ingenieros, and Alfredo Palacios in Argentina—all in one way or another developed the theme of Latin American autonomy. Eventually, the reform itself took up this theme and developed it into a strident anti-imperialism. Haya de la Torre, the founder of APRA in Peru, articulated the political concern of the reform in these words:

> Lest we forget, the decision to participate directly and actively in the Latin American struggle against imperialism is of vital importance. This is a matter of great urgency and yet it is difficult to discuss because it encompasses many others. It is also a subject which leads to hard and fast polemical and political positions. The anti-imperialist attitude might seem to exceed the limits of the Reform, but there is, indeed a close relation between them. The Reform prepared a class of intellectuals, the very first university generation to understand what imperialism in America was, a phenomenon against which some critical voices had already been raised. If one wanted to fit them into some sort of categorical scheme, they would be called "petit bourgeois," those who had felt the early effects of expanding imperialism. These were the intellectual leaders of the Reform movement who carried on their struggle against capitalism and imperialism in the manner of European intellectual orthodoxy. They repeated these ideals and followed tactics, which, while suitable for the place in which they had been developed, were premature and ill-suited for Latin America. Nevertheless, it was these lyric and confused cries of the middle-class intellectuals that pointed to the danger. The Reform had opened the doors for the study of new problems. The first to pass through them were those driven by a desire to see the world afresh.[5]

This new interest in the nature and structure of Latin American societies also precipitated an examination of militarism and clericalism. Clericalism was clearly associated with the enduring traditionalist atmosphere surrounding the university as well as with upper-class conservatism and resistance to social change. Militarism, on the other hand, was just as clearly allied with the coming to power of dictatorships that frustrated the continuing development of the democratic and constitutional norms.

The reform took an adamant stance against militarism and clericalism, manifest in the political activities of the student movements in opposition to dictatorial regimes such as those of José Uriburu in Argentina, Gerardo Machado and Fulgencio Batista in Cuba, and Luis Manuel Sánchez Cerro in Peru. In each case, the government counterattack first took the form of a hostile posture on the part of the military dictatorships toward the reform movement and subsequently toward the universities (which they were forever accusing of being subversive centers).

One of the extrauniversity goals of the reform was the creation of new social elites in the process of change, an educational function that the traditional university had failed to perform. Haya de la Torre described this aspect in strictly political terms:

> The proletariat which was born as a result and as negation of imperialism—if we express ourselves in Hegelian dialectics—is a new class, as imperialism is the advanced stage of industrialism. It seems clear that the proletariat, wherever it exists now in America, needs allies, and in the countries where it does not exist, or is just emerging, it must incorporate itself into the movement of national liberation. The middle classes who have joined in the struggle have done so with greater or less skill. The middle-class intellectuals supported the two causes of anti-imperialism and national liberation. Their petty-bourgeois prejudices notwithstanding, they and the Reformers provided many a good leader to the cause of anti-imperialism, even, indeed, in the extremist groups.[6]

Even the moderate groups of the reform felt that the renewal of the university necessarily involved its playing a role comparable to that formulated by Haya de la Torre: encouraging the formation of new groups of technicians and professionals, politicians and militants, all of which would have a new concept of the social process.

It was charged that the university betrayed society if it limited itself to the mechanical conferral of degrees upon students to serve their advancement as individuals. Contrariwise, the university served society if it prepared men who would place themselves at its service—men who were aware of society's new problems, who were sensitive to the restiveness and needs of the masses, and who accepted and identified with the process of change. The fundamental mission of the university was to create an elite with this new mentality.

It is at this point that the educational and social objectives of the reform converged. The reform movement knew that, despite the transformations of the university, it would still remain the vital center for the training of national elites. It envisaged the university as a catalyst and promoter of change, producing elites to direct and induce the transformations needed in the country and in the continent.

NOTES

1. Hector Ripa Alberdi, "Renacimiento del espíritu argentino." In *La reforma universitaria: Documentos relativos a la propagación del movimiento en América Latina, 1918–1927*, 3 vols., compiled and edited by Gabriel del Mazo (Buenos Aires, 1927):3:29.

2. Luis Alberto Sánchez, "El estudiante, el ciudadano, el intelectual y la reforma universitariaria americana," In ibid.

3. Alejandro Korn, "La Reforma universitaria y la autenticidad argentina." In ibid.

4. Alberto Ciria and Horacio Sanguinetti, *Los Reformistas* (Buenos Aires, 1968), p. 271.

5. V. R. Haya de la Torre, "La reforma universitaria." In del Mazo, ed., *La reforma universitaria*.

6. Ibid.

7

Students in the Latin American University

Alistair Hennessy

Any consideration of Latin American students is unrealistic unless they are first seen in the context of the continuing fascination exerted over successive generations by the reformist mythology. For the influential minority, it provides legitimation of political action and predetermines their conception of the function of the university in society.

The reform is usually considered to have started at the Argentinian university of Córdoba in 1918 (although there had been antecedents) in protest against a university system which had changed little since the beginning of independence, and which was failing to provide the leadership required by the swiftly changing society of early-twentieth-century Argentina.[1] The Córdoba Reform transcended the mere correction of university abuses by also claiming to be a national regeneration movement. It was essentially an assertion of cultural independence from European models and a plea for Latin American solutions to Latin American problems: a nationalist phenomenon, conceived in terms of the Bolivarian ideal of a united continent. The national spirit, and by extension that of Latin America as a whole, in the students' view would find its purest, unsullied expression in the university, which must become the conscience of the nation and a bulwark against North American influence. For the past fifty years the nationalism and antiimperialism enunciated by the early reformers have been integral components of every influential Latin American student movement.

The reformers argued that the university should be a microcosm of the perfect national society. The "democratic university republic," where professors and students shared in the joint pursuit of truth and knowledge, would provide both the model and the leadership for the reform of corrupted societies. The university would be the laboratory of democracy.

Students saw themselves as a regenerating elite whose privileged position obliged them to act as spiritual leaders in the process of regeneration. The generally high level of tolerance shown toward their activities suggests that this view has been widely reciprocated. The history of Latin America since the 1920s is full of examples of students providing the main, and in some cases the only, resistance to dictatorial regimes.

At the core of reformist ideology is the myth of the incorruptibility of youth and the idea that the young nations of the New World require youthful leadership. Because students are not involved in mundane pursuits, their motives must necessarily be purer than those of their professors, whose attitudes are conditioned by humdrum considerations of professionalism and earning a living. The reformists argued, therefore, that students must be involved in university government both to keep a watching brief over professors and to participate as full citizens of the university republic. *Cogobierno*, by which students were to be represented on faculty boards, became a tenet in the reformist program.

Reformists argued that universities must also be closely linked to society and the oppressed by means of "popular universities" and night schools where students would educate the masses.[2] In common with general Latin American middle-class attitudes, reformist ideology has been urban-oriented.

Another aim of the reform was to break down the narrow class character of the university by opening it to lower social strata. This was embodied in the reformists' hostility toward examinations, which, it was argued, unfairly penalized those from underprivileged backgrounds.

The fundamental tenet of reformist ideology has been the conception of the university as a political institution as distinct from the purely vocational, professional university of the colonial and Napoleonic type against which the reform had originally been directed. Universities must become the foci of revolutionary change and instead of passively reflecting the values of society must actively change them.

The university reform movement exemplified the exaggerated importance given to intellectuals in Latin American culture. Reformist ideology was one aspect of the early-twentieth-century reaction against positivism which swept through Latin America; it represented a flight to spirituality in which little appreciation was shown for the technical requirements of a modernized society.[3] Subsequent failure by the reform movement to change the university's basic values reflects an acceptance by the majority of its spokesmen of the literary, idealistic culture of which they were an integral part.

The reformists did not show an adequate appreciation of revolutionary politics. The early success of the movement in Argentina, evidenced by the rapid acquiescence to student demands in the university legislation of the early 1920s, followed the political victory at the polls in 1916 of Hipólito Irigoyen and the Radical party, who, representing the rising middle class, sympathized with student demands. Once the lower-middle-class and middle-class supporters of the radicals were assuaged by access to universities and the evidence of qualifications and increased social mobility they provided, much of the momentum behind the Argentinian reform slackened.[4]

No university in Spanish America during the 1920s and 1930s escaped some degree of politicization of its student body. As social tensions sharpened and the conflicts within outworn social structures became more acute, student organizations argued for universities to become more, not less, political. Not only have these arguments been fortified by recent European and U.S. examples, but as demographic pressures on universities increase, the possibilities of university reform in isolation from more fundamental changes in society recede.

Student Numbers, Selection, and Social Origins

Latin America has not escaped the universal explosion of numbers entering higher education. In 1956 there were 414,000 matriculated students; by 1965 the number had risen to 796,000 and seven years later to 2,201,000. Student registration at Chilean universities in 1950 was 14,917; by 1965 it had risen to 32,995 and by 1973 to 127,238. In Venezuela, between 1957 and 1962 numbers increased by 414 percent and continued to soar in the next decade.

Rapid expansion of higher education is bound to have radical political repercussions unless social structures prove sufficiently flexible to absorb the flow of graduates and unless roused expectations can be satisfied. In common with other developing areas, changes in the structural basis of Latin American society lag behind ideas and aspirations.

In spite of reformists' efforts to widen the social composition of universities, they continue to draw their students overwhelmingly from the middle classes. The proportion of children from working-class or peasant backgrounds who gain admission is somewhere between five and ten percent. Apart from Cuba, where worker faculties have been set up to train skilled laborers and to channel the ablest into the university, the highest proportion of children of workers is in some recently founded institutions, in the Universidad de Oriente in Venezuela, for example, as high as seventy percent.[5]

Middle-class students, especially those from professional groups where there is a tradition of attending university, regard the university as a confirmation of their social status—an important function for a middle class which often feels itself to be socially and economically insecure under conditions of rampant inflation. An acute awareness of the gap between self-identification and aspiration on one side, and economic insecurity and limited opportunities on the other, puts a considerable strain on middle-class students that contributes to their political radicalism. Failure of the university reform to reconstruct universities is evidence of a wider failure by the middle classes to consolidate their political power and to inaugurate dynamic economic and social policies.

For those first-generation university students from humbler backgrounds—children of artisans, petty bureaucrats, and manual workers—the university is a means of social mobility. Merit by itself, though, is no guarantee of advancement. Personalist links and clientage relationships permeate Latin American society. Hence the significance of the all-important *enchufe* or *panelinha* (connection) of Brazilian society.[6] The better connected a student's family, the more these contacts can be taken for granted. For the student from a working-class background, the university opens up possibilities of being introduced to a wider social spectrum, and especially through political activity, of making useful contacts.

The social spread of recruitment remains limited, however, by the inadequacies of the school system. High dropout rates at public primary and secondary schools insure that only a small minority ever get the matriculation qualification that makes them eligible for the university. Those eligible are drawn from private schools attended by higher social strata. Because there are far more applicants than places available, most universities require entrance examinations as well as the baccalaureate.[7] Higher marks are earned by students from private secondary schools, from less overcrowded public secondary schools, and by those from urban rather than rural areas, which have poor educational facilities. It is rare to find many university students from peasant backgrounds except in Cuba and in the highland universities of Peru such as Cuzco or Ayacucho, and even here provincial middle- and lower-middle-class mestizos predominate.[8]

Preselection works also at another level; academic secondary schools, which prepare students for university entrance and thus concentrate on traditional academic disciplines, are rarely attended by children from working-class backgrounds. These children usually go to industrial or commercial schools, where standards are lower and work openings more apparent for those without the necessary contacts to break into an unfamiliar social ambience. It requires very strong achievement motivation, as well as considerable home support, for a child from a manual-worker or peasant background to get into and pass through the university.[9] Visible social mobility is necessary before lower-class families will encourage their children to stay on at school rather than benefit from immediate earning power. Because of the prestige attached to universities as forcing houses for the nation's elite, academic secondary schools are overcrowded while vocational schools are often underutilized, despite society's greater need for middle-grade skilled labor (over nonscientific professionals, who still constitute a large proportion of university graduates). Expenditure on rural schools remains low as governments channel funds to the urban, academic secondary schools used by the nation's elite. Indirectly the mass of the population is subsidizing the middle classes.

A major criticism of the academic secondary schools is that they are helping to perpetuate traditional prestige valuations. But so long as the prestige faculties of law and medicine continue to attract the greatest number of applicants, there will be little incentive for secondary schools to change their literary-oriented syllabuses. The pedagogical benefits gained from a broad general education are partially offset by the need to pass increasingly fierce competitive examinations as the demand for restricted university places rises. The sources of creativity and interest are often dried up by the need to memorize and learn by rote.

Students come to the university with undeveloped critical faculties and a traditional outlook toward the professions, which the school, parents, and the general culture all perpetuate. The root of academic discontent, often both a consequence of poor academic motivation and a cause of political turbulence, must therefore be sought in understaffed and old-fashioned secondary schools. Teachers, underpaid and undervalued, may pass their discontent on to their pupils, and the secondary-school student with firm political views by the time of entering university is a common phenomenon. The lack of adequate preparation is an important contributory factor in the dropout rate at universities; only a small proportion of those who get a place come out with a degree.[10]

Convincing evidence of the inefficiency of universities is provided by the number of students who fail to get a degree. The cause would seem to lie in economic factors that promote low academic motivation and provide poor academic competence.[11] Aldo Solari has shown for the University of Montevideo, comparing 1942–49 and 1957–63 figures, that although the number of entrants rose almost threefold, the number of students graduated remained nearly constant. The part-time nature of the course is an important contributing factor for, as Solari shows, the actual time taken by a student to complete his course is invariably longer than the time scheduled—in some faculties more than double. In no faculty is the average age on graduation lower than twenty-six and in most it is thirty or above. To persist in such a long-drawn-out course requires high academic motivation obviously not shared by many. Uruguay, with its stagnant economy, high urbanization, and large middle class with inflated expectations, is not typical of Latin America, but its high dropout rate is paralleled in other countries.

The part-time nature of the teaching profession and crowded classes make it difficult for professors to convey the excitement of their subject to their students. Nor are there many occasions for the professor to do this by informal contacts. Under such conditions interest withers. A dropout will lose the prestige conferred by having a degree but this need not necessarily inhibit the student from obtaining employment. The fact that so many students also have a job probably contributes to reducing academic motivation. Latin American societies are not meritocracies; in many instances jobs are acquired through informal contacts of family links rather than by ability tested in the examination room.

Attempts have been made by some universities, following the example of the University of Mexico's preparatory schools, to provide preparatory courses to make up for the inadequacies of school training. During this preparatory year, an effort is made to persuade students to transfer from overexpanded faculties like law into faculties needed for economic development, such as agronomy.[12] These preparatory courses are wasteful of scarce university resources and can be self-defeating in that students dislike the extra year's study which may not be relevant to their chosen profession. As some of these basic introductory courses have been financed by U.S. grants, it is easy for resentment to be exploited for political purposes, as happened at the University of San Carlos in Guatemala, at the University of Concepción in Chile, and at the University of San Marcos in Peru. Students and teachers may come together in their hostility to basic study programs. Part-time teachers see their jobs threatened; administrators dislike the threat of diminished faculty autonomy implied by centralization and cross-fertilization; and activist students resent the way in which basic studies marks a trend toward the North American pattern. For these reasons it is often in new institutions like the University of Oriente in Venezuela, geared to the needs of the region, that such programs seem to have the best chance of success.[13]

Universities by themselves cannot change the prestige valuation of faculties although they can attract students into science-based departments by means of a selective scholarship program, as at Buenos Aires. Ultimately, however, society creates the demand which universities attempt to satisfy. In litigious societies, law holds out tempting prospects and is recognized as a springboard into and a complement to a political career. Students find part-time work in lawyers' offices while studying one of the least intellectually exacting disciplines. Whereas a law degree used to offer the widest choice of jobs on graduation, new specializations are now reducing its utility. The demand for economists, statisticians, or empirically trained sociologists is tending to reduce the percentage of those studying law. Even the demands of the bureaucracy, once the lawyer's preserve, are becoming more specialized.

While no country can compare with Cuba's percentage drop in the number of students studying law—from twelve percent in 1959 to two percent in 1963, or with the rise in those studying engineering—from three percent in 1959 to fifteen percent in 1963,[14] the balance is being redressed in most countries.[15] The expansion of economics departments has been one of the most striking developments of recent years. Their popularity is due to the prestige of development economics, to the demand for accountants, and to the feasibility of studying economics part-time. Although job opportunities are highly favorable, the contrast between the rational emphasis of the discipline, with its frequently undisguised value connotations, and the apparent irrational nature of many government decisions may explain the radicalism of many economics students.

The Nature and Impact of Student Subculture

A crucial difference between Latin American students and those in either Britain or the United States is the large proportion who are part-time and undertake employment to supplement themselves while studying. Fees are minimal (one reason why Latin American universities are so poor) but there are few grants or scholarships to help the many students who must cover living expenses. In a study of Brazilian law students, seventy-five percent of those attending day classes and eighty-seven percent at night classes had a job. At the University of Buenos Aires, fifty-eight percent of all students had some form of employment. In economics, eighty percent had jobs, followed by philosophy and letters with seventy-one percent. Employment would seem to leave little time for study. In Caracas, the lower proportion who work—about one-third—reflects the higher standard of living and the generally higher social status of the student body. Faculties such as medicine and most of the sciences, which require full-time attendance, tend for that reason to draw their students from the wealthier segments of society.

Students lack the homogeneity of a full-time student community —a situation exacerbated in those universities where, as in Buenos Aires, faculties are widely separated in different parts of the city; in these cases both university and students lack a focus. There is no counterpart of the English college and few examples of the North American-style campus. There is nothing in the philosophy of Latin American education to correspond to the strongly held British belief in the educational value of students living together, which, of course, presupposes their being full-time. The sheer size of the metropolitan universities militates against a residence-building program which would soak up funds needed elsewhere, and in any case, a large proportion of students live at home.[16] There is, too, a feeling that for political reasons students ought to be dispersed rather than concentrated: the residential blocks on the campus at Caracas became strongholds of radical extremism and had to be closed down in 1967. Residences for women are sometimes run by nuns, but these tend to seal off their inmates from the rest of the student community. The need for a sense of community is even stronger in those universities where a large proportion of students come from the provinces and so live in cheap boarding houses away from their families.

"University cities" like those in Caracas and Mexico City (for which in the Hispanic world the University of Madrid, planned in the 1920s, provided a model), have been designed as total communities (although with few residences) and offer a more developed social life than the smaller metropolitan or provincial university. But the sheer size of university cities militates against homogeneity, and student organizations are on a faculty rather than a university basis. Faculties have their own restaurants and common room facilities; sports events, social activities, and politics are usually organized on a faculty basis. Student unions are federations of faculty centers. The social and political exclusiveness of faculties reflects their academic exclusiveness: it is rare for students from different faculties to attend the same lectures. Compartmentalization of the degree structure makes it difficult to inaugurate new interdisciplinary syllabuses and encourages a myopic, unintegrated vision of cultural development. This leaves a vacuum easily filled by a simplistic Marxism. A major attraction of the reformist ideology was its vision of an integrated culture which, in the absence of any other integrating philosophy, has given meaning and substance to the students' fragmented academic world.

Many of the tensions which gave rise to demands for participation and dialogue derive from the disappointment students feel on discovering the impersonality of the large, anonymous metropolitan university. Much of the original dynamic of the reform movement came from the assertion that a university should be a society of equals, in which professors and students could work closely and harmoniously together. Although this was supposed to find one expression in *cogobierno,* it did not remove basic tensions. The presupposition that the interests of professors and students would coincide was constantly belied by political as well as academic conflicts. As both professors and students continued to be part-time, interests alien to those of the university intruded. This was one consequence of the university's failure to become professionalized. As long as part-time professors taught part-time students, the sense of community among teachers and the sense of commitment to the university (and through it to the wider society) eluded those who were so earnestly seeking it.

Nor is absence of a sense of academic community compensated by sense of community in other spheres of activity. Sport, which plays such an important role in North American universities, does not feature prominently in Latin American universities. Some have excellent facilities, as at Caracas or at UNAM in Mexico, but here they seem to be prestigious rather than functional; and in any case, they are inadequate for their enormous student populations. In many smaller provincial universities, facilities are nonexistent.

In situations of rapid social change where students are agents of modernization and have high elite expectations, we might expect to find them reacting against the restrictions and presuppositions of a traditonal authoritarian family structure. Nor is it surprising that they should be disoriented when, as a result of this rapid change, family ties are weakened. It is too readily assumed that student turbulence in Latin America is an expression of generational conflict. Surveys in the United States have shown that it is often students from the most liberal and permissive family backgrounds who, finding the university both restrictive and depersonalized in contrast, become activists.[17] In Latin America the situation is different if only because the family plays a more important social role, is more authoritarian and does not encourage children to take on the sort of responsibilities their contemporaries do in the United States or in Britain.

Child-rearing patterns may often determine the direction generational conflict will take. It has been suggested, for example, that in Brazil the combination of an authoritarian father, early indulgence by the female members of the family, and adulation by servants is largely responsible for Brazilian boys having a much lower achievement motivation than their North American peers and gives the child an exaggerated sense of his importance and power.[18]

The comparative absence of generational conflict not only reflects the continuing cohesiveness of familial ties in Latin America but also the lack of intergenerational tensions in those countries where social mobility is restricted.

Myron Glazer comments on the remarkable generational continuity in the case of FRAP (Frente Revolucionaria de Acción Popular) and Christian Democrat students—confirming the findings of Frank Bonilla's earlier detailed study on Chilean students. In a Uruguayan study, it has been shown that there is also considerable generational continuity and very little rejection of the values of the student's family.[19] Indeed, it has been suggested that the lack of dynamism in Latin American society may be precisely due to the lack of sharp generational conflicts.[20] Where, however, the pace of change has been swift and accompanied by a rapid expansion of the university population—Venezuela is an example—or, as in prerevolutionary Cuba, a neocolonial economy restricted the openings for an inflated middle class, generational conflict does seem to be a significant factor.

One of the more obvious forms of generational revolt is against the moral code of the older generation—particularly their sexual ethics. Youthful rebellion in western countries frequently takes the form of outraging moral norms, with the justification that the transgressors are more honest than their hypocritical elders. This type of revolt has become formalized in the emergence of a distinctive youth culture, an offshoot of high wages and mass consumption, creating a sense of youthful solidarity which can cut across lines, and erupts in claims for moral autonomy in sexual matters and drug taking, and in antiauthoritarianism. So far this type of youth culture seems to have had comparatively limited impact in Latin America, mainly because of the still considerable influence of the Catholic Church, and the resilience of the family structure, and because traditional attitudes toward sexual relations are slow to change. A dual standard of morality is still accepted; the *macho* complex coexists with the virginity complex and the concepts of *honor* and *vergüenza* are still operative. In western societies, women's emancipation means sexual emancipation but this is dependent on an easy access to contraceptives nonexistent in Latin America. There, while women are coming to play an increasingly important part in public life, sexual mores are slow to change.

The period of sexual adjustment from adolescence to adulthood may coincide with a student's time at the university but one can only guess at the significance of sexual tensions in student subculture. Do Latin American universities fulfill a "marriage market" function as do British or North American universities? Opportunities for women to find suitable mates are never so favorable as when they are at the university. It is a reasonable assumption that considerable energy goes into selection and courtship—perhaps in some instances still ritualized in the Hispanic manner. But because of the narrowness of the social spectrum, it seems unlikely that marriages between students, whereby one of the partners marries into a higher social category, encourage social mobility. It may be (although this is said very tentatively) that sexual frustrations arising from a work situation in which the sexes mix freely and a sexual ethic which inhibits fulfillment contribute to the febrile intensity of political activity and find partial relief in riot and demonstration.[21]

In most analyses of Latin American students, women tend to be ignored;[22] yet they now constitute about forty percent of all students. This high proportion reflects the growing number of women entering public life in the more developed countries. In the less developed countries the proportion is somewhat lower: in Guatemala, for example, about twenty-five percent of students are women and in El Salvador about thirty percent.

Teaching is the profession for which most women students train, followed by pharmacy and dentistry. At Concepción, forty percent of all women students were studying some aspect of education compared with only ten percent of men, while 6.6 percent were studying dentistry (6.5 percent men) and 9.2 percent pharmacy (4.4 percent men). At the University of Buenos Aires women constituted seventy-five, fifty-five, and forty-nine percent, respectively, of the faculties of philosophy and letters, pharmacy, and dentistry. In general, faculties with a large proportion of women tend to be more conservative politically. It may be too that there is a correlation between dropout figures and the increase in the number of women students who leave before taking a degree in order to get married.

Students constitute the most visible subculture in Latin American society. Wide distribution over the city means that students are not hermetically sealed off from the rest of society. Those in part-time employment or living in boarding houses have contacts with the rest of the urban population and fulfill an important function as communications agents in cities where rumor and the spoken word are often more important than the written word. Scarcely a day passes without students being publicized, but it is a narrow, hectic, *political* subculture involving the few and alienating the many. Because secondary associations are weak within student society, and because a sense of academic community is absent, political activity provides a means of finding identity. Membership in a political group or participation in political activity fills a role analogous to that of the *Korporation* in Germany or the fraternity in the United States (although without the latter's exclusiveness). If the group is affiliated with a national political party, membership can also help in furthering career prospects.[23] The annual elections of student representatives are like a ritualized fiesta, but the jarring clash between groups and ideologies underlines the failure of politics as a substitute for a genuine sense of community. The ideal of the early reformers vanishes in the fierce factional conflicts of a student body divided against itself. These divisions reduce the effectiveness of students as a national pressure group and prevent the student subculture from having any lasting impact on society, while to the students themselves and to the army of dropouts the experience of student life can be profoundly disturbing.

Cogobierno

The most striking feature of Spanish American student subculture and the most controversial aspect of the university reform movement has been the principle of *cogobierno,* by which students are represented (usually in a ratio of one to three) on faculty boards. What many students in Brazil (where the principle has not been accepted), North America, and Europe started agitating for in the 1960s has been an accepted part of the Spanish-American state university since the 1920s. Its original purpose was for students to keep some check on professors whose interest in the university was peripheral and who regarded their chairs as personal property and status symbols. The reformists' arguments still retain some of their validity and student programs for reform today (both in Spanish America and in Brazil) suggest that some of the old professorial attitudes continue to exist. Private universities fiercely resist the *cogobierno* principle—a fact to which opponents of the system attribute their comparative freedom from political disturbance.

Student participation in university government is one of the few meaningful roles open to Latin American students and many take their responsibilities seriously. Professional opinion is divided about its desirability and utility. Many old reformists are reluctant to criticize a system they helped to pioneer while others blame *cogobierno* for the intrusion of politics into the university. Scientists, too, are often critical, arguing that the complexity of decisions precludes useful student participation. In the context of the political university it is rare for decisions to be taken on purely academic grounds. Political issues are inextricably mixed with academic considerations in the election of student representatives, who are often expected to push political views as well as to safeguard student interests.

Examinations are a particularly sensitive area where academic and political interests interweave. There are justifiable pedagogical criticisms of their inadequacy in testing knowledge or creative thinking, of their overemphasis on memory, and of their tendency to encourage students to regurgitate a particular professor's lecture notes. Activists go further, regarding them as a bourgeois sickness, an importation into the academic world of the values of free competition, and an insidious obsession with classification and grading. This, it is argued, penalizes students from poor backgrounds with inadequate secondary schooling—because they either are excluded in the first place from coming to the university or, once there, are at a disadvantage in course examinations. This argument ignores the fact that students from working-class backgrounds striving to integrate into society may have a high academic motivation.

The pressure of rising numbers compels universities to weed out students who are occupying places to no purpose (particularly in science faculties, where facilities are limited), but attempts to tighten academic standards are strongly resisted by student organizations. It is difficult to avoid the conclusion that much of the agitation is inspired by "professional students" who fear that they will be the first casualties of any academic improvement. There is also the feeling that examinations impose a rhythm on students' work that frustrates the aim of the activists to keep up constant political pressure.

Political considerations are also believed to enter into entrance examinations in universities where competition for places is particularly stiff or where there may already be a delicate balance of political forces within the university. During course examinations, threats of strike action can intimidate professors, who, in any case, may have qualms at failing students they feel are laboring under severe financial and social difficulties. In such an atmosphere standards get lost, sensitive professors become demoralized, and many students join the army of dropouts.

Cogobierno by itself can solve little. After fifty years of activity, it has failed to effect radical changes in teaching methods, in syllabuses, in admissions procedures, in examination techniques, in administrative structure, or in the organization of the teaching professions—part-time professors still outnumber full-timers. To read student demands of today, it is almost as if those fifty years of reform had never been.

The problem is how to delimit the justifiable area of student participation in university government. This problem exists not because of any intrinsic fault in the original reformist conception of *cogobierno* but because of the way in which the political university has distorted the system by allowing students to feel that its political function is more important than its academic purpose.

Student Criticism of the University Structure

The widespread and continual repetition of criticisms of the present university structure is evidence that the crisis is a general one and that differences among national universities are ones of degree, not of kind. The student president of the National University of Colombia in Bogotá put it succinctly: "The University of Colombia is in a state of crisis because the majority of students do not know how to study and many of the professors do not know how to teach."[24]

Both governments and students want university reform. Governments are interested in the universities' productivity, represented by their ability to produce the modernizing elites increasingly necessary for economic development. They resent the slowness of universities to respond to new requirements, and so where it has been possible—as in Argentina—university autonomy has been whittled away and students removed from participation in university governments.[25] In Brazil, where universities have lacked such autonomy and remained under the close control of federal and state authorities, the attack has been even more direct.[26] The reaction in both cases has been predictable. Students have become government's most bitter opponents and many able staff have been driven away, often taking whole research teams with them, or have gone into voluntary exile. Both staff and students feel that the government's only interest is to emasculate the universities as centers of independent criticism and to turn them into factories of "neutral" technicians. By reducing the universities' freedom of action, activist students feel the government will have removed the last bastion of resistance against imperialism.

This last assertion derives from the considerable help given by U.S. official agencies and individual universities and foundations to assist universities to modernize. Close and fruitful cooperation exists between a growing number of North American and Latin American universities, which have twinning arrangements, and assistance from foundations—particularly in the field of medicine—has served as useful pump priming. Even when such schemes are successful the charge is still made that they are examples of cultural imperialism. Particular hostility is aroused by official aid schemes. Suspicions were considerably increased by the revelation that CIA funds had been channeled into the American National Student Association, which has been trying to strengthen links with Latin American students. Members of the Peace Corps, especially when working in universities, are sometimes suspected of being CIA agents and on occasion have been compelled to leave.[27]

Not all criticism of modernizing schemes are blinkered and paranoic. Some of the more constructive criticism now comes from radical Catholic student organizations and, in the case of Chile, even from Catholic universities. Under the influence of ORMEU

(Oficina Relacionadora de Movimientos Estudiantiles Universitarios)—later renamed Corporación de Promoción Universitaria —with its headquarters in Santiago, and through various conferences organized under its auspices and those of JUDCA (Juventud Democrática Cristiana de América), new ideas were worked out for university reform and for linking universities with radical changes in society.[28] These clashed with official government-sponsored programs of radical reform during Allende's presidency.

There is now conscious rejection of much of the elitism implicit in reformist ideology. In common with other Latin American Christian Democrats, but rejecting the paternalist overtones of the parent parties, Christian Democrat students are inspired by the philosophy of liberal Catholic writers like Jacques Maritain and Mounier: "From our humanist and personalist, communitarian and revolutionary conception of society in general we have deduced a similar conception of the university."[29] Christian Democrats explicitly reject the methods of established left-wing groups. "It is necessary to create new methods of struggling—they must not be mass-oriented, that is, they must previously condition public opinion with a serious and rational job of awakening awareness and not utilize sentimental and superficial mass-oriented methods." This expression by Venezuelan students is very much in line with the stress on *concientizacão* by Acão Popular, the most radical student group in Brazil before it was driven underground in 1964.[30] It also corresponds to the thinking of Acción Popular in Peru. These groups represented a reaction against what they believed to be the manipulative methods of the old left. There are many practical expressions of this new wave in the way students are organizing voluntary social work.[31]

Although many student critiques relate to the general structure of society and the distortions produced by excessive dependence on the United States, there is a growing concentration on problems within the university and on the need to carry through the "Second Reform," as it is sometimes called.[32] The most common criticism is that universities have lost touch with the new needs of society by focusing too much on training professionals whose skills are no longer relevant to the requirements of a developing economy. Increased emphasis is now placed on the improvement of research facilities—especially in the sciences—because only in this way, it is argued, can total dependence on foreign scholarship be reduced. There is also demand for more integrated courses on general culture to offset excessive specialization, to bridge the gap between scientific and humanist studies, and to rouse the social consciousness of scientists, whose interests may be more narrowly professional. Emphasis is also placed in student programs on job counseling and welfare services for students as well as on preuniversity preparation in secondary schools.

Recognition that a major prerequisite for reform is an increase in professors' salaries, so that they can devote themselves entirely to the university, is coupled with a distrust of lifetime professorships. More extreme students want a say in academic appointments. In Chile, for example, when Christian Democrat students' proposals for a modified form of *cogobierno* were accepted by plebiscite in November 1967, communist students occupied the building of the Instituto Pedagógico and agitated for an even larger say in university government and appointments.[33]

The crux of the proposed reforms is financial and many demonstrations in recent years have been concerned with the need for bigger budgetary allocations to universities. Apart from this, it is alleged by students that economies could be made by rationalizing the financial administration, by functional planning, and by pruning chairs duplicated under the fragmented faculty system. Many complaints are leveled against the faculty system and the hardships it creates for students who wish to transfer from one faculty to another. Students also want flexible transfers between universities.

Although some student programs include higher fees for richer students in order to subsidize scholarships to enable poorer students to study in socially exclusive faculties such as medicine that require full-time study, the idea of differential payment runs counter to the tenets of reformist ideology. Objections to fee payment reveal an almost pathological distrust of government motives. Argued the president of UME (União Metropolitano do Estudantes) in Brazil, "Such a system will allow for the greater influence of the large corporations in the educational system directly devoted to meeting the country's requirements."[34] The left suspects a conspiracy by governments to "denationalize the state universities."[35] It is argued that universities, to avoid being compelled to serve the interests of international capitalism, retain cultural autonomy in order to apply science to national rather than international needs.

The establishment of private universities, which has been a cause of many student disturbances in recent years, illustrates an understandable obsession with employment possibilities. The largest demonstration over the foundation of a private university was the 1958 protest in Buenos Aires against Arturo Frondizi's law to legalize Catholic universities. This reflected the strong anticlerical current in the reformist ideology and in the radical tradition, but the creation of new private (especially Catholic) universities also raised fears that these would provide a higher quality education that would lessen the value of national university degrees. This feeling was a motive behind the 1967 demonstrations in Bolivia over the proposed opening of a Catholic university when the country's seven universities were already overproducing graduates.

The hostility is greater because these new universities are dependent on fees and thus recruit from a high social stratum.[36] Some receive financial assistance from abroad, which raises suspicions about the donors' motivation. When financial assistance from governments is given to new universities, much-needed funds are diverted from national universities. It is feared that graduates of these institutions will have better employment prospects because of their contacts in influential circles and hence will preempt key posts in business, planning and institutes, and politics. Students also suspect that private universities will become government-supporting institutions, producing "neutral" technicians who do not share the commitment to social change central to reformist ideology. By supporting private universities, governments can avoid confrontation with national universities, jealous of their autonomy, which refuse to permit the government to dictate their academic policy.

Behind some of the sense of occupational insecurity reflected in this opposition, there is a subconscious realization of the declining social utility of arts graduates—a feeling that society is being divided into a Saint-Simonian dichotomy of *oisifs* and *producteurs*. Resistance to radical changes within universities would be expected from those who are unable, for reasons of temperament or competence to adjust themselves to the requirements of the technologies needed in developing economies. The fact that many of the programs aimed at deflecting students from socially unproductive faculties like law are U.S.-financed enables resistance to them to don the cloak of political respectability. What on one level appears to be politically progressive—resistance to "cultural imperialism"—on another level may be socially regressive.

Reformism was primarily a nationalist ideology. It was a

deliberate attempt to throw off European influences, and to formulate a continental nationalism in order to resist encroaching U.S. influence. Anti-imperialism is integral to student attitudes and although many of the U.S.-inspired and -financed schemes do improve the quality of university teaching and help to produce more highly skilled and competent professionals, the price paid in loss of national self-esteem is considered by many students to be too high.[37]

The main justification given for the multiplication of private universities is that in national universities the distractions of febrile political activity and the disruption caused by strikes, demonstrations, and sit-ins disorient students, making it difficult for them to concentrate on academic study and impeding the reorganization necessary to produce the new professional skills needed in countries undergoing rapid modernization. Another justification is that private universities could be the pacemakers of new syllabuses; the threat from new disciplines, such as business studies, would then force the more traditional national universities to modernize, enabling their graduates to compete on comparable terms. Modernizing these institutions is not simply an academic operation, however, but involves changing a complex of cultural and political attitudes.

One reason why the reform movement has proved so unsuccessful in restructuring universities has been the way in which students, concerned to obtain paper qualifications guaranteeing employment and status, have perpetuated an outworn risk-avoiding mentality. It has been frequently observed that entrepreneurial drive has tended to come from immigrants who have been outside the dominant cultural ethos, or from those who have not been processed by an academic system that still transmits these values.[38]

Prima facie, it might be assumed that declining job opportunities for those trained in prestige disciplines would encourage a flow into more modern specialties. As far as sciences are concerned, financial resources are not adequate to provide the facilities which could soak up any potential demand: even a rich country like Venezuela can scarcely furnish these fast enough.[39] Medical faculties severely limit their admissions for similar reasons, and even were these restrictions relaxed, it is questionable whether those wishing to enter would be prepared to work in rural areas, where their services would be really welcome, rather than in cities, where prestige and money lie.

There is an understandable reluctance to choose courses whose career potentials are not clearly mapped out. Thus, in spite of the need to expand agronomy faculties, lack of confidence in possibilities that only massive agrarian reform programs will open up is a serious deterrent. Similarly, low-paced industrialization is not conducive to the study of science-based technologies.

Another complication is that those countries which have developed reasonable science facilities and produce good scientists are in danger of losing them through emigration. Techniques become more sophisticated and machinery and equipment more expensive, and the abler scientists and graduates want to work where these are available, where specialization is possible, and where research teams can be attracted by the facilities provided. The high cost of supplying these raises the whole question of priorities and educational strategy. Just how far can primary and secondary school needs be sacrificed to the "luxury" of developing expensive scientific research facilities in an effort to keep scientists at home? This is a dilemma common to all developing countries and one which markedly affects the attitude of the student who wants to acquire the best possible scientific training.

The crucial problem that arises from the quickening pace of social and technological changes is that the type of elite now required has changed. Whereas previously a broadly based humanistic culture was an adequate passport to a position of influence, now more specialized skills become necessary. The awareness that the skills taught in universities may no longer be relevant to the needs of society is a major cause of their politicalization and of the intricate interweaving of political and academic affairs which is the distinctive feature of the Latin American student ethos.

Politics within the University

There are many different forms of political activity open to the student. Interest may go no further than café chatter, attendance at an occasional political meeting, or voting in the annual elections for faculty representatives or for the student center. On the other hand, it might consist of nearly full-time political activism. Providing a student is in no hurry to obtain his degree, the university will put few obstacles in his way if he wishes to pursue his political interests on the campus. The larger the university, the more exiguous the control exercised over students by the administration; however, because of the financial pressures under which many students work, it is not uncommon to find leading activists drawn from wealthy families.[40]

The impression created by the press of students in constant turmoil can be misleading. There are frequent protest meetings; demonstrations erupt into strikes over university, national, or international matters, and these can lead to sit-ins and even to university closings. This is both distracting and irritating to the uncommitted students, who are usually in the majority, but it is rare for these to organize in counterprotest. Conservative and politically uninterested students rarely demonstrate; indeed, their passivity is as noteworthy as the activism of radicals. Occasional counterdemonstrations do occur between national and Catholic universities, but rarely between left and right within the same university. There have been few right-wing student organizations. In general, student groups are not repositories of right-wing nationalism (unlike the European experience between the 1890s and the 1930s). Where they have been, they were fringe groups disowned by the student body—for example, the Chilean Nazi students who made a foolhardy attempt at a putsch in 1938 or the Tacuara group in Argentina which, although founded in 1930, is still an active minority exploiting latent anti-Semitism for use against the large and influential Argentinian Jewish community. Otherwise, conflict has been mainly between groups of the left and center, each proposing rival reformist or revolutionary programs. The 1970s, however, have seen some polarization between left- and right-wing groups. Hitherto politically inactive students have started to organize—especially in Argentina—partly as a consequence of the growth of urban terrorism. Anticommunist groups in Argentina and Brazil have initiated witch hunts in universities. But it is difficult to determine how far the students themselves have participated in them.

It has been suggested that the quiescence of conservative students can be related to their "role image," which differs markedly from that of radical students.[41] A radical orientation seems to be connected with an integrated role image; the student does not see his role separated from that of a citizen. For the activist, student life cannot be separated from national life. Politics is not a matter of compartmentalization but an all-embracing experience in which university problems cannot be divorced from those of society as a whole. Students are not merely a sectional pressure group but the conscience of the nation. A progressive university in a backward society is therefore a contradiction in terms, and an apolitical student must be by definition a supporter of the status quo. This is in the reformist tradition and postulates the idea of the political university as distinct from the professional, vocational, academic university.

For the conservative student, on the other hand, the university is sharply separated from society. Its purpose is to provide the best possible professional training judged by criteria independent of politics. Political action is not only irrelevant to the university but positively harmful in that it deflects energies away from the business of learning and professional formation. The university is thus not an instrument for bringing about change so much as a machine for feeding professionals into the system. The university is the guardian of traditional values, not the generator of new ones.

For the conservative student, the university works to preserve status, although many students (particularly those working-class students whose ambition is to be integrated into society rather than to change it) sharing this view of the apolitical university may do so precisely because they see in the acquisition of a professional qualification a means of rising in the social scale. Thus students from different social backgrounds can coalesce in their apolitical passivity. The radical student, however, often concocts his campaign for representation on the faculty board on a platform of promoting student interests and of improving facilities. This as well as political factors helps to explain voting alignments.

As political activity is on a faculty basis, the political mood of a faculty partly conditions whether a student accepts political involvement or rejects it in favor of professional excellence. The mood of a faculty is predetermined by factors such as social origins, family advice, and career prospects, which will have influenced the student's original choice of course. In the case of agronomy faculties, limited openings keep them the preserve of landowners' sons, except in rare instances where agrarian reform has been taken seriously. Pharmacy and dentistry, with their high percentage of women, have a conservative bias. The same is true of philosophy and letters and education, although the implicit value connotations of these subjects, combined with uncertain job opportunities, make them more volatile. Economics and law, providing the main source of recruits for government service and politics, have a high political commitment, while medicine, engineering, and architecture, with their more selective recruitment pattern and full-time course requirements, tend to have a low political commitment.

To explain the different self-images among students studying science and those in arts and social studies, Aldo Soares has hypothesized a threefold identification pattern which he correlates with political attitudes.[42] Those who identify with a scientific or professional role see this in specific terms with their expertise limited to one field, while intellectuals tend to think of their role as involving general competence on a wide spectrum of issues. The intellectual's wide-ranging interests combine with more blurred expectations for employment as well as ambivalence over his precise function and place in society. He is thus impelled toward greater involvement in politics than the professional or the scientist.

To these considerations can be added the more demanding work-discipline required of science students, which excludes them from much of the political activity of nonscience students. There are more full-time students in science faculties, the staff-student ratio is better, the contact with staff is closer, there is a more developed esprit de corps, and subjective value judgments do not play the part they can in sociology or economics, where these are often explicit. Attendance at lectures and practical laboratory classes are necessary if a student is to keep the thread of a course, whereas in nonscience subjects, attendance can be, and often is, casual. Myron Glazer suggests in his study of Chilean students that the greater the intellectual challenge from the curriculum, the lower the probability of student political activity.[43]

The intermingling of university issues with wider national and even international ones makes it difficult to generalize about student elections with any accuracy. Alignments may be determined by local issues—such as, at the University of San Marcos, resentment against APRA's strong-arm tactics, which often swing otherwise uncommited students to support anti-APRA candidates even when these are communists. Student groups which are purely *gremialista*—fulfilling a nonpolitical, trade-union function, concerned with narrow student issues—can muster few votes except in private universities.

The constant forming and re-forming of splinter groups, each with distinctive ideas, suggest that within a comparatively homogeneous political system, differences between groups can only be recognized by ideology. Without the legitimation of ideology, a student group has little chance of survival. "Political interest and participation," suggests Professor Soares, "is associated *not* with a leftist ideology *per se*, but rather with the *strength* of ideological beliefs, regardless of their direction.[44]

Academic issues can easily become political issues charged with ideological overtones. Allegations of discrimination by examiners, rumors of kickbacks like scholarship or travel awards to students of a particular political persuasion, and attempts to raise academic standards by stiffer examinations can all be interpreted in political terms. The point about political deals is not that they are true or apocryphal, but that within a highly charged political atmosphere they too easily seem credible.

The lack of interest in politics among many students stems from disillusion with the politicking of the activists, and this can also breed a cynicism about politics in general extending into later life. Far from being the laboratory of democracy, universities can also be its deathbed. The influence of student politics has been grossly exaggerated. Students' views of their importance have been sanctified by reformist mythology but constant reiteration of these convictions in their publications and on the rostrum has had the effect of sealing them off from a wider public. Incantatory exhortation can lose its magic through overuse. As literacy increases, and as new groups acquire political consciousness and sophistication, student claims to be the articulators of the demands of the unfranchised become less convincing. Students find that they are then reduced to the status of a pressure group, forced to compete with other sectors for scarce available resources.[45]

Although most student groups are self-sustaining, flagging energies are revived by "professional students." The presence of aging students, only nominally following courses and devoting most of their time to political activities, is an accepted part of the Latin American university scene. Student groups suffer from acute discontinuities because of rapid turnover. The professional student is the contact man between a national party and its student affiliates who provides needed continuity. He must register in a faculty to qualify for using facilities and for voting in elections, but if he fails his examinations or does not appear for them, he can take them an indefinite number of times or even reregister in another faculty. Hence the anger at moves by university authorities to introduce nonrepeating rules to weed out those who fail examinations, and the hostility at attempts to limit those who stand for student office to bona fide serious students who have passed their course examinations.

The "professional student" may be on the payroll of a party or indirectly subsidized by holding a job with a party sympathizer.[46] He will be responsible for organizing elections, distributing funds, and coordinating strikes and demonstrations with outside bodies. Some even have a responsibility for organizing urban terrorism or rural guerrilla activity.

Student Politics and National Politics

APRA in Peru, Acción Democrática in Venezuela, the Chilean and Venezuelan Christian Democrat parties, the 26th of July Movement in Cuba, the communist parties in Venezuela and Cuba, as well as others, have had their origins in student groups. Student politics have been the breeding ground where many politicians have served their apprenticeship as student agitators, attracting the attention of national political leaders by their rhetorical skill or organization ability. Latin American student movements serve an important socializing function by preparing participants in them for adult roles in highly political societies. They also provide a way in which new social groups can be injected into the national political system.

There have been cases of students being used by groups marginal to the political process for their own ends—communists during periods when they are illegal or on occasions when they find it easier to capitalize on the discontent of easily accessible students rather than trying to organize inaccessible peasants. Excluded groups might climb into power on the backs of students and then, once in power, try to force them to return to their books. Even sections of the military may seek legitimacy by allying with students—as in Venezuela in 1928 and 1945 and, most strikingly, in Cuba in 1933. By the very narrowness of their social base and numbers, students are vulnerable to alliances of this sort.

At first, communist parties distrusted the reformists: the urban proletariat, not bourgeois students, would lead the revolution. But the attractions of operating from the inviolability of the university campus were difficult to resist. Activity in universities opened up possibilities of placing sympathizers in key posts and, where communist parties were actually banned, university politics could provide a convenient cover. The influence of established communist parties among students should not be exaggerated, however.[47] During the 1930s, cooperation between communist parties and dictatorial governments led to some ambivalence in students' attitudes toward them. But more important was the way in which the reformist concept of students as a regenerating elite militated against their becoming mere appendages of wider political movements.

It is an oversimplification to regard students simply as the passive dupes of outside interests, although a few undoubtedly have been. National parties try to build up student followings, but the latter try to keep their freedom of action. The popularity of Castroist movements among students derives partly from the Castroists' claim to be free from manipulation by the old established communist parties.

Once a revolutionary regime has become established, student groups previously in opposition face absorption into the official political structure, and thus relinquishment of their autonomy. Cuba is a clear case in point. The FEU (Federación de Estudiantes Universitarios), which was founded in 1923 and played crucial roles in the revolt against Muchado in the 1920s, in the revolutionary government of 1933, and in the resistance against Batista in the 1950s, has now been fused with the UJC (Unión de Jóvenes Comunistas), ostensibly to avoid bureaucratic duplication. In practical terms, it has been converted into a branch of the governmental apparatus.[48]

The Bolivian situation provides a contrast. There, the MNR never succeeded in gaining control of the student movement. The government's overthrow in 1964 can be partly explained by this failure, as universities became a major focus of opposition to the revolution.[49]

In Mexico, the history of the student movement has been distinctive if only because students had little effect on the Revolution starting in 1910 (except the unusual case of the art students of the Colegio de San Carlos). In the early 1920s, José Vasconcelos's concept of the national university as the forge of national consciousness was central to the new Mexican nationalism and influential outside Mexico. Many students responded by going as teachers into the countryside. Later the steam went out of this rural populism; reality was too intractable. Mexican students did not join the reform movement until 1929, the year in which the PNR (Partido Nacionalista Revolucionario), the new official party, was formed. Now there was a repository of revolutionary virtue which preempted the regenerative role played by students elsewhere. The 1968 disturbances in Mexico may be seen as an attempt on the part of students there to take on the role hitherto denied them.[50]

One reason for the interest of opposition parties in student politics (an interest reflected in the extraordinary coverage given to student elections in the press) is that they are felt to constitute a barometer indicating the real, as distinct from the artificial, balance of political forces. Where elections can be and usually are influenced by government pressure or by bribery and intimidation, the results of national elections do not necessarily reflect the real state of opinion. In contrast, elections held in the sanctity of the campus are free from government pressures; they may be used as evidence that the government does not represent the real will of the people. Governments must always be the losers since student elections are contests between various opposition factions bidding against each other for the uncommitted, and not contests between pro- and antigovernment groups. Where opposition parties have student affiliates, they therefore look to the university election results for an indication of what their real strength in the country as a whole might be.

A more tangible benefit is the part that students can play in demonstrations and strikes. Where political violence does not carry the opprobrium it does in stable parliamentary societies, a high premium is placed on violent demonstrations.[51] Student demonstrations may be concerned with university matters or with national issues, but it is sometimes difficult to draw the line between the two. A demonstration in Lima in 1963 shows how issues become confused. Student demonstrators set out from San Marcos to present a petition at the presidential palace for a higher budgetary allocation to the university. Leaders addressing the marchers beforehand stressed the importance of not allowing sectarian interests to destroy the united front. The demonstrators moved off peacefully enough, but as they approached the palace square, they were joined by groups of strikers together with their families; by members of La Cantuta teachers' training college, demanding autonomy similar to the university's and freedom from Ministry of Education control; and by students of the Catholic university, wanting to press the case for the inclusion of private universities in any increase of funds. What seemed to start as a reasonable demonstration finished as a political protest against the Ministry of Education, against an unjust social system that allowed the families of striking workers to starve, and against the principle of private education favoring the privileged, and with rival student groups coming to blows. Unanimity was lost and effectiveness dissipated.

A constant feature of student politics is the failure of governments to control them. Efforts have been made during periods of military rule to pass legislation which would limit student political activity by making it obligatory for all students to vote in their elections. This rule would work to tap the apathetic and presumably conservatively inclined majority and to limit the influence of "professional students" by requiring evidence of academic competence from those standing for student office. But these measures meet with strong resistance from student organizations as an unwarrantable infringement of their liberty. In Argentina, under General Juan Carlos Onganía, and in Brazil since 1964, efforts have been made to establish new student organizations, but these have enjoyed only limited support. In Brazil, the DNE (Directorio Nacional do Estudantes, which replaced UNE, União Nacional do Estudantes), has never enjoyed more than minority support, and major efforts have been made by Brazilian students since 1964 to reestablish UNE as the genuine mouthpiece of student opinion.

Attempts to establish student groups affiliated to the governing party have been unsuccessful. It is uncommon for an opposition party, once in office, to keep the support of its student affiliate. The PRI has little influence in Mexican student politics; Acción

Democrática's support in Venezuela is almost nonexistent; Juan Bosch's student following in the Dominican Republic dropped sharply once he came to power. Chilean Christian Democrat students were reluctant to be too closely associated with the government of President Eduardo Frei lest any of its unpopularity rub off on them. Acción Popular in Peru was unable to win much support, and its small student following was forced to ally either with Christian Democrats or with communists in their common opposition to APRA. In Colombia's consensus politics, neither liberals nor conservatives have substantial student followings.

Part of the explanation for this situation lies in the difficulties of psychological adaptation from an opposition role to that of an establishment group, but more important has been the challenge from the various Castroist groups that emerged in the wake of the Cuban Revolution. Under this challenge, the youth movements of the democratic parties moved left, while the old-guard leadership grew more conservative. The year 1961 marked the break between the student wings and the leadership of these parties. In Venezuela the failure of Acción Democrática (which came to power in 1958 contemporary with Castro's victory in Cuba) to initiate changes on the Cuban pattern caused the majority of its student supporters to break away and form the MIR (Movimiento Izquierdista Revolucionario). In Peru the cooling of APRA's support for Castro resulted in the formation of Apra Rebelde.[52]

Successful resistance to the United States and the assertion of nationalism, combined with Castro's charisma, have a compulsive fascination for the vocal activist minority. A crucial feature of this attraction is the important role played by students in the revolutionary struggle in Cuba (although a greater number were active in the urban resistance, it is rural guerrilla activity that has the real appeal). This confirms activists in their belief in the vanguard role of students. Reformist tradition crystallized the concept; Cuban success sanctified it.

Many Latin American students (in common with their Western European counterparts) have sought a "third way," rejecting both capitalism and communism. This may take the form of Castroism with its subjective, voluntarist Marxism, as exemplified in Guevara's and Debray's writings, or it may take the form of the communitarianism of radical Catholics.

The concept of alienation is integral to both Castroist and radical Catholic theorizing. Castroists find salvation in identification with peasants. Castroism is wedded to violent revolution; the Christian Democrats to a "revolution in liberty." In both cases a key role is assigned to students. Castroist students see themselves as the "small motor" of Debray's thesis, who by their revolutionary example will set off the larger motor of a general rising by deprived and suppressed classes hitherto unaware that society could be changed. For radical Catholics the function of students is to awaken the masses to their predicament so that they can find a solution of their own choosing instead of passively accepting one imposed from above. Radical Catholic students see another role in their radicalizing Christian Democrat parties, which are more cautious than their youth affiliates. When the party fails to respond, the more extreme students break away, much as extremist groups did from Acción Democrática and APRA during the early 1960s. In Venezuela and Chile, far-left Catholics have broken away from the official Christian Democratic student organizations in order to cooperate with Castroists. They accept the necessity of violence much as Camilo Torres did in Colombia.[53]

Students by themselves can only be political catalysts or detonators of wider revolutionary outbursts. Their numerical basis is too small, their social base too narrow, their career as students too short, and their interests too diverse for them to implement the ambitious role assigned them by the reform movement. Reformists have become aware of students' social isolation and sought to break it down by educating urban workers in the night schools of the "popular universities"—the González Prada in Lima, the José Martí in Havana, or the Tupac Katiri in La Paz—but only minimal numbers were touched by this. In the early 1920s, students in Lima implemented educational links by supporting the agitation for an eight-hour day, and at the same time in Chile, students gave priority to social and political problems over university reform.[54]

In the formative stages of labor movements, students have played an important informal organizational and educational role, but this declines as labor bureaucratization increases. Once trade unions have been set up, the relationship between them and students can be institutionalized—as in the 1966 Mineworker-Student Pact in Bolivia, and in Uruguay, where the Students' Federation (closely linked to the pro-Soviet Communist party) made a "permanent pact" with labor leaders to coordinate strike activity. In Argentina, however, student approaches met with little union response, at least until the Córdoba rising of 1969.[55] This is partly a legacy of the Peronist period between 1945 and 1955, when students were an important focal point of opposition to the regime. The confrontation between Peronists and the military has seen the emergence of Peronist student groups sympathetic to guerrillas, such as the Montoneros. (Similarly, students helped the Tupamaros in Uruguay.)

Until ten years ago student lack of interest in rural problems was evidenced by the absence of the Russian *narodnik* type of rural populism (with the important exception of Mexico in the 1920s). It is only since the Cuban Revolution's emphasis on agrarian reform has been coupled with the myth of the rural guerrilla, that rural issues have impinged on the student conscience; now the leadership and cadres of rural guerrilla movements often consist of students. Another aspect of this rural emphasis may be seen in government-sponsored schemes in which students work in depressed rural regions during vacations.[56] Whatever the criticisms of the left against the Peace Corps (the commonest accusation that of their being CIA agents), the example of young North Americans working in poverty-stricken areas has acted as a spur to many Latin American students to do the same. The breaking down of taboos about doing manual labor and working in rural areas may well be the Peace Corps's most important contribution to development. One consequence of the new consciousness of rural poverty is a deeper appreciation of the complexities of social change and of the inapplicability of simplistic political notions bred in the rarified atmosphere of an academic environment.

The slow response of student subculture to the challenges of modernization, and the inability of universities to provide modernizing elites, have encouraged governments to question the previously accepted assumptions on which university autonomy rested. Intervention has provoked resistance from students and staff alike but public tolerance of their tactics can no longer be taken for granted. Nor can students depend on widespread support from other social groups. Only when students are prepared to abandon their position *qua* students by crossing the cultural and social gap separating them from the dispossessed can they command respect and a following, and even then only if they have something more practical to offer than book-learned theories of revolution.

Even within universities the gap between activists and the apolitical majority is widening. Factionalism on the left is reducing the effectiveness for positive action that students can take to reform the university; at the same time, their influence as a national pressure group is declining. By rejecting compromise in favor of messianic visions, the activists have restricted the possibilities of an academic community and condemned the university to a marginal role in national development.

Whereas in Europe and the United States student activism has been directed against their impersonal, bureaucratic, technological societies, in Latin America it is directed against the threat to established values from the imminence of technological advance. Yet it is only through technology that poverty can be overcome and economic prosperity assured. Technology is essentially international, and so far in Latin America it has been largely dependent on foreign inventions and on foreign technical aid. The imperatives of technological advance, without which Latin American societies must remain underdeveloped, strike at the very essence of the nationalist ethos fundamental to student attitudes.

In the difficult resolution of this issue students can play a constructive role only if they accept a modification of many long-cherished illusions. The traditional student role as defender of democratic freedoms, however, has by no means lost its relevance to the Latin America of the 1970s, which has been swinging far to the right.

NOTES

1. M. van Aken, "University Reform before Córdoba," *Hispanic American Historical Review* (1971). There is a huge literature on the reform movement in Spanish but very little in English. See Gabriel del Mazo, *Estudiantes y gobierno universitario* (Buenos Aires, 1955), and in English, R. J. Walter, *Student Politics in Argentina: the University Reform and Its Effects, 1918–1964* (New York, 1968). There is a useful selection of translated documents in *University Reform in Latin America*, edited by International Student Conference (Leyden, 1961). The key concept of the "political university" is succinctly discussed in J. P. Harrison's "The Confrontation with the Political University," *The Annals of the American Academy of Political and Social Science* (1961). An important overview on students in selected countries, though curiously insensitive to the issues of reformist ideology, is A. Liebman, K. N. Walker, and M. Glazer, *Latin American University Students: A Six-Nation Study* (Cambridge, Mass.,

1972; the six nations are Colombia, Mexico, Panama, Paraguay, Puerto Rico, and Uruguay). For a longer bibliography, see J. J. Petersen, "Recent Research on Latin American Students," *Latin American Research Review* (1970).

2. For the case of Peru, where the popular university idea has been an important part of the APRA's strategy, see, J. L. Klaiber, "The Popular University and the Origins of Aprismo," *Hispanic American Historical Review* 55 (1975).

3. For intellectual influences see R. J. Walter, "The Intellectual Background of the 1918 University Reform Movement in Argentina," *Hispanic American Historical Review,* 49 (1969).

4. For the Argentinian case see Jorge Graciarena, "Classes medias y movimiento estudiantil: el reformismo argentino (1918–1966)." In *Estudiantes y Política* (Santiago, 1970).

5. R. Arnove, *Student Alienation: A Venezuelan Study* (New York, 1972), p. 21. This is the most detailed analysis of a particular university's student body.

6. A. Leeds analyzes the significance of personal contacts in Brazil in "Brazilian Careers and Social Structure in Brazilian Society," *American Anthropologist* 66 (1964).

7. In Chile in 1964, 64 percent of 13,600 passed the entrance exam. The Department of Philosophy and Education admitted 1,100 out of 3,100 applicants, the Medical School admitted 160 out of 1,200, and the School of Agriculture 55 out of 400 (*El Siglo*, April 12, 1964). In 1968 in Venezuela, 23,604 eligible students competed for 12,500 available places. The number of applicants had increased threefold in seven years (*Elite*, Caracas, September 21, 1968).

8. G. Soares in "El mundo del ideología," *Aportes*, 5 (1967), note 18 observes that out of six countries studied (Colombia, Mexico, Paraguay, Panama, Puerto Rico, and Uruguay) not more than one percent of the students came from peasant stock. Even in postrevolutionary Bolivia the proportion is minimal; only 1.7 percent of the 19–24 age group were studying in universities in 1963 (*La situación de la educación superior en Bolivia* [La Paz, 1962], p. 85). At Caracas, 118 out of 15,595 gave their father's occupation as agricultural laborer and 1,103 as urban worker (F. de Venanzi, p. 180).

9. See the general discussion for Latin America by A. Solari, "Secondary Education and Elite Development," in *Elites in Latin America,* edited by Aldo Solari and Seymour Martin Lipset (New York: Oxford University Press, 1967). The inadequacies of Argentinian secondary schooling either for the university or for nonuniversity activity are analyzed by J. O. Inglese, "El poder socializador de las instituciones educativas argentinas," *Aprotes* 5 (1967). The case of Brazil is analyzed by F. Bonilla in *Education and Political Development,* edited by J. M. Coleman (Princeton, 1965), where secondary-level schooling is summarized as "narrowly utilitarian, compartmentalized, mechanical, dogmatic and pretentious" (p. 203), and "almost totally unresponsive to the man-power needs of the nation" (p. 201). See R. J. Havighurst, "Secondary Schooling and Socio-Economic Structure in Brazil," *Social and Economic Studies* 14 (1965), where he tentatively concludes that secondary education provides a substantial degree of opportunity for working-class youth.

10. A study by the University of Chile's Institute of Statistical Research showed in December 1962 that, of all students enrolled, 48.4 percent withdrew at the end of the first year in private universities and 54.9 percent in state universities—the highest percentage being in law, pedagogy, and engineering. At Concepción the figure for 1964 was 28 percent (*Memoria presentada por el Directorio de la Universidad de Concepción,* 1964, p. 114). At the University of Buenos Aires in 1958 only 3,324 degrees were granted. Drop-out rates were as high as 80 percent in architecture, 64 percent in law, and 44 percent in medicine. In Mexico, UNAM granted only 7,532 degrees between 1931 and 1943 (K. Silvert, "The University Student." In *Continuity and Change in Latin America,* edited by J. J. Johnson [Stanford, 1964], pp. 214, 272 n 16).

11. *Memoria . . . de Concepción,* p. 99; *Boletín de la U. de Buenos Aires,* p. 12; Venanzi, *op. cit.,* p. 181; L. R. Scheman, "The Brazilian Law Student: Background, Habits,

Attitudes," *Journal of Inter-American Studies* 5 (1963). Between 1953 and 1959, 47 percent of the enrolled students at the University of Buenos Aires withdrew. Fewer than half of these gave economic or job difficulties as their motive: 31.5 percent gave "personal reasons" and only five percent found university studies too strenuous [R. C. Newton, "Students and the Political System of the University of Buenos Aires," *Journal of Inter-American Studies* 8 (1966)].

12. According the Felipe Herrera, in *Obstacles to Change in Latin America*, edited by C. Veliz (London, 1967), p. 249, Latin America had only 26,000 agronomists in 1962 but would need at least 60,000 by 1970 to meet the needs of agrarian reform programs; yet all the agricultural schools put together graduated only 2,000 agronomists a year. Similarly in forestry: in 1962 there were only 600 forestry engineers, but 5,000 would be needed by 1970. Five hundred new sanitary engineers are needed each year, but only 100 are produced.

13. R. Arnove, *Student Alienation*.

14. Solari in *Elites*, p. 478, and *Boletín de la U. de Buenos Aires* (October 1965). Some insight into the new scale of revolutionary values of different occupations is shown by a survey among Cuban youth published in *Bohemia* (Havana, December 20, 1963), where preferences were listed in order of popularity as: scientists, teachers, professors; engineers and related technicians; doctors and related professions; humanist and literary occupations; technical office workers; artisans and skilled workers; social workers; agricultural and livestock workers; white-collar workers; lawyers and related professions; *government officials in administrative* posts. These ratings were probably expected by the questioners.

15. *Aportes* 2 (1966) figures on pp. 46–41. The only countries showing a percentage increase in those studying law were Haiti and Paraguay. An interesting analysis, using data from the 1958 Buenos Aires University census, showing the correlation between social class and faculty choice is Izaguirre de Cairoli, "Estratificación y orientación professional en la Universidad de Buenos Aires," *Revista Latinoamericana de Sociología* 3 (1965).

16. At Caracas UCV, out of 15,595 students, 11,374 lived with parents or relatives and only 971 in residences. At Concepción, out of 4,048, 2,045 lived at home, or with relatives, 1,005 in pensions, and 734 in residences. The University of Concepción has built some imaginative chalet-type residences, grouping students into small self-contained units. Approximately nine-tenths of Buenos Aires University students lived at home (Newton, "Students"). A rare example of an integrated residential university is the Universidad Técnica Federico Santa María at Valparaíso, although the accommodation is austere and barrackslike.

17. See the articles in the Special Issue "Stirrings out of Apathy: Student Activism and the Decade of Protest," *Journal of Social Issues* 23 (1967).

18. B. C. Rosen, "Socialization and Achievement Motivation in Brazil," *American Sociology Review* 27 (1962), and E. Willems, "The Structure of the Brazilian Family," *Social Forces* 31 (1953).

19. M. Glazer, "Student Politics in a Chilean University," in the Special Issue "Students and Politics" of *Daedalus* (1968), p. 105. For a thorough study of Chilean students in the pre-Allende period see F. Bonilla and M. Glazer, *Student Activism in Chile* (New York, 1970). See also Bonilla's article "The Student Federation of Chile: Fifty Years of Political Action," *Journal of Inter-American Studies* 2 (1960). It is perhaps misleading to generalize about generational continuity based on identity of political views between Christian Democrat supporters and their children. Christian Democracy is an elastic term. For many of the older generation it was a preferable alternative to the secular left—either FRAP or Unidad Popular—precisely because they believed it would not promote social change. For many students, in contrast, Christian Democracy was attractive because it appeared a radical alternative to the secular left that could work within a Latin American cultural ethos with populist rather than manipulative overtones. During Allende's presidency the most radical wing of Christian Democracy was represented by MAPU (*Movimiento de Acción*

Popular Unitaria), which had a strong student base. For the tensions within Christian Democracy see E. de Kadt, "Paternalists and Populists: Views on Catholicism in Latin America," *Journal of Contemporary History* (1967). For a full if at times far-fetched Freudian interpretation of student movements with some Latin American examples see L. S. Feuer, *Conflict between Generations* (New York, 1969).

20. Solari, in Preliminary Introduction to *Aportes* 5 (1967), p. 7.

21. I know of no studies, in contrast to the situation in the United States, on Latin American students' sexual behavior, or of any study as to where students meet their future spouses. In the absence of sociological information it is impossible to say what proportion of Latin American male students experience sexual initiation in brothels—a higher number, one would assume, than in more permissive societies. It can be argued that in more permissive societies the removal of guilt over premarital sexual intercourse and of fears over pregnancy releases a store of psychic energy which can be turned into political channels. Not that many Latin American students would be inhibited by a Puritan sexual ethic.

22. See M. Knaster, "Women in Latin America: The State of Research, 1975," *Latin American Research Review* 11 (1976).

23. The APRA party in Peru is the clearest example, with its own self-contained subculture.

24. *El Tiempo* (Bogotá), May 12, 1965.

25. By Law 16912, of July 29, 1966. For the Argentine situation in the mid 1960s see *A Report to the American Academic Community on the Present Argentine University Situation*, prepared for the Latin American Studies Association (Austin, 1967).

26. For Brazil see Marialice Foracchi, *O Estudante e a Transformação de Sociedade Brasiliera* (Rio de Janeiro, 1965), especially pp. 252–88, and by the same author, "El radicalismo vinculado al sistema: condiciones sociales de la politización del estudiante brasileño," *Revista Latinoamericana de Sociología* 3 (1966); also see V. Durand Ponte, "Análisis del movimiento estudiantil brasileño," *Revista Mexicana de Sociología* (1967). In English the most accessible accounts are L. T. Gierry, "Dominant Power Components in the Brazilian University Student Movement Prior to April 1964," *Journal of Inter-American Studies* 7 (1965); R. O. Myhr, "Brazil," in *Students and Politics in Developing Nation*, edited by D. K. Emmerson (New York, 1968); and the author's "Nationalism in the Brazilian University Student Movement," *Inter-American Economic Affairs* 22 (1969).

27. For one example of a leftist view of the Peace Corps see the article by Mario Mencia in the Chilean review *Plan* 2 (1967). Reference is made to fifteen Peace Corpsmen expelled from Concepción University on October 26, 1966, "for being spies and the instruments of ideological penetration." The Bolivian film *Blood of the Condor* exemplifies the suspicion with which the Peace Corps is regarded by the left.

28. The Chilean case was unusual in that students at the Catholic University sparked off the campaign for *cogobierno* in the University of Chile. See articles in *El Mercurio* (November 1967). The campaign began in the Catholic University in Valparaíso but soon spread to Santiago. The best source for radical Catholic theorizing about university reform are the forty or so issues of the *Boletín* published by ORMEU and the CPU in Santiago. See especially no. 32. During Allende's presidency, Catholic universities, represented by such extremist groups as MIR, moved further left.

29. *Democracia Cristiana—Reforma Universitaria*, published by a group of Christian Democrat students in Venezuela (no date), from which this quotation is taken, is a cogent and succinct summary of Catholic aims. See also *Voz Universitaria* (Quito, 1965) for a similar but less precise summary.

30. For Acão Popular see Gierry, "cominant Power Components." See also E. de Kadt, *Catholic Radicals in Brazil* (London, 1970).

31. This may take the form of medical students setting up clinics in slum areas on their own initiative, as they have done in Bogotá, or providing extramural teaching in "popular

universities." In Chile a group known as MUPT (*Movimiento Universitaria para Todos*) was set up to teach, on a voluntary basis, some of the 18,500 eligible applicants who did not get a university place in 1965 (*Ultima Hora*, February 12, 1967). This type of activity became common during the Allende period.

32. For the need for a new reform see the article by the "grand old man" of the original reform movement in 1918, Gabriel del Mazo, *La crisis universitaria en América Latina*, published in *Estudios y Documentos*, no. 9, by the *Centro de Estudios y Documentación Social* (Mexico City, 1964).

33. The agreement between UFUCH, the student federation, and the acting rector made provision for one-fifth to one-third student representation, with full voting rights, in the administration of the university and one-quarter representation on boards connected with appointments and elections. Also, university employees would be represented through their own union on administrative organs concerned with their affairs. This agreement, concluded in June 1968, went further than the original proposals agreed to by an earlier plebiscite, due to a number of factors—reforms in the Catholic University, communist pressure, and possibly the influence of European student revolts.

34. *Jornal do Brasil* (April 9, 1968).

35. This is a theme running through left-wing writings on universities; see *Ultima Hora* (January 20, 1968) and a Cuban formulation by M. Mencia, "Complot contra las universidades latinoamericanas," *Casa de las Américas* (1968). The case for the cultural autonomy of universities as a defense against their denationalization is argued by Darcy Ribeiro in "Universities and Social Development," in *Elites in Latin America*.

36. For a discussion of fees and of government assistance to private universities see L. Scherz García, "Relations between Public and Private Universities," in *Elites in Latin America*. The threat to state universities from private universities does not come from numbers; in Buenos Aires, for example, Catholic universities in the mid 1960s had a total enrollment of some 5,000 in comparison with some 70,000 at the University of Buenos Aires.

37. The relevance of the U.S. university model to Latin America is posed by the example of the University of Puerto Rico, which, since its foundation in 1903, has had a practical orientation and drawn students from a far wider social spectrum than is true in Latin America. So long as the benefits of the acquisitive society are available to its graduates, radicalism is dampened, in spite of FUPI, the vocal independista group. See A. Liebman, *The Politics of Puerto Rican University Students* (Austin, 1970).

38. For a general discussion of the problem see S. M. Lipset, "Values, Education and Entrepreneurship" in *Elites in Latin America*. F. Bonilla's chapter "Cultural Elites" in the same volume analyzes the literary orientation of Latin American intellectuals, as does W. S. Stokes, "The Drag of the Pensadores," in *Foreign Aid Re-examined*, edited by J. W. Riggins and H. Schoek (Washington, D.C., 1958). An interesting analysis showing how immigrants into Argentina were attracted to technical schools in contrast to the traditional humanist orientation of Creoles is J. C. Tedesco, "Educación, sociedad y economía en Argentina (1880–1900)," *Aportes* 15 (1970). A penetrating analysis of intellectuals in Argentina and Mexico is J. Marsal, *La Sombra del Poder* (Madrid, 1975).

39. High professional expectation came before financial remuneration as a motive for the scientific brain drain from Chile, according to S. Gutiérrez Olives and J. Riquelme Pérez, "La emigración de recursos humanos chilenos de alto nivel a los Estados Unidos," *Ciencia Interamericana* 6 (1965) writing before the fall of Allende. Political factors have been a prime cause of brain drain from many countries.

40. For a general theoretical discussion see D. B. Thomas and R. B. Craig, "Student Dissent in Latin America: Toward a Comparative Analysis," *Latin American Research Review* 8 (1973).

41. Soares in "The Active Few: Student Ideology and Participation in Developing Countries," in *Comparative Education Review* 10 (1966).

42. Soares, "Intellectual Identity and Political Ideology among University Students," in *Elites in Latin America.*

43. Glazer, in "Students and Politics" issue of *Daedalus.*

44. Soares, "The Active Few."

45. The relationship between students's political effectiveness and level of national political maturity is traced by K. Silvert, "The University Student," in *Continuity and Change*, pp. 221–24.

46. For some indication of communist influence see *Communist Infiltration in Latin American Educational Systems* (Washington, D.C., 1965). The real threat does not come from strongly entrenched communist parties—which tend in Latin America to be conservative—but from a fragmented left with each faction striving to outbid the others. One consequence of the Cuban Revolution has been to divide the left, not to unite it. Universities have suffered from this as Maoists, Trotskyists, Castroists, and so on, struggle for power and influence. See A. Hennessy, "Las raíces del radicalismo estudiantil en los útimos años," in *Estudiantes y Política* and his "The New Radicalism in Latin America," *Journal of Contemporary History* 7 (1972).

47. See the Hennessy articles cited in note 46 *supra.*

48. The justification for this move is in *Granma* (Havana, November 23, 1967). Two background articles on Cuban students are J. Suchlicki, "El estudiantado de la Universidad de La Habana en la política Cubana, 1956–7," *Journal of Inter-American Studies* 9 (1967), and his "Stirrings of Cuban Nationalism: The Student Generation of 1930," in the same journal 10 (1968). See also his *University Students and Revolution in Cuba, 1920–68* (Coral Gables, 1969).

49. This is discussed briefly in A. Hennessy, "University Students and National Politics." In *The Politics of Conformity in Latin America*, edited by C. Veliz (London, 1968).

50. For 1968 see E. Poniatowska, *Massacre in Mexico* (New York, 1971) and R. Ramírez, *El movimiento estudiantil en México*, 2 vols. (Mexico, 1969).

51. For violence see B. Wedge, "A Case Study of Student Political Violence: Brazil, 1964, and the Dominican Republic, 1965," *World Politics* 21 (1969). For a general discussion see J. Suchlicki, "Sources of Student Violence in Latin America: An Analysis of the Literature," *Latin American Research Review* 7 (1972). The extraordinary atmosphere of student violence in prerevolutionary Havana University is caught in N. Valdés and R. Bonachea, "Fidel Castro y la política estudiantil de 1947–52," *Aportes* 22 (1971).

52. Venezuelan student politics have been comprehensively covered by O. Albornoz in "Activismo político estudiantil en Venezuela," *Aportes* 5 (1967), and "Universidad, política y estudiantes en Venezuela," *Estudiantes y Política.*

53. Camilo Torres was a Colombian priest from a wealthy background who, after a period as sociology lecturer and chaplain at the National University in Bogotá, became a guerrilla. He was killed in 1966 and has been a major inspiration of extreme-left Catholic groups ever since.

54. For Chile see M. J. Barrera Romero, "Trayectoria del movimiento de Reforma Universitaria en Chile," *Journal of Inter-American Studies* 10 (1968). The Tupac Katari Popular University in La Paz was set up as a result of the Bolivian "university revolution" of 1954.

55. See C. Agulla, "Protesta, subversión y cambio de estructuras," *Aportes* 15 (1970).

56. Among others may be mentioned the Cooperación Popular of Acción Popular in Peru when it was in power, the Chilean Promoción Popular of the Christian Democrats during Frei's presidency, and the activity of Chilean students during Allende's presidency.

8

The Rector, the University, and Society

Luis Manuel Peñalver

Inevitably, the rector is a product of the university and the social environment. As the leader of an academic community in which intellectual and ideological currents and contemporary social problems of the nation are debated, he represents one of the actors in the mix of forces producing change within the university and the society it serves.

The rector must be seen as the professional advocate of certain intellectual concepts, trends, and opinions generated in the university and projected upon society at large. The rector is not merely a caretaker of an institution, nor an apologist for the status quo, but a catalyst for change and a dynamic figure on the national and international fronts of education.

The Social Setting

Latin America continues to be subject to a violent process of social and economic transformation. One may with some assurance say that it will not follow the same courses taken by the developed nations. Instead, progressive movement will consist of sudden leaps from one stage to several above, then of excessive concentration upon a specific economic or social sector, followed by an acceleration in one particular direction with what would appear to be not only disagreeable but unhealthy speed. The unevenness of these developmental trends is a response to such factors as the population growth throughout the region, the awakening of a mass or popular consciousness (with all of its political implications), the seemingly geometrical progression of technological and scientific invention, the high proportion of youth in the total population, the backwardness of educational facilities, the inequities between wealth and poverty, a cruelly underdeveloped agricultural base, and an insufficiently capitalized and inexpertly managed industrial organization. As a result, the production of goods and services and the availability of foodstuffs (the whole matter of nutrition and health upon which an effective social apparatus must in the end depend) are woefully inadequate. Moreover, today's media, as a means of instantaneous communication, convey alluring images of a better life, and serve to aggravate the situation by augmenting the potential for social unrest and violence.

Among all these problems, there is one of special importance both to society and to the university—what one may call the frightening "deficit" in human resources in both qualitative and quantitative terms. Latin America lacks sufficient talent—in the form of technicians, skilled laborers, and artisans, educators on all levels, and adequately developed rational organizations—to exploit fully the natural resources of the continent, or to permit a successive development of democracy from top to bottom in our societies.

It is even more important in Latin America than in the developed countries—not without university problems of their own—that the university develop a philosophy about society, a constructive outlook upon the material and organizational problems of man, which will allow it, in conjunction with other segments of society, to provide solutions, or, at the very least, alternatives to existing situations. Equipped with a "philosophy," the university must also have the means to put it into action; in short, the university must have adequate structures and mechanisms both to implement its philosophy and to be responsive to outside social pressures. It is this dilemma, the mission of the university and its social responsibilities, that most perplexes educational leaders in Latin America today.

The University Environment

Most Latin American universities are as yet unfinished in form, have a hybrid physiognomy in which some of the older inherited forms from Europe (from Spain or Portugal, principally), clash with the more recently introduced variations and reforms—always with whatever educational vices and virtues native to Latin America. This picture is made all the more complex by events of the nineteenth and twentieth centuries, in which traditionalisms were commingled with the demands of the 1918 Córdoba Reform and with North American innovations. The university, hence, is set in a vortex of pressures, forces, demands, problems, and complexities that make it arduous indeed to practice in a purely academic way. It does not seem too much to say that the university is hampered by anachronistic attitudes and apparatuses. In the end, there is always the question of "autonomy," *sui generis* in concept and practice in Latin America—sometimes carried to illogical extremes, sometimes reduced to ineffectuality. Sometimes, insistence on autonomy (but what other choice does a university have?) has led it into feckless isolation, and at other times, into grave confrontation with the state.

These characteristics of the university parallel an inherent tendency on the part of most academe to withdraw from the world, to concentrate on its own intellectual, organizational, and administrative concerns. As a result of this tendency, the university grows less receptive to outside influences, new ideas from abroad, and the social changes brought on by the scientific and technological revolution.

The present-day Latin American university is the product of the ideological and social struggle surrounding the academic uprisings at Córdoba in 1918. It was characterized by a dogmatic insistence upon certain principles (perhaps often elevated to the status of unquestionable truths) such as university autonomy, renovation of the *cátedra, cogobierno,* and a special electoral system for administrators. Many of those who were committed to the Córdoba tenets later rose to high political posts and in this subsequent capacity were to translate concepts of university reform into broad social legislation. One of the weaknesses of the reform, however, was that, although the university itself went on taking "progressive" stands on controversial issues, it failed to provide mechanisms for continuing the reform impulse in society. In effect, the university had become a liberal institution in a conservative society. Despite this apparent antagonism between university and society, there have rarely occurred drastic encounters—or "confrontations"—between the university and rightist or leftist groups, simply because neither wanted to be cast as an "enemy of the university." Thus, even though both groups have proclaimed all sorts of radical "solutions," they have still, in the end, supported the Córdoba university reforms as basic to the survival of the university.

Locked in an educational machinery whose practical goal is to confer a degree rather than to educate, the student in almost every instance will defend the existing structures and procedures. He will follow the line of least resistance in the face of modernization that, if accepted and implemented, would not only reduce his importance but would lead directly to uncomfortable adjustments, particularly in the area of selecting students for admissions.

Because legally the private universities are part of the general educational system, they suffer from the defects of the law and its inherent inadaptability to changes in society. Because, as a social group, these universities are more homogeneous and, in such matters as organization and internal discipline, more stable, they are less vulnerable than the public universities to political and social controversies. As a direct result of their homogeneity and relative insulation from external pressure, therefore, the private universities tend to reflect the status quo, to take on a distinct conservative appearance, and are much less likely to be sources of innovation and reform.

The rector of a university, apart from discharging his daily administrative activities, is confronted with an unstable world, inside and outside the university, which not only makes it difficult for him to perform the prescribed duties of his office, but can lead to his fall from office before his term is over. Even the most recent history of the Latin American university is filled with examples of rectors toppled by dictatorships, or by political revolutions on or off the campus. In strikes and demonstrations, sectors of the student body and the professors—the latter sometimes playing the Pied Piper, but more frequently giving support to or simply following student agitators and groups—have overwhelmed university authorities, generally for overt political reasons, although sometimes for ones with academic pretexts.

It is perhaps enough to say that Latin America is a region where any democratic system of government faces a difficult battle against a tradition of barbaric or "civilized" dictatorships supported by the oligarchies and maintained by the military. There seems to be a historical cycle in which dictatorships rise and democracies decline—as when, in 1964, the military took over in Brazil, inaugurating a new cycle of authoritarian rule. In this confrontation between the democratic and the authoritarian forces, the university almost always plays a leading role. At this point, the rector finds himself in an untenable position: either he yields to outside pressure in an effort to save the institution he presides over, provoking violent opposition from the students and faculty; or else he joins those opposed to the dictatorships and stoutly rejects any attempt to coerce the university. Such a dilemma explains why the university and/or the rector is almost invariably the first victim of a newly established dictatorship. The rector is either dismissed by those responsible for the *golpe militar* or repudiated by the university community. The private universities, however, with a lower involvement in social and political issues and with a somewhat more apathetic student body, are generally less affected by military regimes, although they too have fallen prey to them.

The pervasive insecurity of society and of the university creates a situation unheard of, perhaps until recently, in Western Europe and the United States. In Latin America the rector, the vice-rector, and the secretary-general, who hold the administrative responsibility of the university, are forced to keep a watchful eye on the centers of power—the government, the political parties, the faculty, the students, and even the labor unions—that impinge, to varying degrees, on almost every aspect of the institution. Consequently, too much attention is given to these factors by the university authorities and the rector as he attempts to manage them. For whatever reasons—out of necessity, political ambition, or the rector's own inclinations—the time normally given to the conduct of university business is devoted to other matters, to the impairment of the university.

The precariousness of the internal power structure of the university acts as a restraint upon any rector who would try to

reform its politics and its organization. The organization of the
university is spelled out in the constitution, statutes, and various
regulations, and it is a matter of great moment—and instant
controversy—to try to modify them. Autonomy, as it is defined in
most Latin American universities, often becomes autarchy *vis-à-vis*
society. There are autarchies internally as well. Rudolf Atcon, in
his study of the Latin American university, quite accurately
compares the rector with a monarch of the Middle Ages—holding
few real powers, surrounded by dukes, barons, counts, lords, and
seigneurs jealous of their prerogatives, privileges, and immunities,
who operate in specific "fiefdoms" of activities such as the *facultad*,
the school, the *instituto*, and the *cátedra*, and look upon the rector
more as *primus inter pares* than as a leader capable of ruling.

Most of the rectors govern through the *consejo universitario*, a
form of collegiate governance, with deans and delegates. It is this
body that discusses and reaches decisions on the most important
university matters, with only routine and ceremonial acts left to the
rector. The *facultades*, *institutos*, schools, departments, and the
cátedras, by law or by custom, have certain prerogatives and
exclusive areas for decision making, which makes for a university
structure highly impervious to change that would weaken the
status quo or undermine the strength of vested interests. Thus, the
rector faces the dilemma either of acting as a sort of musical
director who leads his orchestra in the performance of a well-
known score and takes no risks at all; or of attempting to introduce
certain changes (much as a politician would in a democratic
system—recognizing his limitations and the expectations of his
peers) by persuasion, by building up a supportive consensus, and, in
general, by pursuing the "art of the possible."

The Rector and the University Community

The chances of a rector introducing a new policy depend upon
his ability to get support from the other university power groups,
the faculty, and the students. As previously observed, the road to a
rector's obtaining such backing is indeed a rocky one. Even where
there is a strong sense of community and little difference of opinion
on policy matters, it is common for deans and heads of departments
to have conflicting political persuasions and objectives and, thus,

for them to sponsor a course of action within their bailiwick, not in agreement with the rector's policy for the university. This clash of opinions and platforms is reflected in the sessions of the *consejo universitario*, where blocks are arrayed for or against the rector and where student representation tends to play a decisive part—as an important "swing" block.

The rector's ability to exert decisive influence upon the faculty, to enlist the professors in a program of university reform, to arouse a sense of commitment to academic and institutional progress is, at the very best, limited. The traditional Latin American concept of the "university" is an abstract notion, and the individual allegiances of the members of this community are not equally strong to the institution as a whole. Because they are rather narrowly bound to the *cátedra*, the *escuela*, and the *facultad*, the members view their relationship to the university through the prism of these interests. One might say that their loyalties are "regional"—rooted in the particular divisions of the university—and not "national," construing the university as a nation. The governing impetus and specific ideas that flow from the *rectoría* are more often than not obstructed by lack of faculty communication and by institutional provincialism. Only in times of crisis or under the leadership of an especially dynamic and politic rector can these barriers be broken down. The rector's capacity to lead is often further complicated by associations of professors, with their guildlike tendencies and factional politics.

The thorniest of all the rector's relationships, however, is with the students. The principal goal of a rector is to find ways of developing influence among students for administrative purposes and for effecting needed university reform. The Latin American student reaches the university as the product of a schooling system in which he has been inadequately socialized: although he has received information of all sorts, little attention has been given to developing in him a sense of social responsibility. Within the university, the student becomes almost at once the object of a propaganda campaign waged by outside political groups who use the university as a sounding board or loudspeaker to advertise their programs and enlist adherents. In this cacophonous atmosphere the students are factionalized and politicized. Ignoring the appeals of the rector, professors, or deans, they respond to political slogans. Because of their experience and sophistication, political groups, even though in the minority, are able to manipulate the generous feelings and idealism of the students. Such sentiments as rebellion and comradeship, more alluring to the young than to the old, are commingled with "democracy," "freedom," and "autonomy" by outside political groups intent on gaining student sympathy for their own ends. The majority of students are led by a relatively small minority of activists who skillfully brandish slogans, carry about petitions to be signed, or start violent and headline-making demonstrations.

Not so long ago it was generally assumed that the attributes of Latin American student culture were unique to the area. Recent events in traditional upper-class and middle-class universities in the United States and Western Europe, and even in some of the socialist countries, however, make us doubt the uniqueness of the characteristics to Latin America. Perhaps student unrest stems not only from dissatisfaction with the blight of underdevelopment, but also from a more pervasive discontent reflecting disenchantment with an affluent society.

In Latin America the phenomenon of youth rebellion may come full circle, so to speak, by rekindling the spirit of reform within our universities. The "latinamericanization" of universities in Europe and the United States, with demands paralleling the principles proclaimed in Córdoba in 1918, may be a powerful factor in restimulating student discontent in Latin America. Any rector attempting to direct this movement and the energies of its ardent participants must begin by understanding what propels them to action.

The administrative sector of the university, composed of its white-collar employees and maintenance workers and bound together by the laws of the land, has undergone profound changes in recent years. Somewhat in response to the guildlike structure of other groups in the university and as a result of misunderstandings as to what constitutes "autonomy," this sector, too, has formed pressure groups to be taken into account by the rector. Although there are means of influence over these groups, their "syndicalization" and readiness to join other groups in internal political activity pose new and serious problems for the rector. The administrative framework of the university depends upon these employees, and if they fail to perform their essential functions, the result is decay.

Economic, financial, and budgetary problems limit the rector's freedom to innovate and make structural changes. The pressures for expanding all aspects of the university grow at a geometrical rate—the student-age population explosion; the underdeveloped country's need for diversification of careers and professions; the modernization of teaching techniques; and the increased demands for more research and specialization—while the wherewithal to meet these pressures increases at best in an arithmetic proportion. No reform of any significance can be effected within a chronically impecunious institution; visible structural reforms, new buildings and the like, prepare the way for less tangible structural reforms. Thus, even though annual income to the universities has grown enormously over the past ten years, there are still serious limitations in programs of expansion and improvement.

Demands for social reform continually force the democratically inclined governments to spend more on such services as education, public health, and social security. At the same time, the imperative of economic development requires the state to make massive investments in capital improvements. The education item in the budget of most countries has reached what appears to be its upper limits of somewhere between ten and twenty percent. The cost of higher education has already reached about twenty-five percent of the total educational budget, a fact that makes it difficult for universities to find new sources of revenue. There have been occasions when the state has felt itself the victim of a university's aggression, causing government officials to turn a slightly deaf ear to the budgetary importunities of the rector.

The Latin American tradition of free university education makes it doubtful that, even in countries with sizable upper and middle classes that could afford to pay for the education of their sons and daughters, tuition would result in a significant source of revenue to the university. Support from the private sector has been hard to come by, in contrast with the United States, where private support has always been a key factor in university growth, including even the state universities. There have been some recent instances of universities finding ways of overcoming this old attitude and gaining private support. Financial help from abroad, in the form of loans from the Inter-American Development Bank and grants from the foundations, have been of great assistance in initiating new programs; however, they are not an unalloyed boon because with new programs come new needs, new allocation requirements, which may end up by throwing off balance the university's precarious economy.

The economic conundrum is a persistent challenge to a rector's ingenuity. Because the university is an institution hellbent on growth, matters attendant on the budget usurp more and more of the rector's time and demand more and more of the *rectoría*.

The Rector and the Outside World

In all societies, the university is a central institution; but in developing societies, where there are relatively few institutions of comparable social prestige, and, as in Latin America, where it has played a vital political role, the university has acquired great importance indeed. Words and actions occurring within the university, whether sane or not, have repercussions affecting all sectors of society. Because, in a significant sense, the university shapes opinions and exerts pressure, political parties seek to capture it in one way or another; the university is, in short, an institution capable of strong influence over the course of social and political development.

Much of the power of the university—almost all of the institutional prerogatives and prestige—are lodged in the *rectoría*. The rector not only is faced with a vast array of responsibilities, but also is surrounded by temptations and opportunities leading to even higher positions in the realms of diplomacy and politics. Seats in the parliament, ambassadorships, ministerial posts, and even the presidency of the republic might be discovered as immanent possibilities among the insignia and robes the rector wears. It is not always necessary, of course, for the rector to graduate to the presidency of his country for his importance as a social figure to be recognized.

Obviously, not all rectors are interested merely in self-promotion. The *rectoría* is an equally vital office for the university as an institution, and for a nation experiencing profound social unrest and, one hopes, a progressive upward trend. How a rector understands the functions of his office, the way he outlines his policy, the sources in the university he might rely upon for support, the sense of mission he imparts to his colleagues, the dignity he confers to his office—all these matters and others are determined both by the *rectoría* as an office, and by the rector as an individual.

The university has been simultaneoulsy a revolutionary and a conservative institution: revolutionary, as a source of idealism denouncing social hypocrisies and injustice and calling for enlightenment and reform in society; conservative as its concerns focus on self-administration and providing education to its members. The rector, again, plays the leading role in the radicalism and the conservatism of the institution over which he presides.

In the past two generations, the rector has been at the center of forces that have remade the university. One such force has been the unrelenting demands beginning at Córdoba for internal reform and for new attitudes by those living and working close to the university. The second force has been the physical restructuring of the university in almost every particular: educational theories, mass education, scientific knowledge—and bigness, bigness everywhere. Largely depending on the rector's response to these forces, the university has fared well or badly.

The Qualifications and Election of the Rector

In almost all cases, before assuming office the rector has been a professor and frequently a dean of a *facultad* or a director of an institute or school in the university. Either as a student or as a faculty member, the rector has participated in the struggles and politics of the university and is identified with one side or another. Although this identification and support have contributed to his election, the rector's dependency on these groups and commitment to certain issues restrain his freedom of movement. In addition, the rector's background as a teacher and as a professional educator as a rule does little to teach him administrative techniques for the *rectoría* and leaves him ill prepared to deal with the complex government of the university.

The rector of a public university, like the vice-rector and the secretary-general, reaches his post through an electoral process. The election can be direct or indirect, though it is generally the former, with the vote taken in the *claustro*—a governing body composed of professors, students, and alumni. In an indirect election the designation takes place in such bodies as the permanent *consejo universitario*. In Latin American universities these elections are very serious matters. The political temperature suddenly rises above normal, and the rational climate of the university is disrupted by strident choruses claiming this virtue for themselves and impugning that vice to all the others. Candidates for the office of rector become real politicians. They build up support for themselves among groups within the university and look to the established political parties for guidance and help of all sorts in winning the game. Elections are held generally every three or five years, a frequency that leaves a relatively brief period for holding office. In some university statutes reelection is prohibited, probably reflecting the national distaste for military dictatorships and the practice of civilian *continuismo*. Of course, such a short term in office with no possibility of reelection makes planning on a broad scale virtually impossible. Where reelection is permitted, rectors and their administrative colleagues are plunged into politics repeating all of the excesses in which they indulged to get the post in the first place. Most rectors believe that only where reelection is practiced do they have any chance of developing and overseeing really effective plans for their universities' development. In some public and private universities the rector is appointed by the minister of education, the president of the republic, or some governing body of the university. In the case of public universities, the appointment of the rector is always subject to highly political considerations.

The Rector as Educator and Leader of the University

The orientation and training of students, the philosophy of higher education and the means for transmitting it, and internal restructuring and adjustments are all aspects of a rector's job, which is partly political and partly administrative. However he formulates his policy, the rector's basic concern should always be educational.

The rector must be the sort of person who can lead all of the components of the university community—especially the students, in their pursuit of knowledge and human and civic fulfillment. By example as much as by policy, the rector's influence upon his colleagues and the students can have a decisive and long-term effect. The rector is obliged to see to it that the university turns out competent professionals; but the professional man should not be a captive of his own narrow training. Rather, he should have talents—and wisdom—that will enrich all of society. What the rector does or fails to do in his leading role as the first educator in the university community will have a determining influence upon the technological and civic progress of the society. Within the university as well, the rector is responsible for devising a policy that will promote a true sense of community throughout all of its departments, *facultades*, schools, and even *cátedras*.

Because the university is the apex of the total educational enterprise, what has been said should not imply a categorical separation between secondary and vocational training on the one hand and higher education on the other. While the secondary schools and the university are usually closely related in purpose and function, vocational and technical training generally is terminal and not related to university education. One of the principal tasks of the *rectoría* must be to open new channels for talented professionals to continue their education and training in the university. Furthermore, in order to enhance the intellectual development at the secondary and university levels, broad courses of general education might successfully be introduced.

In a catalogue of qualities the rector needs as the leader of the university community, the following items, at least, would have to be included: a sense of the university's mission; an administrative capacity; an arbiter's impartiality; a diplomatic flair for dealing with real or potential dissidents; and an ability, derived from character or background or both, to develop a sound rapport with the student body.

At the pinnacle of a large and complex bureaucratic structure, the rector must be an effective policy formulator, the chief decision maker, and an inspiring leader of his immediate administrative staff. As the university's leader, at times he must employ and deploy diplomatic or manipulative skills in dealing with the particularistic and egocentric wills of the university—from the *facultad* to the *cátedra*. If the rector has such skills, their successful exercise depends to a large extent upon his also having an overview of every part of the institution, thus enabling him to get all of its components to function together. There are always operational problems confronting the rector, and his ability to surmount them depends to a degree upon his conception of his role; his sources of information and channels of communication; the relationships he has built up among the *rectoría,* the professors, and the students; and his ability to isolate the problems and present persuasively his intended solutions to them.

Perhaps the most difficult of the rector's relationships is the one with the various components of the student body. The first rule for a successful rectorship is to avoid either of two simplistic attitudes toward the students. The first view holds that the student should be merely a passive recipient of knowledge accepted uncritically and respectfully. The other view sees the student as an object of adulation who must be either coaxed or enticed to learn or allowed "to do his own thing." Examples of both attitudes have been demonstrated in too many Latin American universities. If a rector has the wit to escape embracing these outlooks, he can then go on to develop an effective rapport with his students. He should convey his sense of the university's mission; the students should feel the force and integrity of his character and, hence, his policies within the university. The rector should come across as a unifying agent in a social institution of heterogeneous parts and often heterodox beliefs; and the rector and students together should recognize their greater responsibilities—beyond learning and preserving the institution—to the improvement of the society in which they are physically and spiritually located.

The modern university with its tremendous growth and complexity has imposed a whole new range of administrative chores upon the rector. Just as there has been a population explosion and an urban explosion, so too there has been an "executive explosion." In almost all of our vital social institutions there has been a sudden enlargement of the administrative functions of the executive. The rector, in addition to performing his traditional duties, now must act as chief of a large administrative staff; as fund raiser; as controller of a web of relationships with the government, other universities, and international organizations; and as a master planner of the university. The effects of this executive explosion are perhaps exaggerated in Latin America, where there is a *presidencialista* tendency in most organizations. By this is meant that power tends to concentrate and subsequently accumulate in one main executive office. There is a presumption in favor of having the head man dispose of matters, certainly the most important ones, before they are considered finally resolved. Even though there are fine flowing lines of divisional and operating responsibility on the organizational charts, what usually counts is the executive's imprimatur. This rule, the large increase in bureaucratic size notwithstanding, applies to the presidency of a Latin American country just as much as it does to the *rectoría*.

One may single out five areas in which the rector's administrative functions have been enormously expanded in recent years: planning, financing, management, operations, and evaluation. The art of planning has undergone a scientific revolution that relies as much upon time-tested methods of cost projections and accounting procedures as upon the science of "computerology." The planning for a university does not only involve a year-to-year budget forecast, but also a long-range program incorporating the budget as a main item among many other important considerations.

Given the current university's massive size, financing is a major activity requiring its own department of specialists. Basically, the problem involves, first, expanding the university's assets and revenues, and second, enlisting the support of the traditional sources of income and tapping new ones, in both the public and the private sectors. The Latin American rector is rapidly coming to resemble the president of a North American university, among whose constant preoccupations are fund-raising and staving off deficits.

The changes that have taken place in the university make it resemble more and more a big corporation of the business world. "Management" becomes a chief concern of the rector. As an executive of a vast operation, the rector has a goal to "maximize" productivity and efficiency at all levels. This is not to say that a rector should or could view his institution only in stark terms of profit and loss. What is implied here is that the university, too, has been affected by the "managerial revolution" of the last thirty or forty years. There have been some promising recent experiments in university management and organization in Venezuela and elsewhere in Latin America. It would seem that pilot projects in this sensitive area of the university ought to be expanded. Such experiments, when distilled, would be most helpful to current and future rectors.

By "operations" two things are meant: first, an administrative overseeing of the organization; second, an intensification of coordination and cooperation among rectors in the country and among rectors throughout Latin America. Meetings of rectors and their staff executives, allowing an interchange of their experiences, mistakes and all, could provide remedies and solutions to all sorts of administrative problems. As yet, Latin American university executives are not working and consulting with one another as much as they should, nor to the extent envisioned by the Inter-American Cultural Council created in 1964 at the Punta del Este Conference.

It is safe to say that institutions survive in proportion to their capacity for self-scrutiny. The science of evaluation has only recently developed in Latin American universities; however, where practiced, not only has it led to improved efficiency, but it has also stimulated a desire to experiment with the university's organization. Such attempts at institutional evaluation are the inevitable first steps of progress, and could have the advantage of removing some of the rector's present responsibility for "auditing" the institution.

In addition to his administrative duties, the rector has three extrainstitutional roles: as representative of the university; as politician and/or statesman; and as leader of the community. Regardless of how much of his time is devoted to the conduct of the university's internal affairs, the rector is nevertheless the most visible of all the university *personae*. Whatever the university does, the rector is the main recipient of praise or blame. What in Spanish is known as *la masificación de la universidad* has dramatically enlarged all aspects of the rector's existing duties of external relations and has gone on to add new burdens. The *rectoría* has, in many cases, adopted some of the techniques of public relations in its dealings with other sectors of society. Indeed, at many institutions there have appeared departments of public relations to inform the outside world of what the university is up to. Being the chief actor of the university, the rector is in intimate contact with the powerful leaders of other national and even international institutions. One of the insistent demands facing all rectors in Latin America is the development of greater and more effective coordination of interuniversity efforts: local and regional planning, exchanges of faculty and students, regular staff meetings of various administrative levels, and the reinforcement of existing machinery are lines of action which should be pursued vigorously by the Latin American universities.

The rector's job, in a broadly construed "political"sense, is not to seek the eradication or suppression of politics in the university, but rather to prevent disruptive political activity from upsetting the academic affairs of his institution. Of course, this is a rule much easier to state than to implement, especially when one takes into account the historical tendency toward *"la politización"* of the university. There is, however, a fine line to be walked between chaos and order, and this second role of the rector—that of politician and/or statesman—is perhaps his most exacting. There are several measures he can take to keep his and the university's balance. He can create a climate within the university that is hospitable to a diversity of attitudes and in which there is no tyranny of any given opinion. As leader of the university community, the rector should presumably possess enough political acumen to deal effectively with its sectors—such as professors, administrative staff, and students—and to keep the ties and the lines of communication among them open and civil. Presumably, also, the rector will have initiated a university policy more inclined to educational ends than political ones and will have majority backing for it. With such support in hand he can then contend with the intrusions of outside political parties and politicians. Except during times of great popular emotion on certain issues or moments of national crisis, the rector stands a better than average chance for fending off overzealous parties, or cliques within parties, in their attempts to politicize the university and to recruit young adherents.

All of this does not mean that the rector should remain so neutral and aloof from the politics of the university that he ends up with virtually no power to influence the course of events. The rector must have the abilities of an umpire, but at the same time he should have the shrewdness of Solomon in rendering decisions on political matters. The danger in *la politización* is not so much in politics *per se*—in fact, the dialectics of political discussion are an extension of the learning process. The peril lies, rather, in the progressive fragmentation of the university into cliques and groups whose existence leads to intense and distracting animosities and to institutional disintegration—should the rector allow such a state to come to pass.

The Challenges of the Past and the Future

The *rectoría* has been treated here as a sort of institution within an institution: almost as a microcosm of the university. The university itself is an institution performing special services for society, responding to a whole gamut of outside influences. We have in effect set up a scheme—*rectoría,* university, and society —that would permit us to see as much of the particular educational setting as a general view would allow.

The university will be increasingly called upon to give more and more services to the national, regional, and even international society in which it finds itself. These services may range from literacy programs to highly sophisticated research activities, and will in one way or another be related to the society's economic, social, and political development. In the coming years, the institutionalization and growth of the university will be more regional than national, paralleling the tendency to see problems as broad units of land and people not sealed off by the political boundaries of nation-states.

Another challenge that will probably become more acute in future years involves the relationship of the rector to his university constituents, especially the students. Their numbers will undoubtedly continue to rise; their concern with immediate social, economic, and political issues will be undiminished; the old custom of the students forming "nations" will take on renewed significance, but in an international context, not merely within the narrow ambit of the university as it was once understood. In addition there is the possibility that students not only will be better organized in their response to immediate issues, but in fact also may be better educated in the future than ever before. Their increased numbers will lead to keener competition, and teaching methods will be improved by the absorption of advanced technology. Students, now devoting more of their lives to the refinement of the intellect than ever before, may find new ways to combine their education in the university with their real experiences in the outside world.

A third challenge that will weigh heavily on the *rectoría* in the next decades is the set of relationships it will be able to establish among the university and the other nerve centers of society—the church, the labor movement, the business world, the political parties, the agrarian interests, and various cultural and international organizations. Not only will the pace and progress of advancement be determined by such relationships, but so, also, will its evenness and quality.

The question of maintaining and justifying the exercise of authority lies at the core of any institution. This is a question pertinent at all times for the survival of any institution. The ability to deal with grave or minor challenges to the university's authority —from within by *la politización*, from without by attacks upon its *autonomía*—will depend principally on the rector's philsophical understanding of the university's mission in society, his professionalism in the discharge of the duties of the *rectoría*, and the qualities of excellence he brings to the university community.

9

The Professor and the Cátedra

Gino Germani

Departments have replaced the traditional chairs; full-time professorships have been established, curricula and degrees modernized, and the educational methods brought up-to-date. In the majority of the universities where these and other innovations have been introduced, however, they cannot be considered more than token concessions to current fashion, or attempts to appease growing demands for reform that are supported by students, progressive intellectuals, scholars, professors, and sectors of other modernizing elites in the national society.

The university was, and still is, divided into *facultades* (schools consisting of semiindependent units), each devoted to one or more careers and awarding professional degrees, with *cátedras* for specific subjects endowed with a high degree of independence. The *catedrático* (titular or full professor) was appointed for life, invested with great authority, and had few if any limitations imposed upon the exercise of his prerogatives. The *cátedra* could include a varying number of assistants of different status, from the rank of adjunct or associate professor to teaching assistant, as well as clerical and service personnel. The staff of the *cátedra* could be large or small depending upon the ambition and personality of the incumbent, preexisting traditions, or the nature of the *cátedra's* subject. In many universities departmentalization has occurred but, especially in the older and more traditional professional schools like medicine and law, the autonomy of the *cátedra* persists. Particularly in the more recently created schools, such as the schools of social sciences, real departmentalization has been introduced. Where the system of the *cátedra* still exists, it is being challenged and its legitimacy questioned. In a number of universities, life tenure has been abolished.

Although the *cátedra* in many ways retains its old prestige, and the professor may enjoy his teaching or maintain some positive approach to his discipline, he may find his roots in any specific university too shallow to make him an active participant in university life. Even if he devotes a considerable part of his time to teaching, he may be employed simultaneously by several institutions, often at the secondary-school level.

Commitment to a particular institution is a recent phenomenon that did not develop within the traditional university. Although the role of the professor was formally differentiated, the fact that it tended to be allied to other positions of power and prestige in the society blurred its distinctiveness, both in the public mind and in the mind of the incumbent himself. The traditional university professor was a member of the oligarchy; a member of the legal or medical professions (rather than the teaching profession); an aspirant to higher public office; and, as an honorific appendage to this conglomerate of diverse roles, proprietory holder of a *cátedra*. In a different social context these roles might appear disparate, and at times even conflicting; however, in a highly stratified society, dominated by the landed oligarchy, they tended naturally to merge. Such diffusiveness permitted expression of commitment to a social class rather than to a single institution.

To the extent that the university and the social order were stable, the special commitment demanded by the role of professor *qua* professor could not be experienced. Stability must be understood in the Latin American sense; the ideal type of traditional university was not incompatible with political cleavages and struggles within the elites, with palace revolts or military coups. The *cátedra*, life appointment, and university autonomy were part of the nineteenth-century European heritage which tended to function as adaptive mechanisms to these recurrent patterns of political life in Latin America.

The culmination of a professor's career came with his accession to the *cátedra*. Afterward few demands were made of the *catedrá-*

tico, who then was virtually the seigneur of his domain. As Rudolf Atcon has written, emphasizing the contrasting demands of the past with the transitional stage of the present:

> When a chair becomes vacant due to retirement or death of its previous owner, the university sooner or later calls for a competitive examination to find a successor. In many places this examination is called a *"concurso."* In most cases it is a formal procedure. The candidates who appear on certain fixed dates are obliged to submit to a series of examinations and tests before they present and defend a thesis. Depending on the country, varying degrees of importance are placed on the different steps taken under law before a Board of Examiners. . . . A man prepares himself for years with an eye towards a possible future vacancy in his field at some university. He writes a book, publishes it at his own expense, and then submits it as a thesis at the proper time and place. Though it is supposed to be an original piece of work it is not always of outstanding value. When a candidate has won his "nomination" for life, he usually feels so exhausted that he is likely to look on this event as the true culmination point of his university career.[1]

All the university demanded of the *catedrático* until about 1950 was a few hours of teaching and giving examinations; it did not provide him with office space, libraries, laboratories, and other facilities that would encourage research. The higher administrative offices of the university were in the hands of the professors—and they indeed absorb time—but even the more demanding positions, such as those of dean or rector, were less complex and burdensome than they are today. These offices, also, tended to merge with the political and personal ambitions of the *catedrático* as a member of the ruling elite.

Although in some countries or regions the traditional university still persists, the modern transitional university recruits its professional personnel from many social strata. The social origins of today's *catedrático* differ as much from those of his traditional counterpart as do his economic situation and outlook, social obligations, and life-style. In the major universities in most countries of Latin America, the "social register" of traditional families no longer represents the majority or even an important segment of the total teaching staff in the universities. In the more traditional faculties, such as law, there is still a concentration of upper-class personnel, but for the most part it is the urban middle-class that provides the main source of recruitment for both the teaching staff and the student body.

In Argentina, Uruguay, and Chile since the turn of the century, and since the 1930s in most other Latin American countries, a substantial urban middle class has emerged. Although in most of Latin America there is hardly any rural middle class, social stratification in the cities has changed significantly. If one compares the degree of economic development and modernization of each country with the historical experience of the western world, he discovers that the growth of the middle sectors is higher than expected. In Argentina and Uruguay, certainly extreme cases, nonmanual groups make up more than forty-five percent of the total urban working population. In the majority of the other countries, the corresponding figure would be thirty-three percent or more. These proportions are not much lower than the levels reached by the more advanced western countries,[2] although in Latin America the industrial sectors and the corresponding social institutions lag far behind.

Although most of the professors depend increasingly on what they earn for their living, full-time professors remain scarce in the universities. The table below provides the total number of teachers in higher education in practically all of Latin America (with the exception of Cuba and some of the newly independent countries), and for most of them a distinction is made between "full-time" and "other" teachers. Unfortunately, the data do not provide a breakdown for each category. They include all teaching staff from titular professors to teaching assistants, and it is quite possible that the definitions used and included in the totals are not uniform or comparable. Also, since an unknown number of professors teach simultaneously in different universities or in other institutions of higher education, their number may be overestimated. Nevertheless, data seem to confirm the small proportion of full-time teachers. Only in two countries is this proportion above one-third (Chile and Colombia); in three others it is in the range of one-fourth and just over one-fifth of the total (Panama, Venezuela, and Peru); and in all others it is less than 17.3 percent, with

TABLE
Members of the Teaching Staff in Latin American Universities
and Other Institutions of Higher Learning

Country	Total	Full-time	Other	Percentage Full-time
Argentina	17,171	--	--	--
Bolivia	1,706	105	1,601	6.1
Brazil	30,862	--	--	--
Chile	11,220	4,210	7,010	37.5
Colombia	6,453	2,370	4,083	36.7
Costa Rica	659	114	545	17.3
Dominican Republic	722	73	649	10.1
Ecuador	1,417	89	1,328	6.3
El Salvador	352	45	307	12.7
Guatemala	587	80	507	14.5
Haiti	226	--	--	--
Honduras	308	44	264	14.3
Mexico	16,346	1,018	15,328	6.2
Nicaragua	355	55	300	15.8
Panama	260	65	195	25.0
Paraguay	945	10	935	1.0
Peru	7,125	1,589	5,536	22.3
Trinidad Tobago	50	--	--	--
Uruguay	2,308	167	2,141	7.6
Venezuela	4,754	1,396	3,358	25.5
Total	104,451	--	--	--

-- No information

SOURCE: Inter-American Development Bank, *Socio-Economic Progress in Latin America* (Washington, D.C., 1968). Even though the total figures have increased, even doubled in most cases, during the last ten years, the percentage of full-time teachers has remained about the same.

Paraguay (of those countries reporting) having the lowest percentage of full-time professors. Unfortunately, no aggregate information is available for two major countries, Argentina and Brazil. For Argentina the proportion is certainly very low. For instance, at the University of Buenos Aires, the most modern in the country, in 1965 (before the military take-over) the proportion of full-time teaching staff (all categories) was only four percent. If we consider only the professors, however, the percentage increases to 13.4. Of the four other national universities whose data are available (of a total of ten), the proportions are lower, with the exception of the University of Cuyo with the highest rate of twenty-seven percent.

It is interesting to note that in the private universities in Argentina there are even fewer full-time teachers. The rather scanty information on Brazil, provided by the *Censo Universitario Latino Americano*, suggests that the overall picture is about the same as in Argentina.[3]

Although the salaries of full-time professors are higher than those of other teachers, they still remain far below the usual relative level prevailing in the United States. There are also considerable differences from country to country and among universities in the same country. Simple conversions from local currencies to dollars would be misleading inasmuch as the level of domestic prices varies greatly and in general the standard of living is so much lower than in the United States. The full-time salaries must be supplemented by consulting and writing or other activities permitted under the regulations governing full-time employment at the university.[4]

Although the exercise of a liberal profession is still frequent enough for the part-time university professor, it is common for him to have one or several jobs unrelated to his university work.[5] The social and psychological consequences of this multiplicity of occupational roles may create status incongruity. For example, a professor may have a relatively low clerical position in some public or private administration; or he may own and operate a small bookstore; or, as in the case of a distinguished professor of philosophy, run a small restaurant in a summer resort.

The demands placed on the time and energy of the professor are likely to be heavy. The attempt to fulfill different and sometimes disparate tasks may exercise a negative influence on the academic performance of the professor. To the extent that the university is modernizing (at least in some aspects), its requirements may be more exacting than those of the traditional institutions of higher learning. The number of students has increased enormously and in the large universities, especially in the first years, the enrollment in many courses may be described as massive. Thus the classrooms are terribly crowded and the examination period seems interminable. For each course, most examinations are still oral, taking place at the beginning and end of the academic year or semester, and in some cases even every month. Despite efforts to simplify the procedure, in many places the regulations still require *comisiones*, or committees of three professors for each examination.

A discrepancy between legal forms and social realities has always been common in Latin America but in the present transitional universities this phenomenon tends to increase confusion and disintegration. Regulations governing examinations have been modified; still, when written exams have been required, they have been merely perfunctory. In a number of faculties and schools, partial written exams given by teaching assistants at intervals during the academic year or semester have been introduced. The grades obtained in these examinations are then combined with the final oral exams, for which the professors are entirely responsible.

Although attendance is often not mandatory, and many students do not in fact attend classes, still the classroom may be extremely crowded. Necessarily, the lecture system prevails; the professor engages in monologues with little or no discussion or interaction with the students. Since the 1918 *reforma*, however, and increasingly in recent years, the so-called *clase magistral*,the pure lecture *ex cathedra*, the rituals, and the typical physical and social distance between the professor and the students have been sharply criticized and in many cases theoretically abolished. In several faculties, sections have been added in which a limited number of students under the guidance of a teaching assistant discuss topics and make reports. Careful training and supervision of his teaching assistants are very important, but it may be impossible for a part-time professor, whose interests and time are dispersed in several teaching or nonteaching jobs, to assure their competence.

Another problem both the professor and the student face in reshaping their educational environment is the tradition of *apuntes* and the frequent scarcity of textbooks and other reading materials. In the past the typical solution to this problem was provided by lecture notes (*apuntes*). They were a text or a summary of the lectures usually published in mimeograph form by the student union, a private organization, or, in some cases, by the professor himself. Their quality in content and structure was often substandard because, with few exceptions, the professor accepted no editorial responsibility. The *apuntes* were used as the main, or even the only, reading material to prepare for the final exam. The professor suggested a bibliography for his course, but often it was not of much use to the students because of the unavailability of many books and journals. Sometimes these reading lists looked more like an exhibition of erudition than a practical study guide for the student.

Nowadays, this situation is not as readily tolerated. Many students and the most advanced educators reject the use of *apuntes* to be memorized and repeated at exam time. They demand instead that the readings consist of good textbooks and a variety of bibliographical sources. The new ideal emphasizes both individual and joint efforts by students and instructors. It is expected that the student will be helped by guidance from the professor and by discussions in small groups or by other appropriate means. The poverty of library resources, the insufficiency of competent staff at the teaching assistant level, and the limitations on the time of the professor, however, frustrate the realization of such innovations.

During the last decade the publication of textbooks and scientific works has increased a great deal, and this may improve the situation considerably. In law and medicine, the conditions are certainly better. Even in the more recently established areas there is a constant flow of new publications. Yet it remains difficult for Latin American students and professors to keep up-to-date with the scientific production of the advanced countries. Exchange programs, fellowships, and travel abroad partly help the situation and it is not unusual for a conscientious Latin American professor to have a large private library at home. But radical measures will have to be taken if the problems affecting documentation and bibliography are to be solved.

The professor oriented toward research faces perhaps more formidable obstacles than the professor as teacher-scholar. Laboratories, space, and research facilities are scarce and woefully inadequate to the present requirements of scientific work. In the few countries where national science councils have been established, they have made a positive contribution to scientific research in universities and in other institutions. In some countries, as in Argentina, they supplement the salary of the professor engaged in research, but generally they are still operating at too reduced a level to make a substantial impact.

Among the important aspects in the life of the professor are the effects upon him of his relationships with colleagues, academic authorities, students, and groups outside the university, and of public opinion and political events at the national or local level. One of the characteristics of the Latin American university is the relatively high incidence of intergroup and interpersonal conflicts. Such tensions, of course, exist in every complex organization or social group. What strikes one as peculiar to the Latin American university is the high intensity and visibility of such conflicts, and the threat they pose to the new structures in the institutions of higher learning. Consider, for instance, the several schools and research institutes in sociology that have been created in a number of countries in the last fifteen years. They represent an important innovation and in many ways have been successful. Most of them, however, have suffered severe internal crises. Sociology is perhaps especially susceptible to controversy, and comes under attack from many quarters: the older humanistic disciplines, the extreme right or the extreme left, and sectors of the military and the church. If sociology is an extreme case, it is by no means an isolated example: at all levels—*cátedras*, institutes, faculties, and universities—factionalism, deep cleavages, and interpersonal conflicts are common enough. A relatively small incident may set off a chain reaction leading to a major conflict. Discord tends to spread and become more complex so that ultimately its origins may be completely forgotten. At one time or another, most faculty members have been personally affected by such conflicts; for some of them they may represent an aspect of everyday life.

Although the specific causes and the actors involved may change, the game remains essentially the same. Special meetings and many casual conversations are devoted to it and tend to absorb considerable time and energy. It is fairly common for the teaching staff of a university—from teaching assistants to titular professors—to form cliques and factions. Such groupings are especially cultivated and courted at election time, when the officers of the department, the *facultad,* or the university council are to be reelected to or reconfirmed in their posts. Solution or easing of the conflict is rendered more difficult by the considerable publicity given it by the mass media through the circulation of manifestos, declarations, public letters, and notices of resignation.

Such recurring conflicts contribute to the lack of continuity in the functioning and efficiency of institutions so typical of Latin America. A given period characterized by a high degree of growth, success, and achievement may be followed by one of deterioration and stagnation, both at the institutional and at the personal levels. This discontinuity may be explained by a general instability in the social environment, particularly political instability. Extreme fragmentation in the political parties and other institutions has a disruptive influence on the universities, especially the public universities.

The university's internal organization should be viewed as the principal source of its conflicts. In Latin America the administrative function is complicated by an organization that is incapable of meeting the needs occasioned by the enormous growth in enrollment, and the creation of new areas of study and careers. The lack of a clear-cut separation between educational and purely academic matters and administrative functions is a continuing source of strife. Politicization of the university is yet another cause of institutional discontinuity, and some observers attribute this discontinuity solely to the participation of students and alumni in university government. Although there is a long tradition of politicization of the university and of *cogobierno* in Latin America—with factions and cliques among professors antedating the university's politicization—nevertheless the students' participation both creates and magnifies problems and difficulties in what has become a complex administrative process.

In Latin America there is no open national market for the academic profession. There are complicated regulations not only for the *concurso* (the special competition required for an appointment to a *cátedra*) but also for obtaining a contract or yearly employment. To climb the ladder of success one must consider personal connections and the right channels to the powerful cliques or factions. The part-time nature of much university teaching limits job mobility, since a person cannot easily transfer *all* his interests from one city to another (it would be a rare occurrence to find alternate openings in another university—if indeed there should be more than one). The professor's extremely restricted range of choices, or even the practical absence of any choice outside his current position, tends to increase the psychological investment in what looks like the professor's only chance in the academic profession. Thus, it may be understood why conflicts and tensions are more acute in an environment that lacks the safety valve offered by the possibility of relocating.

In recent times this situation has been eased in some academic fields at the regional level. For example, specialists may be hired as researchers by international organizations located in Latin America. Some professors have been able to find teaching positions outside their own countries, in other Latin American universities. For instance, in 1966, when the military regime sheared many of the Argentine universities of their traditional freedoms, quite a few professors were invited to join academic institutions elsewhere. Twenty years earlier, the Peronist purge of the Argentine university failed to generate a similar continental response. This change is not only a sign of increasing continental solidarity in the academic world, but also a reflection of the emergence of an academic market.

The Latin American tends to express his emotions strongly, indeed vehemently. Opinions and feelings are almost always manifested with little or no restraint. There is a particular tendency to indulge in intrigue, to feel persecuted, and to overreact to real or imaginary threats. Throughout all socioeconomic strata in Latin America, factors generating frustration, alienation, fear, and insecurity seem more frequent than in more stable societies.

Often the outcome of an important issue may depend on the votes of the student representatives on the council of the faculty, the department, or the university. Some professors concentrate too much on their popularity with the students, out of an exaggerated need to be accepted by them. The students are frequently skillful in manipulating situations of this type. Although in face-to-face relationships a certain distance and respect are generally maintained, the professors are often exposed to severe criticism and even vicious attacks from the students—in mass meetings, in the student press, and by other means. The attitudes reflecting a professor's acceptance and popularity or his rejection and disfavor wax and wane with political events and changing fashions in the university or the wider national scene. Since most of the activism occurs during the students' first two or three years, the succession of new students entering the university each year contributes to the rather sudden shifts in attitudes toward the professors.

The university professor is very much in the public eye. Many political groups, especially those on the extreme right and the extreme left, are deeply interested in university affairs and devote much attention to them in their publications. Usually these groups are unrestrained in their attacks, mounted mostly on ideological or personal grounds. The innovative or modernizing university leader is the most vulnerable. The rightists accuse him of being a communist and a terrible threat to the social order, while the leftists, with the same hostility, condemn him as an agent of Yankee imperialism. Both extremes oppose modernizing reforms. This is true not only for the social sciences but also for the natural sciences and the professional schools. Everywhere in Latin America the creative academic leader is labeled a *cientificista* or some equivalent word designating a person who, in the name of modern science and technology, tries to create conditions facilitating foreign domination and suffocating the emerging national consciousness and the people's will to achieve liberation. Foreign-sponsored social science research is under especially heavy suspicion.

National politics exercise a varying influence—often disruptive—on the university and on the personal life of the professor. It is not a question of his active participation in party politics, although this may be one of his roles aside from his academic activity. All political parties (not only the left extremists, as usually believed) attempt to turn university problems and student unrest to their own advantage. This is especially true when it becomes desirable to create or increase agitation in the streets. A major student conflict in the university may offer favorable conditions for inciting further complications elsewhere. Student strikes and riots may help produce a climate of widespread public disorder that in turn may invite a military coup.

Except in the few Latin American countries that have remained relatively immune to military regimes, it is the *golpe de estado* that remains a permanent threat to the university and its professors. With the coming of mass politics, the role of the army has profoundly changed; the *raison d'être* of the military regime has become "internal security" and the defense of what has been called the "ideological frontier." The university as a source of extreme left agitation is considered an immediate threat to the stability of the social order and the "western" and "Christian" way of life. Liberal professors are considered dangerous to the security of the nation, and many of them are fired, forbidden to teach, or obliged to resign their *cátedras*. If they try to resist the suppression of university autonomy and of academic freedom, as well as any strict police control over university life, they may be obliged to abandon their profession as teachers and scholars or go into exile. In several Latin American nations the anxiety created by these political crises must be considered one of the negative aspects of the life of the university professor.

This is a transitional phase for both the university and society. The old society and the old university are disappearing. We are in the midst of the conflict between disintegration and re-creation. The insecurity, the fears, the struggles, and the tensions are all symptoms of drastic changes taking place. Because all deep and real change is conflictive and painful, the persons involved in it cannot avoid the shattering effects of such transition on their individual lives and destinies.[6]

NOTES

1. Rudolf P. Atcon, *The Latin American University* (Bogotá, 1966), p. 74

2. G. Germani, *Sociología de la Modernización* (Buenos Aires, 1969), p. 201.

3. Unión de Universidades de América Latina, *Censo Universitario Latinoamericano 1962–1965* (Mexico City, 1967).

4. *Censo Universitario,* and Harold R. W. Benjamin, *Higher Education in the Latin American Republics* (New York, 1965), provide some information on the salaries of the professors in the Latin American universities.

5. Atcon, *The Latin American University,* p. 81.

6. The only specific work I know of on the Latin American Professor is a research project, conducted by Dr. Richard Kind of Harvard University, devoted to the professors in the Mexican universities.

List of Contributors

Joseph Maier, beside being a professor of sociology at Rutgers University, is a Vico and Hegel scholar.

Richard W. Weatherhead is president of the Midgard Foundation and has taught history and sociology at Rutgers and Columbia.

Mario Góngora is a Chilean historian whose writings examine many facets of Spanish-American colonial society.

Anisio Teixeira was a distinguished educator and social philosopher in Brazil and was often compared with John Dewey.

Hanns-Albert Steger is a German Latin Americanist concerned with comparative intellectual history.

Orlando Albornoz is a Venezuelan sociologist who has written numerous critiques on the phenomenon of underdevelopment.

José Luis Romero was an Argentinian student of intellectual history and the impact of the bourgeoisie on urbanization in Latin America.

Alistair Hennessy, professor of history at the University of Warwick in England, is interested in student politics and more recently in frontier studies in Latin America.

Luis Manuel Peñalver, former rector of the Universidad de Oriente, is a recognized authority on education in Venezuela.

Gino Germani is a sociologist at Harvard University and a former director at the Instituto Torcuato di Tella in Buenos Aires.

A Select Bibliography

The following books and articles are divided into two major sections. The first includes works dealing with the place of the university in human society. The second is devoted to the Latin American area and the university there. For the most part, this bibliography is intended to supplement the titles cited in the footnotes of the various chapters.

Part One: The University and the Social Order

"American Higher Education," *Daedalus* 1 (1974).

"American Higher Education," *Daedalus* 1 (1975).

Ashby, Eric. *African Universities and Western Tradition.* Cambridge, Mass.: Harvard University Press, 1964.

————. *Technology and the Academics.* London and New York: Macmillan & Co., 1959.

————. *Community of Universities.* Cambridge: Cambridge University Press, 1963.

Baran, P. A. "The Commitment of the Intellectual." *Monthly Review*, May 1961.

Barzun, Jacques. *The American University.* New York: Harper and Row, 1968.

Behrendt, R. F. *Soziale Strategie für Entwicklungsländer.* Frankfurt: S. Fischer, 1965.

Ben-David, J. *American Higher Education: Directions Old and New.* New York: McGraw-Hill, 1972.

Ben-David, J. and Zloczonver, A. "Universities and Academic Systems in Modern Societies." *Archives Europeennes de Sociologie* 3 (1962).

Bourdieu, P. and Passeron, J-C. *Los estudiantes y la cultura.* Barcelona: Editorial Labor, 1967.

Busia, K. A. "Education and Social Mobility in Economically Underdeveloped Countries," *Transactions of the Third World Congress of Sociology.* Vol. 5. London: International Sociological Association, 1956.

Caplow, Theodore and McGee, R. J. *The Academic Marketplace.* New York: Basic Books, 1958.

Coleman, J. S., ed. *Education and Political Development.* Princeton: Princeton University Press, 1965.

Corson, J. R. *The Governance of Colleges and Universities.* New York: McGraw-Hill, 1975.

Dedijer, S. "Underdeveloped Science in Underdeveloped Countries." *Minerva* 2 (1963).

De Huszar, G. B. *The Intellectuals: A Controversial Portrait.* Glencoe, Ill.: The Free Press, 1960.

De Vane, William Clyde. *Higher Education in Twentieth Century America.* Cambridge, Mass.: Harvard University Press, 1965.

Dreitzel, Hans P. *Elitebegriff und Sozialstruktur.* Stuttgart: Ferdinand Enke, 1962.

Duke, Benjamin C. *Japan's Militant Teachers.* Honolulu: University Press of Hawaii, 1973.

Eisenstadt, S. N. *From Generation to Generation.* New York: The Free Press, 1971.

Cummings, William K. "The Aftermath of the University Crisis." *The Japan Interpreter* 10 (1976).

Feuer, Lewis. *The Conflict of Generation.* New York: Basic Books, 1969.

Flexner, Abraham. *Universities: American, English, German.* Rev. ed. London: Oxford University Press, 1968.

Frankel, Charles. *Education and the Barricades.* New York: W. W. Norton, 1968.

Fürstenberg, Friedrich. *Das Aufstiegsproblem in der Modernen Gesellschaft.* Stuttgart: Ferdinand Enke, 1962.

Giner de los Ríos, Francisco. *La universidad española.* Vol. 2 in *Obras Completas.* Madrid: Imprenta Clásica, 1916.

Grant-Robertson, Sir Charles. *The British Universities.* London: Benn, 1930.

Green, V. H. H. *A History of Oxford University.* London: B. T. Batsford, 1974.

————. *The Universities.* Middlesex: Penquin Books, 1969.

Habermas, Jürgen, et al. *Student und Politik.* Berlin: Hermann Luchterhand, 1961.

Halsey, A. H., et al. *Education, Economy and Society.* Glencoe, Ill.: The Free Press, 1961.

Harbison, Frederick and Myers, Charles A. *Education, Manpower, and Economic Growth; Strategies of Human Resource Development.* New York: McGraw-Hill, 1964.

Haskins, Charles Homer. *The Rise of Universities.* Ithaca, N.Y.: Cornell University Press, 1957.

Herr, Richard. *The Eighteenth-Century Revolution in Spain.* Princeton: Princeton University Press, 1958.

Hobhouse, Christopher. *Oxford.* 4th ed. London: B. T. Batsford, Ltd., 1948.

Hofstadter, R. and Metzger, W. P. *The Development of Academic Freedom in the United States.* New York: Columbia University Press, 1955.

Hutchins, Robert M. *The Learning Society.* New York: The New American Library, 1969.

Jaspers, Karl. *The Idea of the University.* London: Peter Owen Ltd., 1965.

Jericks, C. and Riesucan, D. *The Academic Revolution.* New York: Doubleday, 1968.

Jiménez, A. *Selección y reforma: ensayo sobre la universidad renacentista española.* Mexico City: Colegio de México, 1944.

————. *Ensayo sobre la universidad española moderna, ocaso y restauración.* Mexico City: Colegio de México, 1948.

Kerr, Clark. *The Uses of the University.* Cambridge, Mass.: Harvard University Press, 1963.

King, Alexander. "Higher Education, Professional Manpower, and the State." *Minerva* 1 (n.d.).

Krauss, Ellis S. *Japanese Radicals Revisited: Student Protest in Postwar Japan.* Berkeley: University of California Press, 1975.

Laín Entralgo, Pedro. *La universidad, el intelectual y Europa.* Madrid: Editorial Cultura Hispánica, 1950.

————. *La universidad en la vida española, 1961. Sobre la universidad hispánica.* Madrid: Editorial Cultural Hispánica, 1953.

Latorre, Angel. *Universidad y sociedad.* Barcelona: Ediciones Ariel, 1964.

Lazarsfeld, P. F. and Thielens, W. *The Academic Mind.* Glencoe, Ill.: The Free Press, 1958.

Leff, Gordon. *Paris and Oxford Universities in the Thirteenth and Fourteenth Centuries.* New York: John Wiley and Anis, Inc., 1968.

Lind, Andrew W. *Nanyang Perspective: Chinese Students in Multiracial Singapore.* Honolulu: University Press of Hawaii, 1974.

Lipset, Seymour M. "University Students and Politics in Underdeveloped Countries." *Minerva* 44 (1964).

Llavero, Francisco. *La repoblación cerebral en España: universidad y sociedad.* Madrid: V. M. Molina, 1962.

Löwenthal, Richard. *Der romantische Rückfall.* Stuttgart: W. Kohlhammer, 1970.

Machlup, Fritz. *Education and Economic Growth.* Lincoln: University of Nebraska Press, 1970.

MacIver, R. M. *Academic Freedom in our Time.* New York: Columbia University Press, 1955.

McClelland, David C. *The Achieving Society.* Princeton: Van Nostrand, 1961.

————. "The Achievement Motive in Economic Growth." In *Industrialization and Society*, Bert Hoselitz and Wilbert Moore, eds. Paris: UNESCO-Mouton, 1963.

Merton, Robert K. "Role of the Intellectual in Public Bureaucracy." In *Social Theory and Social Structure*. Glencoe Ill.: The Free Press, 1957.

Moberly, Sir Walter. *The Crisis in the University*. London: SCM Press, 1949.

Morison, Robert S., ed. *The Contemporary University: U.S.A.* Boston: Houghton Mifflin Company, 1966.

Morison, Samuel E. *Three Centuries of Harvard 1636–1936.* Cambridge, Mass.: Harvard University Press, 1965.

Morris, Jan. *Oxford*. Oxford: Oxford University Press, 1978.

Myers, Charles N. "U.S. Activity Abroad: Implications of the Mexican Case." New York: Education and World Affairs, Occasional Report No. 5, 1968.

Myint, H. "Education and Economic Development" *Social and Economic Studies* 14 (1965).

Newman, Cardinal John Henry. *The Idea of the University*. London and New York: Longsman, Green and Company, 1947.

Nisbet, Robert. *The Degradation of the Academic Dogma*. New York: Basic Books, 1971.

————. *Tradition and Revolt*. New York: Random House, 1970.

Ortega y Gasset, José. *Misión de la universidad*. 3d ed. Madrid: Revista de Occidente, 1960.

Ottaway, A. K. C. *Education and Society*. London: Routledge and Kegan Paul, 1960.

Parsons, Talcott and Platt, G. M. *The American University*. Cambridge, Mass.: Harvard University Press, 1973.

Passin, Herbert. *Society and Education in Japan*. New York: Teachers College Press, 1966.

Perkins, James A. *The University in Transition*. Princeton: Princeton University Press, 1966.

————. "Is the University an Agent for Social Reform?" New York: International Council for Educational Development, 1973.

Pierson, G. W. *Yale: The University College 1921–1937*. New Haven: Yale University Press, 1955.

Pusey, Nathan M. *The Age of the Scholar*. New York: Harper and Row, 1964.

Rashdall, H. *The Universities of Europe in the Middle Ages*. London: Oxford University Press, 1936.

Rieff, Philip. *The Intellectuals*. New York: Doubleday, 1970.

Ross, Murray G. *The University: The Anatomy of Academia*. New York: McGraw-Hill, 1976.

Rothblatt, Sheldon. *The Revolution of the Dons: Cambridge and Society in Victorian England*. New York: Basic Books, 1968.

Rudolph, Frederick. *The American College and University: A History*. New York: Random House, 1962.

Salmen, Stanley. *Duties of Administration in Higher Education*. New York: The MacMillan Company, 1971.

Schelsky, Helmut. *Erziehung und Schule in der industriellen Gesellschaft*. Würzburg: Werkbund, 1959.

Shils, Edward. "The Intellectuals in the Political Development of New States." *World Politics*. 12 (1960).

————. *The Intellectuals and the Powers and other Essays*. Chicago: University of Chicago Press, 1972.

Silvert, K. H. and Bonilla, Frank. *Education and the Social Meaning of Development*. New York: American Universities Field Staff, 1961.

Snow, C. P. *The Two Cultures: A Second Look*. New York: Cambridge University Press, 1964.

Tannenbaum, Frank, ed. *A Community of Scholars*. New York: Frederick A. Praeger, 1965.

Tinbergen, J. and Bos, H. C. "The Global Demand for Higher and Secondary Education in the Underdeveloped Countries in the Next Decade," O.E.C.D., *Policy Conference on Economic Growth and Investment in Education, III, The Challenge of Aid to Newly Developing Countries*. Paris: O.E.C.D., 1962.

Touraine, A. *The Academic System in American Society.* New York: McGraw-Hill, 1974.
Trow, Martin. "The Democratization of Higher Education in America." *Archives Eurepeennes de Sociologie* 3 (n.d.).
———. "The Second Transformation of American Secondary Education." *The International Journal of Comparative Sociology.* 2 (1961).
Ulam, A. *The Fall of the American University.* New York: The Library Press, 1972.
Various authors. *La idea de la universidad alemana.* Traducción de A. del Campo. Buenos Aires: Editorial Sudamericana, 1959.
Veblen, Thorsten. *The Higher Learning in America.* New York: Sentez Press, 1965.
von Friedeburg, Ludwig. *Jugend in der modernen Gesellschaft.* Köln-Berlin: Kiepenheuer, 1965.
Wallerstein, Immanuel. *University in Turmoil.* New York: Atheneum, 1969.

Part Two: The University in Latin America

Agramonte, Roberto. *Sociologia de la universidad.* 2d ed. Mexico City: Biblioteca de ensayos sociológicos, Instituto de Investigaciones Sociales, Universidad Nacional, 1957.
Agudo Freites, Raul. *Vida de un adelantado.* Caracas: Universidad Central de Venezuela, 1948.
Aguirre Beltrán, Gonzalo. *La Universidad Latinoamericana.* Jalapa, Mex.: Universidad Veracruzana, 1961.
Arciniegas, Germán. *El estudiante de la mesa redonda.* 3d ed. Buenos Aires: E.D.H.A.S.A., 1959.
Atcon, Rudolf P. *La universidad Latinoamericana.* Bogotá, Colombia: ECO, Revista de la cultura de Occidente, 1966.
———. *Proposta para a reestrutuacão do Pontificia Universidade Catolica do Rio de Janeiro.* Bogotá, Colombia: ECO, Revista de la cultura de Occidente, 1966.
———. *Rumo a reformulação estrutural de universidade brasileira.* Bogotá, Colombia: ECO, Revista de la cultural de Occidente, 1966.
Ayala, Francisco. "Universidad y sociedad de masas," in *Temas de Pedagogía Universitaria,* Santa Fe, Arg.: n.p., 1957.
Azevedo, Fernando de. *Sociología educacional.* 4th ed. São Paulo: Ed. Melhoramentos, n.d.
Bakke, E. W. "Students on the March: The cases of Mexico and Colombia." *Sociology of Education* 37 (1964).
Belaúnde, Víctor Andrés. *La realidad nacional.* Lima, Peru: Talleres Gráficos, 1964. See especially the chapter, "El problema universitario."
Benítez, Jaime. *Etica y estilo de la universidad.* Madrid: Aguilar, 1964.
Benjamin, Harold. *Higher Education in the American Republics.* New York: McGraw-Hill, 1965.
Bermann, Gregorio. *Juventud de América: Sentido histórico de los movimientos juveniles.* Mexico City: Ediciones Cuadernos Americanos, 1946.
Bonilla, Frank. "The Student Federation of Chile: Fifty Years of Political Action." *Journal of Inter-American Studies.* 2 (1960).
Burns, R. W. "Social Class and Education in Latin America." *Comparative Education Review.* 6 (1963).
Cardoso, Fernando Henrique, and Ianni, Octavio. "As exigencias educacionais do processo de industrializacão." *Revista Brasiliense.* 26 (1959).
Carreño, Alberto M. *La Fundación de la Real y Pontificia Universidad de México.* Granada: Universidad de Granada, 1958.
Chagas, Valmir. "A luta pela universidade no Brazil." Rio de Janeiro: Ministerio de Educação e Cultura, 1967.

Chiappo, Leopoldo. "Principios y bases de la renovación universitaria." *Revista de la Asociación de Estudiantes de Medicina "Cayetano Heredia,"* 2 (1965).

———. "El estudiante y la universidad para el desarrollo." *Desarrolo y Democracia,* 7 (1966).

Comparative Education Review. 10 (1966). Special issue on students and politics.

Cockcroft, James D. *Intellectual Precursors of the Mexican Revolution, 1910–1917.* Austin: University of Texas Press, 1968.

Collier, Simon. *Ideas and Politics of Chilean Independence 1808–1833.* Cambridge: Cambridge University Press, 1967.

Crawford, William Rex. *A Century of Latin American Thought.* New York: Frederick A. Praeger, 1966.

Cuenca, Humberto. *La universidad revolucionaria.* Caracas: n.p. 1964.

———. *Ejército, Universidad y Revolución.* Buenos Aires: n.p., 1962.

Cuento Fernandini, Carlos. *La universidad en el siglo xx.* Lima: n.p., 1951.

Dalurzo, Beatriz F. "El professor universitario." *Universidad.* Universidad del Litoral. Argentina, 1954, pp. 161–186.

del Río, Angel, ed. *Responsible Freedom in the Americas.* New York: Doubleday, 1955.

———. *El mundo hispánico y el mundo anglosajón en las Américas.* Buenos Aires: Asociación Argentina Libertad de la Cultura, 1960.

Febres Cordero, Foción. *Autonomía universitaria.* Caracas: Universidad Central de Venezuela, 1959.

———. *Reforma universitaria.* Caracas: Universidad Central de Venezuela, 1960.

Fernandes, Florestán. *Educação e sociedade no Brasil.* São Paulo: Dominus Editora, Universidade de São Paulo, 1966.

Freyre, Gilberto. *The Masters and the Slaves.* New York: Alfred A. Knopf, 1956.

———. *The Mansions ad the Shanties.* New York: Alfred A. Knopf, 1963.

Friedman, John. "Intellectuals in Developing Societies." *Kyklos,* 13 (1960).

———. *Venezuela, From Doctrine to Dialogue.* Syracuse, N.Y.: Syracuse University Press, n.d.

Frondizi, R. "Presentation," in Council on Higher Education in the Americas, *National Development and the University.* New York: Institute of International Education, 1965.

———. "Raíz filosófica de los males universitarios." *Universidad.* 9 (1958).

Germani, Gino. *Política y sociedad en una época de transición.* Buenos Aires: Editorial Paidos, 1962.

Gibson, Charles. *Spain in America.* New York: Harper and Row, 1967.

Gonzalez A. Alpuche, Juan. *La universidad de México.* Mexico City: Asociación Mexicana de Sociología, 1960.

González Ginovés, I. *Educación superior latinoamericana.* Concepción, Chile: Universidad de Concepción, 1966.

Graña, César. "Cultural Nationalism: The Idea of Historical Destiny in Spanish America." *Social Research* 29 (   ).

Grompone, A. *Universidad official y universidad viva.* Mexico City: Biblioteca de ensayos sociológicos, n.d.

Halperin Donghi, Tulio. *Historia de la Universidad de Buenos Aires.* Buenos Aires: Eudeba, 1962.

Haring, C. H. *The Spanish Empire in America.* New York: Harcourt, Brace & World, 1963. See especially chapters 11 and 12: "School and Society," and "Literature, Scholarship and the Fine Arts."

Harrison, John F. "The Confrontation with the Political University." *The Annals, American Academy of Political and Social Sciences,* 334 (1961).

———. "The Role of the Intellectual in Formenting Change: The University," in *Explosive Forces in Latin America,* J. J. Te Paske and S. Nettleton, eds. Columbus: Ohio State University Press, 1964.

———. "Learning and Politics in Latin American Universities." *Proceedings of the Academy of Political Science*, 28 (1964).

Haussman, Fay and Haar, Jerry. *Education in Brazil*. Hamden, Conn.: Archon Books, 1978.

Havighurst, R. J., et al. *A Cross-National Study of Buenos Aires and Chicago Adolescents*. Basil: S. Karger, 1965.

———. *La sociedad y la educación en América Latina*. Buenos Aires: Eudeba, 1962.

Herring, Hubert. *A History of Latin America*. 3d ed. New York: Alfred A. Knopf, 1968.

Hutchinson, B. *Mobilidade e Trabalho*. Rio de Janeiro: Centro Brasileiro de Pesquisas Educacionais, Ministerio de Educação e Cultura, 1960. Especially in the chapters on, "A origem socio-economica dos estudantes universitarios."

Imaz, José de. *Los que mandan*. Buenos Aires: Eudeba, 1965.

Johnson, John J. *Continuity and Change in Latin America*. Stanford: Stanford University Press, 1965.

———. *Political Change in Latin America: The Emergence of the Middle Sectors*. Stanford: Stanford University Press, 1958.

Kneller, G. F. *The Education of the Mexican Nation*. New York: Columbia University Press, 1951.

Labarca Hubertson, Amanda. "Educational Development in Latin America." In *Concerning Latin American Culture*. Various authors. New York: Columbia University Press, 1939.

Lambert, Jacques. *Latin America: Social Structure and Political Institutions*. Berkeley: University of California Press, 1967.

Lanning, John Tate. *The Eighteenth Century Enlightenment in the University of San Carlos de Guatemala*. Ithaca, N.Y.: Cornell University Press, 1956.

———. *Academic Culture in the Spanish Colonies*. New York: Oxford University Press, 1956.

Latin American Studies Association. "A Report to the American Academic Community on the Present Argentine University Situation." Austin, Texas, 1967.

Leonard, Irving A. *Baroque Times in Old Mexico*. Ann Arbor: University of Michigan Press, 1959.

———. *Books of the Brave*. Cambridge, Mass.: Harvard University Press, 1949.

Liebman, Arthur, et al. *Latin American University Students: A Six-Nation Study*. Cambridge, Mass.: Harvard University Press, 1972.

Lipset, Seymour M. and Solari, Aldo. *Elites in Latin America*. New York: Oxford University Press, 1967.

MacLean y Estenós, Roberto. *La crisis universitaria en hispanoamérica*. Mexico City: Biblioteca de ensayos sociológicos, Instituto de Investigaciones Sociales, Universidad Nacional, 1956.

Mander, John. *The Unrevolutionary Society*. New York: Alfred A. Knopf, 1969.

Mantovani, Juan. "Idea, forma y misión de las universidades en los países latinoamericanos." *Política* 21 (1962).

Mariátegui, José Carlos. *Siete Ensayos de Interpretación de la Realidad Peruana*. Lima, Peru: Biblioteca Amauta, 1959. See especially chapter entitled "El Proceso de la Instrucción Pública."

Marsal, Juan F. "Los intelectuales latinoamericanos y el cambio social." *Desarrollo Económico* 6 (1966).

Mazo, Gabriel del. *Reforma universitaria y cultura nacional*. Buenos Aires: Editorial Raigal, 1955.

———. *La reforma universitaria y la universidad latinoamericana*. Resistencia, Argentina: Universidad Nacional del Nordeste, 1957.

———. *La reforma universitaria*. 3 vols. La Plata, Argentina: n.d.

Medina Echevarría, José. *Filosofía educación y desarrollo*. Mexico City: Siglo Veintiuno, Editores, 1967.

————. *Responsabilidad de la inteligencia.* Mexico City: Fondo de Cultural Económica, 1943.

————. *La universidad ante el desarrollo económico.* Santiago, Chile: Instituto Latinoamericano de Planificación Económica y Social, 1966

Mencarini Foracchi, M. *O Estudante e a transformação de sociedade brasileira.* São Paulo: Companhia Editora Nacional, 1965.

Mendieta y Núñez, Lucio and Gómez Robledo, José. *Problemas de la universidad.* Mexico City, 1948.

Mercier Vega, Luis. *Mecanismos del poder en América Latina.* Buenos Aires: Editorial Sur, 1967.

Miró Quesada, Francisco. "The University and Society." *Americas* 12 (1960).

Moreira, Roberto J. "O problema da autonomia das universidades latinoamericanas." *Boletín del Centro Latino-Americano de Pesquisas em Ciencias Sociais* 4 (1961).

————. *Educação e Desenvolvimento no Brasil.* Rio de Janeiro: Centro Latino-Americano de Pesquisas em Ciencias Sociais, 1961.

Moses, Bernard. *South America on the Eve of Emancipation.* New York: Cooper Square Publishers, Inc., 1965, especially chap. 7, "A Colonial University."

————. *The Intellectual Background of the Revolution in South America, 1810–1824.* New York: Russell and Russell, 1966.

Myers, Charles Nash. *Education and National Development in Mexico.* Princeton, N.J.: Dept. of Economics, Princeton University, 1965.

Nasatir, David "Estudio sobre la Juventud Argentina," Introducción, *Trabajos e Investigaciones del Instutio de Sociología.* Buenos Aires: Publicación Interna No. 69, Universidad de Buenos Aires.

O'Gorman, Edmundo. *La Supervivencia Politica Novo-Hispana.* Mexico City: Fundación Cultural de Condumex, 1969.

Pacheco Gómez, Máximo. *La Universidad de Chile.* Santiago de Chile: Editorial Jurídica de Chile, 1953.

Palacios, A. L. *Espríritu y técnica de la universidad.* La Plata: Universidad de La Plata, 1943.

Paz, Octavio. *El laberinto de la soledad.* Mexico City: Fondo de Cultural Economica, 1959. See especially chapter on the "Inteligencia mexicana."

Peñalver, Luis Manuel. "El papel del rector en la universidad latinoamericana." *Política,* 6 (1967).

Picón-Salas, Mariano. *De la conquista a la independencia.* Mexico City: Fondo de Cultura Económica, 1958.

Putnam, Samuel. *Marvelous Journey: Four Centuries of Brazilian Literature.* New York: Alfred A. Knopf, 1948.

Ramírez Novoa, E. *La reforma universitaria.* Buenos Aires: Ediciones Atahualpa, 1956.

Ramos, Samuel. *El perfil del hombre y la cultura en México.* Mexico City: Espasa-Calpe, 1951. See especially chapter on "La cultura criolla."

Revista Latinoamericana de Sociología 2 (1966). Various articles on the sociology of the Latin American university.

Rogers, Francis M. *The University of San Marcos in Lima, Peru.* Lima, Peru: n.p., 1961.

Romanell, Patrick. *Making of the Mexican Mind.* Lincoln, Neb.: University of Nebraska Press, 1952.

Rotblat, M. "The Latin American Student Movement." *New University Thought* (1961).

Salazar Larrain, Arturo. *San Marcos: Entre la ley y el caos.* Lima, Peru: Juan Mejia Baca & P. L. Villanueva, Editores, 1956.

Sanchez, G. I. *The Development of Higher Education in Mexico.* New York: King's Crown Press, 1944.

Sánchez, Luis Alberto. *La universidad latinoamericana.* Guatemala: Editorial Universitaria de Guatemala, 1949.

————. *La universidad no es una isla.* Lima, Peru: Ediciones Peru, 1961.

————. *¿Tuvimos maestros en muestra America?* Buenos Aires: Editorial Raigal, 1955.

Salas y Egidio Orellana, Irma. *Correlación entre el Liceo y la Universidad.* Santiago de Chile: n.p. 1960.

Salazar, Bondy, Augusto. *En torno a la educación.* Lima, Peru: Universidad Nacional Mayor de San Marcos, 1965.

Scheman, R. "The Brazilian Law Student: Background, Habits, Attitudes." *Journal of Inter-American Studies,* 5 (1963).

Silvert, Kalman H. *The Conflict Society.* New Orleans: The Hauser Press, 1961.

Spencer, David, ed. *Student Politics in Latin America.* Washington, D.C.: United States National Students Association, 1965.

Steger, H. A., ed. *Grundzüge des lateinamerikanischen Hochschulwesens.* Dortmund: Sozialforschungsstelle, 1965.

Stitchkin Branover, David. *La tarea urgente de la universidad.* Concepción, Chile: Universidad de Concepción, 1959.

Stokes, W. S. "The Drag of the Pensadores." In *Foreign Aid Re-Examined.* J. W. Wiggins and H. Schoeck, eds. Washington, D.C.: Public Affairs Press, 1958.

Tannenbaum, Frank. *Ten Keys to Latin America.* New York: Alfred A. Knopf, 1962. See especially Chapter 6, on education.

Teixeira, Anisio. *Educação não e Privilegio.* Rio de Janeiro: Liv. José Olympio Ed., 1957.

————. *Educação para a Democracia.* São Paulo: Cia. Ed. Nacional, 1952.

Torrealba Silva, Virgilio. *Universidad y Autonomía.* Caracas: Universidad Central de Venezuela, 1964.

Trend, J. B. *Bolívar and the Independence of Spanish America.* New York: Harper and Row, 1968.

Various authors. *La universidad en tiempos de cambio.* Santiago de Chile: Editorial del Pacífico, 1965.

Wagley, Charles. *An Introduction to Brazil.* New York: Columbia University Press, 1963. See especially the chapter on "Family and Education."

Whitaker, Arthur P., ed. *Latin America and the Enlightenment.* Ithaca, N.Y.: Cornell University Press, 1961.

Zea, Leopoldo. *El pensamiento Latino-americano.* 2 vols. Mexico City: Editorial Promaca, 1965.

Index